CANTICLES
III
(MMXXII)

ESSENTIAL POETS SERIES 298

**Canada Council   Conseil des Arts
for the Arts   du Canada**

**ONTARIO ARTS COUNCIL
CONSEIL DES ARTS DE L'ONTARIO**

an Ontario government agency
un organisme du gouvernement de l'Ontario

Canadä

Guernica Editions Inc. acknowledges the support of the Canada Council
for the Arts and the Ontario Arts Council. The Ontario Arts Council
is an agency of the Government of Ontario.

We acknowledge the financial support of the Government of Canada.

GEORGE ELLIOTT CLARKE

CANTICLES

III
(MMXXII)

(CONTEXTS OF AFRICADIAN THEOLOGICAL PRAXIS)

**GUERNICA
EDITIONS**
TORONTO • CHICAGO • BUFFALO • LANCASTER (U.K.)
2022

Michael Mirolla, editor
David Moratto, cover and interior design
Cover font, interior drop caps: Bill Clarke Caps
Guernica Editions Inc.
287 Templemead Drive, Hamilton (ON), Canada L8W 2W4
2250 Military Road, Tonawanda, N.Y. 14150-6000 U.S.A.
www.guernicaeditions.com

Distributors:
Independent Publishers Group (IPG)
600 North Pulaski Road, Chicago IL 60624
University of Toronto Press Distribution (UTP)
5201 Dufferin Street, Toronto (ON), Canada M3H 5T8
Gazelle Book Services, White Cross Mills
High Town, Lancaster LA1 4XS U.K.

First edition.
Printed in Canada.

Legal Deposit—Third Quarter
Library of Congress Catalog Card Number: 2022934715
Library and Archives Canada Cataloguing in Publication
Title: Canticles. III / George Elliott Clarke
Names: Clarke, George Elliott, author.
Series: Essential poets ; 298.
Description: Series statement: Essential poets series ; 298 | Poems.
Identifiers: Canadiana 20220202621 | ISBN 9781771837538 (v. 1 ; softcover)
Classification: LCC PS8555.L3748 C363 2022 | DDC C811/.54—dc23

The beauty of holiness,
if this it be,

is the only beauty
visible in this place....
—William Carlos Williams, *Paterson*

∽

Aren't you ashamed at distancing yourself from this beautiful
moral consensus that is nothing less than the foundation
of a new world order?
—Juan Goytisolo, *Quarantine* [trans. Peter Bush]

∽

For Geraldine Elizabeth Clarke (1939–2000)
& William Lloyd Clarke (1935–2005):
Adepts, Believers, African Baptists.

& For Emily Waller, Matilda Brooks, Helen Claiborne,
& Sahar Bennett, and Elisabeth Benson:
*The Founders of Grace [African] Baptist Church
(Mount Vernon, New York), 1888.*[*]

~⁓

---

[*] Cf. Rachel J. Pilgrim.

THE BOOK OF BAPTISM

Saltwater Spirituals

Princes shall come out of Egypt; Ethiopia shall soon stretch out her hands unto God.
—Psalm 68:31

⟳

Finally, God is simply a white man, a white "idea," in this society....
—LeRoi Jones, *The System of Dante's Hell*

⟳

An epic poetry cannot exist without a religion.
—Derek Walcott, "The Muse of History"

⟳

INTRODUCTION

(To Be Read.)

*For what speaks to me
is what I speak....*
—Rev. Pier Giorgio Di Cicco, *Mediterranea*

THESE *Canticles* (and associate poems) have their origin in the increasing conviction of the Author, through decades of study and use of the annals of the African (United) Baptist Association of Nova Scotia as teacher, poet, and lecturer (*never* upon theological themes), that all of the many excellent and practical histories and literary works leave something to be desired. Chiefly, no thorough *Theology* is produced in these works, although it is a miracle that a few thousand poor, illiterate, publicly cheated, and loathed ex-slaves, separated from the mass of their so-called "Black Atlantic" brethren and sistren, managed to construct, amid hostile white Christians and a bitter, wintry climate, a few dozen churches and chapels, representing their own distinct school of Baptism, in a marginal, hardscrabble province of the British North American "Raj." Moreover, this accomplishment was the feat of primarily one man, Richard Preston, of Virginia, of whom little else is known and of whom no clear, legitimate, pictorial representation exists. After landing in Halifax, Nova Scotia, in 1816, as an obscure, African-American ex-slave, Preston organized, by 1832, the first African-Nova Scotian congregation to be housed in its own church—in Halifax, and then, by 1853, had proclaimed the existence of the African Baptist Association. In 1861, on his deathbed, Preston prophesized that his clutch of churches would one day take its place among the great nations of the world. I believe that the *imagined* history of the constitution of this church, plus the deeds of Preston and his congregation, merits celebration in poetry, even in epic, and thus this ecclesiastical narrative *essays* to conclude my trilogic epic, *Canticles*.

True: Epic in English demands, typically, the treatment of a grand theme involving a larger-than-life hero or heroes. My story, foregrounding a mysterious, itinerant preacher and his life's work, the herding of a few thousand impoverished and oppressed black folk into a never-self-sufficient church, brooks no classicism. Yet, it may border on the epical, for it must consider the unencompassable history of African enslavement (partly the basis of my own genealogy), the intellectual and theological arguments for and against it, and the acts of preachers, mystics, rebels, and lovers in offering resistance. Thus, my collected inklings navigate—in *Canticles I*—among interconnected, sovereign histories; revisit—in *Canticles II*—signal scriptures; and then home—in *Canticles III*—to Africadia.

I should specify that *everything* in the poetry is fictitious, even where real historical actors appear. Moreover, my poetic treatment of the history of the African Baptist Association of Nova Scotia and its historical ministers must not be confused with any *actual* history. The Reader should read my African-Nova Scotians as "Africadians," and thus their Baptist Church as the "Africadian Baptist Association," just so as to scotch any confusion.

January 1, 2009*   George Elliott Clarke

---

* Cf. C.I. Scofield, January 1, 1909.

HISTORY DIRECTORY

Vicissitudes of Race Vice(s) (Caucasian)
and the Backing (Backward) Theology
(Even in Nova Scotia)

Sketch of Life of Rev. Richard Preston, D.D.
1816 to 1832

Selections from The Afrocentric Bible:
Passages Crucial to Africadian Baptism
or *Decisive* for the Missionary Labours
of Richard Preston

Preston Organizes the
Africadian Baptist Association of Nova Scotia
1832 to 1861

The Death of Preston
1861

VICISSITUDES

OF RACE VICE(S)

(CAUCASIAN)

AND THE BACKING

(BACKWARD)

THEOLOGY

(EVEN IN

NOVA SCOTIA)

I didn't want this information
to remain
in the archives
waiting for a time
when it would no longer
be of interest
to anyone.
—Fidel Castro, *Obama y el imperio* [trans. Anonymous]

We are waiting for a new God.
—Jean Toomer, "Blue Meridian"

The new God belonged to the white man and could therefore
listen to none but a man with a white skin.
—Ngũgĩ wa Thiong'o, "The Village Priest"

First, the misery, then the miracle, then the saint;
first the miracles, then the misery, then the poet.
—Boyd Warren Chubbs, *The Birth and Burial Grounds*

Pertinent Personages of this Passage...

Prince Edward Augustus (Royal Libertine)

Alexander Ochterloney (Merchant & Libertine)

William Colley (Africadian Non-Baptist & Libertine)

John Wentworth (Governor of Nova Scotia & Libertine)

Lady Wentworth (Libertine)

Confessions of St. Augustine, of Hippo, in the Roman Province, Africa

I.

Now, my mother was, is, a saint—
warning, "Revels drain to Perversions,"
for she feared I was too much like the man
unsanctified enough to do himself pleasures,
and wrong her further;
i.e., that scoundrel who made her shit brats,
and then sired *encore* behind-her-back bastards.

But I was my father's shadow—
his mottled mirror.
I agreed,
"*Chastity* befits cradle and Kindergarten,
but suits no boy sprouting bristles,
no girl come to bleed."

Nor is college a monastery.

II.

My beloved inamorata, the concubine
I wept to abandon,
I sloughed off for a gal aged nine,
my fiancée;
and while I awaited her maturation—
to see hair crown her blood—
I wore out a second concubine.

(Such praxis is African, biblical—
if not "Catholic."
Eccentricity only becomes *Vice*
if publicly indulged, eh?)

In the end, I wed nil,
was nugatory,
annihilating all my seed
to bleed instead this ink you read.

(Thus, I'm patron to vintners and poets,
printers and pupils—
of God and of eyes.)

III.

To err, and not correct *Error*,
is foolhardy,

and so I bedded no bride.

This *Sacrifice* decided,
I could ascend to government *Intellectual*—
although children be justly suspicious of men
who disdain wives.

Worse, love affairs always breed factions
and *Love* sours into quarrels.
(Raise up Caesar and ask his opinion.)

IV.

I don't yield to *Conjecture*
regarding conjugal could-have-beens.

Whatever is *Invisible* is unaccountable.
(Except God!)

The *Future* we decide, witlessly,
keeps odd subtlety in the *Present*:
We figure our *Fate*;
we undertake superabundant machinations
to engine and engineer and architect
results,
but what befalls is *Surprise*,
Accident,
and yet such always haunts
our foolproof and most explicitly ordered designs.

V.

To look now on my *Youth*—
(rude sports and crude games—
and how *Lechery*
had me jumping—
audacious, predacious)—

and lisp now *Derogation*,

would prove untimely *Disgust*,
quite disgusting in itself.

It is virtuous to speak of *Vice*,
its enticements,
for how can the innocent know
how beautiful the delights of *Innocence*,
otherwise,
since they cannot access
The Library of Prohibited Books
à Praha?

Anyway, the years have a flow that carries us,
no matter our tacking and keeling,

and it is *absurd* to leave off delicacies
seldom injurious.

VI.

When I recall my lovers—
how I used one as a workhorse,
another as a clothes-horse,
and how I could be spleeny,*
or spleenful,**
and do uninhibited evil
to *Chastity*
(and, yes, to table manners)—
I don't assign a faultless epithet
to mitigate my sins,

but admit my pagan spirit—
the malady of maladjusting tropics—
such as Carthage—

where women are marketed "on-the-hoof"
and Apollo laurelled and Venus venerated
and blazing libations preface no grievous meal,
and the best songs rollick jazzy out the brothels—
those sparkling lairs—
and gold hair is combed out upon ivory shoulders
and *Love* is as fresh and naked as sunlight
and grapes turn gold or garnet wine once crushed
and every black doll's sex is a tight
          smoke-ring-in-the-flesh
and a poet takes to long measures—
to glug wine and chug cake long.

I confess:
The gut be the wellspring of *Verse*.

[LHR (England) 19 *avril* / *Nisan (Paques)* mmxiv]

---

* Peevish.
** Passionate.

A Chronicle of the Cadaver Synod
(Synodus Horrenda) (897)

That Throne that Formosus stank upon was an open crypt,
and "he"–or it–was a rat, disinterred from dust,
though embellished in papal purple and gold;
and those are worms that were his eyes,
his aspect so outstandingly downcast,
due to the successor pope Stephen VI's outraged
and outsized harangues—
spittle baptizing the swarming, teeming worms
eating the remains of Formosus's half-decayed face,
so that witnesses were forced to concur:
Religion be the root of all *Evil*.

Exhumed from "his"—or its—dusty turf,
the sat-up bones looked ambergris-plastered
whenever a robe got swept aside
to reveal a heartless skeleton,
a state befitting a once-bishop
known for his astonishing non-neutrality
in theological questions,
and his alleged ambitious usurpation of the papacy
upon the decease of John VIII.

Thus, Pope Stephen VI was contemptuous and derisive
in berating his predecessor's corrupt masquerade
as a bishop
when he was only a plebe.
The living pope, in chivvying the odoriferous corpse
of Formosus
to confess his advocacy of *Blasphemy*—
spectated scraps—
a mannequin of bones—
and a throne unhelpful to lumbago—
and audited a studied, insolent *Silence* as unsound as Pig Latin.

Not that Stephen expected 100% agreement
with his indictment of Formosus;
yet, he confronted gross *Divergence*—
atrocious *Impertinence*—
as he attempted to dissect—
via flaying *Argument*—
a show-pony corpse,
with its dynamically bony visage
so impervious to fault-finding.

Useless was Pope Stephen's fanatical raving—
his pious *Hatred*!
Each new rhetorical *Vengeance*—
even genuine lines, ideal lies—
could not make Formosus flinch.

Some gag shrouded the dead pontiff's words!

Pointless also was the attempt to serve Communion:
Ferried to the holy table as if a fragile idol,
Formosus dishonoured his blood-stained Saviour,
because, non-participating,
the rich-robed thing seemed to deem the bread dry
and the wine poison,
thus turning up its bony nostrils at the fare.

The Synod was becoming an echo chamber
of doggerel–
of self-gratifying hullabaloo—
of unnecessary scurrility.

Stephen could only briskly ruffle, brutally tousle,
Formosus' cold silk garb
by entering the zone of stink
and pumping out croaks, tinny cricks,
or throaty chortles
directly into the model carcass's half-gone face,
the whole big and dirty cadaver—

so volcanically asleep–
its only reply was bombinating flies,
a hum akin to snoring.

(But how could any diatribe arouse
"this gutter rat of a Christian"?
Caustic was this obvious *Whimsy*!
This bungled Inquisition!)

Stephen took indecent swallows of wine
to egg himself on—
to infuse and channel his *Wit*—
to take liberties with a dug-up, *de facto* saint.

Yet, Formsus was so formidable an adversary—
so prodigally cynical–
that "his" retort to *Sturm-und-Drang Theology*
was a hold-my-tongue *Psychology*—
to act rigidly innocent of the jeremiad.
No matter how diagnostic or forensic
was Stephen's "poetry"
versus mouldered bones in stately garb—
encased in a halo of flies
and ensconced in laurels of stench,
Formosus was as sullen as he was decrepit:
Never could "his" tongue be traitor to his heart.

(For "he" now possessed neither:
Half a replica saviour,
"he" was also a half-carbonized fossil.)

How could Stephen bother wrestling
further with these well-dressed, dry bones?
To snarl *Virtue* with *Madness*?

Time to tussle the thing and its shadow
across the cathedral threshold
and toss it into a graveyard for foreign souls.
But first disrobe the cadaver
and chop three fingers from its dexterous hand
to invalidate Formosus' blessings of others.

Not long did Formosus continue to rot
in the earth:
A Roman mob, directed by Pope Stephen,
dug up the cadaver
and flung it into the Tiber River.

Next, it surfaced, slumbering amid shore-strewn trash,
but healing any who touched its grisly bones.

Now understanding Formosus to have been a martyr,
the Roman rabble dragged Stephen VI off his throne,
cast him in prison,
where he was swift strangled by unidentified hands.

[Ketch Harbour (Nova Scotia) 8/8/mmxxii
& 9 *août* mmxxii]

Johannes Gutenberg Prints The Holy Bible (1455)

Dewy handwriting, sketching imagoes—
mirages of definitions—
the indifferent anarchy of wishy-washy palsy—
illegible tracery
or illicit mirroring—
these ideas impossible to set down straight—
the deformed letters that confuse—
that render *Theology* miasmic ooze
slouching from a pen, slurring,
tender unexpurgated bilge.

Via Print, I terminate misreading.

Feelings need to be fixed
to set free—uncensored—*Thought*;
my apparatus presses lines, angles, curves—
incarnates the apparition of *Speech*....

Feathers—quills—whistle upon—or rustle—pages;
Intelligence has always been dredged from ink.

But these works pass before priestly, half-wit eyes,
whose *Theology* becomes a branch of *Zoology*.
These are fellows, fond of incineration,
who name rival clerics as "heretics,"
and lash them to stakes and set them afire,
while fronting as "scholars"
to gullible schoolboys.

The alphabet is a palette of letters—
Greco-Roman—
that, given firm impress in ink got from wine,
leads our *Nature*-naked bodies
from cavernous *Darkness*
to accelerated *Light*—
to suns and stars as round and as definite as a period.

The wet tip of the plume—
the splendid burning of ink—
now becomes the solar brilliance
of laid out, leaden letters—
each line an intoxicating parallel
to sped-up dawn light.

My printing press erects a lighthouse
of books—
a shouting fire—

yet not of "witches" and "non-conformists"
(for that's the perfidy of *That* drat Church);
but the brazen torch of *Enlightenment*.

A pen in a pot is old,
ordinary *History*, unsound.

The Gutenberg Press
shouts back at the dark
in courageous echoes of prose—
the private glamour of the volume.

It isn't sketchy,
nor as bluffing, puffing, or blustery
as the lisping plumage
of a murder of crow-black quills.

Nor is it wasteful of *Silence,*
but presses pages
as incisive as an incision,
whose unspoken *Violence*
is brutal, raw, vehement *Truth*
that scalpels out
Church-controlled eyes,
or the earthy lungs
of maggot-halo theologians,
their black, cadaverous translucence.

The Press is always extra-parliamentary,
Unparliamentary.

No more the glosses as opaque as taverns.
No more the potty mouths of well-fed clerics,
roaring calumnies upon the poor
at each chirrup of the rich.
(The poor go begging to the deaf plutocrats
who heed only the airy hiss
of their own mass-impoverishment schemes.)

This press is newborn lungs:
Howls of *Discord*! Wails of *Dissonance*!

[Funchal (Madeira) **17** & **18** *décembre* mmxv]

The Progress of Servitude

One part of *Humanity*
saddled the backs of the other parts,
who ate gruel,
while their riders feasted on sugar—
edible diamonds.

Cane got tapped on three continents—
and in the Carib and Indo seas.

Sugar's juices fuel th'Americas,
sweeten and tonic Europe,
so all swallow coffee, tea, chocolate,
too-digestible commodities.

Gold squeezed from sugar
firms coal mining,
iron works,

guinea circulation.

Sugar throws a railway cross Haiti.

Sugar transfuses blood of (black) Haiti
into once faltering, now gleaming, white banks *de France*.

Slave-grown sugar, turned rum,
pays for "slave pennies,"
Barbados' first coins.

In Brazil, gold sugar inaugurates gold mines;
white-diamond sugar opens up diamond mines.

Sugar, got from Haiti, transforms to asphalt,
railway steel ties,
even dredged canals,
so British ships and trains and subways
can make the world go round Piccadilly Circus.

To tear sugar outta New World soil,
Africans are traded for glass beads, guns, trinkets, whiskey,
then herded aboard vessels.
(Are they cargo or cattle or furniture?)

Slavery equals *Caucasian-Sugar'd Centuries.*

If the Middle Passage don't drown or disease-to-*Death* most—
jettison'd like sick horses—
"Negroes" anchor on "American," Euro-Zone seaboards
(from which "Indians" have been cleared,
killed off),

then are scoured, de-loused,
shaved, skin oiled,
then measured, graded,

white fingers stuck into their orifices

to test teeth-strength,
or guess at *Fertility*,

Labour health,

and then auctioned off
or marketed by "scramble"
(buyers snatching whoever they want),

and, once bought, are branded,
by wrought—hot—iron,

then coffled—chained—or carted off
to the owner's plantation(s),

while protestors (resisters) are "seasoned"—
i.e., whipped into *Subservience*,
lashed into "good behaviour."

["Likely Slaves For Sale"

sold alongside livestock
and dry goods,

enriched the buyer thus:

1—Rice hand, bad eyesight;
2—Good cook;
3—Fair carpenter;
4—Rice hand and blacksmith;
5—Seamstress, infirm;
6—Nurse;
7—Prime Cotton man;
8—Mule-handler (answers to "Bills");
9—Boy ($400 value);
10—Prime girl (named "Honey"; $850 value);
11—Blacksmith (called "Happy," approx. 60 years; $500 value);
12—Studman ("George"; $100 value—likely to run off).]

Soon, the conch shell is blown afore daylight,
and all hands gotta jump to their feet
for roll call,

then go, beaten, half-fed, to *Toil*:
This retinue of slaves.

(Sugar cultivation takes muscles, sweat.
Sap spoils lickety-split.
Must be processed inside a day.
Night shifts help.

Boiling sugar requires infernal heat,
so water gets gushed upon mill roofs
to forbid fire springing up.

Overseers brandish whips but also emergency machetes:
In case a drowsy slave slips into machinery,
the hefty blade handily lops a cropped hand
or bags a snagged foot.)

Everywhere, sugar-financed slaves
seed forests, burn bush,
pave roads and build houses,
dig canals and latrines,

and drop down into mines,
to work-work-work there,

gettin solid light out the darkness.

[Regina (Saskatchewan) 28 *novembre* mmxiv]

The Deposition of Sally Bassett:
Notes for the Defence (1730)

I.

Frost-haired—feisty—I sling salty
riposte to peppery, sassy queries!

Anyway, I like my apples sour—
or nipped with salt—
Scotian-style—

tart,
as be my *Truth*.

II.

Th'Atlantic's reflex sparkles don't hint
at slaves' badly dressed tables.

(Lower-class life? Snouts
rubbed distinctly in dirt.)

The dismal brilliance of soup that's just water—
is too often our pallid gruel;
we slurp brine tasty as bravura tears.

Satisfyin beef be out of reach—
like black sausage, like mackerel.

Our fowl chow
be scrawny chicken, maggoty pork,
malefic bread.

Palm trees, chopped up, do for charcoal.

III.

We raze sugarcane by raisin machetes
and decapitatin cane.

So many legs, ankles, toes, get in the way of whackin cane,
see black folks tappin canes everywhere.
(Even banjos gotta double for crutches!)

IV.

My grandmother picked slavin over sugarcane
over being studded,
but no matter:

The capital formula got applied—
unblanchingly—
so her black flesh whelped my brown mama;

next, the same *blanco* who sacked her mama
plundered her—

so my mama is also my sister.

V.

My job? To be a tar-black, black-heart "Valentine,"
and squirt out babes;

and it was no easy calypso.

What man ever did my quicksand tears slow down?

Anguished was meself entire—
from my skull's hair
to my feet's soles—
and aching—cracking—my very soul.

To seek out sleep, I had to rest my eyes
on the painting of a bed.

I tried to shield my heart
while yielding only raw *Hatred*

unto the massacr'in pirates massa done fielded,

to saddle me to cross-breed.

So much grog watered the yahoos,
their mouths drooled, slobbered after,
ourselves—prey—
for their *strafexpeditioni.*˙

VI.

I wed meself to "Hannibal"—
a master of stallions, really,
and a sugar-tongued, banjo-plucker;

so between all the enforced beddings—
rude, crude rapes—

I gave meself to Hannibal
and he gave me my only son—
black as iron.

I sang to him,
"Thunder: The rain roars.
Thunder: The rain pours."

Too soon I left him in his cradle—
his handsome, onyx-black body,
swaddled in lily-pale cotton;

---

* Military Italian: Punitive raids.

so, when I retrieved him later,
I saw that massa had slathered
his dark face with so much spittle,
twas a miracle my pickney still breathed!

When Hannibal heard of this *Discourtesy*,
he went straight to massa's Mrs—
her face dull and her heart dark—
to fissure her with vents
so herself sprung tar pools.

I wager you know his fate—
infamous:

He was hanged alive
from a hook through his ribs—

the whole friggin rib cage—

with ivory skulls and bones—
all the skeletal "rubbish"—
the dead collection of our insolent brave—

litterin the soil under his wheezing form.

Our son got sold off—
in the same lot
as Billyum Shakespeare's plays,
plus pepper sauce, needles, ale....

VII.

I got whipped for the first time—
age set at 19—

until my breath came out as dissolute sculpture.

The whip hit like a dirty hammer.
I felt my heart pop out my chest.
Thorns were dragging open,
dredging,
already scalding wounds!

The whip guffawed, lapping my back—
hee-haw, hee-haw;
the heavy cow-skin ate at me—
20 lashes, 50 lashes.

Well, this nigger had to holler.

But massa?
His ecstasy uncorked buttery, smelling of rum.

VIII.

After my mandatory healing,
I got packed off to a new breeding stable,

and there were no velvet whip-cracks:
Nosiree.

There hurricaned a chaos of whippings—
repeated desecrations and whippings.

I got to prefer being constantly pregnant
to stagger the constant whippings!

IX.

Next came gossip outta Jamaica
bout "Nanny"—
merciless Joan-of-Arc of dem Maroons.

This was about 1720,
and I was 40.

I took up Maroon thoughts....

I learned of potions to be gotten
out lambs and cows.

X.

I don't say I slew any animal.

Still, the judge commanded,
"Hew her hue
with ruddy stripes."

Lathered was I studiously,
as if the overseer was copying
a miser at an orgy—
to be fastidious, but comprehensive.

He unfastened lightning.

Lashed was I so hard,
chopped to smithereens, I felt.

Blood burst out in measureless welts.
So much gore as to be disturbing.

The leather had me jigging
like an eel outta water.

I was told, though, I was difficult to mutilate:
Too old, too black, too tough.

XI.

Next, my daughters and granddaughters got sold off.
To be dirtied and befouled, besmirched and polluted—

because you whites
believe in bitches, believe in *Bastardy*.

It's so filthy
everywhere you is!

How could ya dare think I'd forgive you buckaroo
*güeros**

just because I got sold to—
and one granddaughter got bought by—

the "good Mr. Foster"?!!

XII.

I assure you, my attorneys,
the strokes I took were
as profound and incisive as acid.

And yet, I'm old:
My feet hardly hold up my legs!

You want to burn me to ashes
for allegedly trying to murder
Mr. & Mrs. Foster
& Anansi ("Nancy," you say)—
that violently stuttering liar—
that loathsome issue!

---

* Mexican Spanish: Whites.

I's a prisoner in your padlocks,
but I piss on all your type.

Make me a human bonfire. Fine.

But you can't kill a volcano!

You have to suck up the fumes, the flames,
the hot, blazing flow!

My proof?
Outta my ashes will spring a new flower—
violet,
as my soul's inviolate.

[Grotto Bay, Hamilton Parish (Bermuda)
17 *décembre* mmxiv]

Napoléon Broods on the Saint-Domingue Revolt

I.

The "Haitian" Negrory revert to beasts,
unashamed of what they do—
arranging tapestries of corpses,

so France's lilies, heaped bout Saint-Domingue,
look like terraces of drifted snow.
At sea, toys—blobs—of chopped boys bob in brine.

Toussaint L'Ouverture schemed a ceaseless
Dynasty, but the nigger saviour,
let himself dream himself as honourable

as an aristocrat, whom I'd show luxurious
bonhomie. But my letters shaped daggers,
and he faces prompt *Extinction*,

chided by chains:
When he dies, he'll see my image—
patriotic marble—

upbraiding his Sambo *Gullibility*—
just as he's slid face down,
on the guillotine bed, his neck

awaiting a razor-thin, final shave.
L'Ouverture forgot blacks are furniture—
just stools, chamber pots, and steps.

He reared a counterface
Republic to France. So I dispatched
Le Clerc to oust em,

to unbridle hoof and charge warhorses
trample as they gallop,
so the rebels, pure bones anyway,

slicing rations from rats and horses,
would get crushed, literally,
spurt everywhere a glistening red.

Suave marching bests persuasive shouting.
Le Clerc's forces were excellent belligerents,
riding—dire—among the negroes,

and giggling when they buckled,
wriggling under horse hooves.
But now black skin and Yellow Fever

turn my 20,000 troops
into skedaddling plumes,
trotting and tumbling dead into trenches.

I have L'Ouverture in my custody,
but his rabble cavalry
have brought Le Clerc a babbling shattering.

L'Ouverture opined he'd end up
in the Pantheon, a civil inscription
lettering his name and deeds.

But he suits best a tombstone,
not a warrior's memorial.
His strategy forces my forces

to creep through swamp
or sink in the miasma,
and too many flounder amid vipers.

How strange that my ice-shiny *Flattery*
enticed L'Ouverture so much,
he gave up his feeble *Tyranny*,

rather than turn down *moi*, his Emperor.
Now, he'll perish in Jura—
his breath throbbing from rags—

until one is spent and the other gone.
If I can't squash Haitians vehemently,
still I'll harass the licentious brutes,

so that their liberal government
becomes a dusky pantomime
of Greece and Rome, Washington and Paris,

their legislatures echoing with idle rumbles.
(Only G.III.R. is worse—
at *War* and at imperial rule.

Well, ain't L'Ouverture provisionally regal?
Say that for the monkey?
The British King's maladroit countenance

and laws—
those inexplicable mouthfuls of words—
those leaden blots on parchment—

revolted so the Yanks that they revolted.)
L'Ouverture, to his credit,
was no oligarch-at-large.

A decent foe, his tactics
ripped apart flesh, broke up bones,
rendered uniforms sundry bandages,

and now I'm forced to sell Louisiana
to Jefferson so as to remedy
exsanguinations unimaginable

and uncountable exchequering,
bloodshed adding up to *Bankruptcy*.
My revenues bleeding just like ruins....

II.

Wine lunges from the bottle,
plunges down my throat.
I have L'Ouverture—the "opening"—

immersed in ice,
a fortress of Jura snow,
his jail cell duress'd by chill.

I keep him alive only so as to prove
to his lieutenant, Dessalines,
that I will triumph ultimately,

prepare a fresh subjugation *des negres*,
and impose on Saint-Domingue
my wanton *Sovereignty*.

I want Dessalines to recognize *Prophecy*:
L'Ouverture's damnable visage—
the ashamed face of overthrown kings—

flung down, disembodied, in a sewer.
I do parade L'Ouverture as an expedient effigy—
conspicuous as a bullet in the head—

to coax Dessalines to *Suicide* or *Surrender*.
Still, he has my soldiery mired in ruts,
while his hooves accost the earth

at a gallop. Gore-minded, Dessalines
butchers a corps of troops into tripe,
so glittering, bleeding limbs pile up,

and hosts of entrails grace tree limbs.
France is beaten back, pell-mell,
though we crack and crush black brains.

Regard our corpses, streaming,
to log-jam rivers,
so dams leak blood.

Dessalines is clearly monstrous,
monotonously monstrous,
while L'Ouverture was just a maniac.

III.

Dead in his frigid niche, L'Ouverture
is a black head ejecting from France's womb—
an odd god,

a floppy shadow of our *Enlightenment*!
He wouldn't survive as a fugitive.
He leaves—as he arrived—on a breath,

this molten "nigguh,"
this vomited manuscript.
Beware his sulphurous *Immortality*!

Beware his cannibal auxiliaries!
Beware his Mandingo crimes, his defiant melanin!
He is the Negro as basalt—

a godly masterpiece—
a man who incubates *Mutilation*,
just as he presses medicine outta feces.

[Ilonojaa (Finland) 3 *juillet* mmxiv]

Fragment

The Africans and the 'Scotians'
Compose peoples never broken,
Yet always breaking into song.
(They're *righteous*, even when they're wrong.)

Mid peas porridge poverty,
They dream up custard luxury.

[Unguja City (Zanzibar) 20 *février* mmviii]

The Murder of Jude*

Second day of 1801, a groove of a grave
turfed up Jude's corpse,
a dog sniffed at, snuffled.

Dirt covered her only 96 hours
before disinterred she was.
Death struck her down as the last century got struck

from the calendars.
The Coroner's Jury was unanimous,
harmonious: *Murder!*

Dr. Joe Bond fingered four bruises
to Jude's noggin,
and multiple gashes to her corpse.

A hammer had bashed through the skin
of her skull, denting
the bone; venting *Exsanguination.*

Doc Bond disclosed a history of wounds—
a backlog of scars—
on Jude's back, face, bones.

Called to court, Massa Sammy Andrews explained,
"Ma boys had to thrash Jude!
Quite good-naturedly, I say:

"To correct her crooked, cussin mouth!
Thus her death was due to her own malpractice;
was on her own bottom!

---

* Cf. Lynn Murphy, "Nova Scotia slaveowners acquitted of murder" (*Pandora*).

"Din't I stuff her maw
with cod and nigger-toe taters?
So, why was her belly always growlin?

"*Fakery?* And she'd not only steal taters,
but steal the very dirt outta which they whelped.
Thus, the whip became as much a part of her wardrobe

"as was her monthly blood-cloth.
Come December 28, 1800,
as the previous century was groaning to its close,

"my wife right-angled from sleep, screeling,
'Jude's in the house, stealing again!'
Well, I heard glass splashing:

"The slave gal had cannonaded herself through a window
some five feet in the air;
likely to skulk and sulk among free Negresses.

"Us good Caucasian citizens went back
to snoozing.
But the next day, boys sent to salve calves with grains,

"uncovered extra groaning in the barn.
They pulled aside the hay:
Jude stood—bloody—and dropped.

"(The hay about her was stickily scarlet.)
Our pale boys—facing Negro *Recalcitrance*—
broke switches upon the black bitch.

"She skedaddled to the Big House and collapsed.
Three hours later, she was as dead as dust.
"Our sons sang, 'Twas not our fault—

her thieving fingers purloined her of breath!'
Corroboration? Daughter Mary
at sun-up, saw Jude rigidly vertical in a field.

"She was 'much carved' about her neck and ears—
bleeding very liberally—
and then my brother John struck her thrice—

"with something like a hammer,
penetrating her woolly head despite her naps
cushioning the blow (against our prayers)."

[YUL—Dorval (Québec) *Xmas* mmxxi]

The Coroner's Report

I peer at a parish
where countless Negroes perish,
all deemed "infant" unless at least aged 21—
and categorized as akin to sheep.

Thus, Jude was thrashed, punched, hammered in the noggin.
Thus, March, a black boy—
procured after some "pains"—
was forced to gather together a mile-long stone fence—
extending from pasture to a beach—
and died in the doing,
his spine so busted that each trestle
resembled broken pottery shards.
(In truth, the lash had crashed so much upon his back,
the cowskin—bad as rebar—
had burst the skin and fountained gore.)

Lookit! Any Negro caught—no, suspected of—stealing
has to be hanged—absolutely;
but first cross-hatched on the bare back
about 50 times.

Nothin's so byzantine or labyrinthine
as a slave massa's heart!

Their *Charity* is always carceral;
their *Christianity* is always carnal.
Their *Liberalism* is a bewitching—but repellent—*Ideology*,
so grotesquely horrific!

Liberals are libertines—
chronic parasites upon the poor;
they screech "Free Speech"
to trivialize black *Suffering*—
the bull-penis whip visited upon a black belle's back
in unalleviated grating,
thunking up ruddy gunk,
materially spooky,
diagnosably lethal.

[**New Orleans (Louisiana) 25/3/22**]

Statement from Hegel (1807)

Africa can never triumph over Europa,
for they are *Die Hunde*—
black dogs,

whose souls are as invisible
as is their *Innocence.*

But the subsequent remains untested,
for their realms are jungles—
natural, green ruins.

All of Africa is a slimy and grimy prison,
and their *Eternity* looks dusty,
perceptible only as fossils....

One cannot spy in Africa
even the deformities
of our pagan divinities.

Where is the evidence that Africans
can even char or scorch wood,
let alone score and chisel metal?

Their barbarously babbling priests
enact a soiled *Sensibility*:
They're a clack of rabid gravediggers.

[Saint John (New Brunswick) 6 *novembre* mmxv]

John Wentworth, Governor of
Nova Scotia: Libertine

I.

My Lady's Champagne sex—
bubbly, prickly,
toasts a garden-party
orgy.

Madame sports cake-frosting lace,
but she's rose-perfumed pork.

Dark, greasy vermin
rapture her flesh.
They hold her; cuckold me.

Don't she love to pivot upon
a bull-headed, bull-thighed, bull-cock black?

His lamb's tongue rams her slit;
his "log" hogs her till she's soggy.

If his "pumping" balloons her belly,
my gubernatorial sword will tap his blood,
smear her sticky with his ruddy shit.

(I'll end his life just as briskly
as wine slinks down a drunkard's throat.)

II.

My Lady parades the stink of her Maroon Moor
so it daubs all our pious house.

(She adores his "rock core,"
his igneous genius,
his ape-part that—gleaming—plungers her.)

I think he gores her beautifully,
looses an obstinate musk.

When she straddles his length,
she looks every inch
a butterfly atop a crocodile's nose.

Her normally parsimonious mouth
O's charitably.

Enthroned upon his thighs,
her body fidgets—

like a diamond
tossed bout in a black hand.

III.

I'll invest myself in small-tit black chits
(whose legs mirror soft, skinny scissors),

or spend in their luscious, mammoth mamas,
whose rumps insist on strenuous routines.

(The only deficiency in a whorehouse?
Sleep!)

I need wine and a woman—
to have *pleasure* and forget *Death*.

(We don't die like gold—
to be buried, then unearthed.)

Send me a cargo of *petun**
and a payload of *putains*
(much confected dirt).

Lemme bust the *Virginity*
prized by every brothel.

To govern is to execute:
To impregnate *une femme*,
to castrate *un homme*....

[Halifax (Nova Scotia) 3–4 *février* mmxi]

---

* Brazilian: Tobacco.

Portrait d'une femme

That blacked-up, Bluenose bluestocking—
Angela Colley, a Maroon,
ex-Jamaica—
slings a bitch temper
being Wentworth's slut....

The figurehead of our silvery, mercurial
"Golden Age,"
she is a preening *putana*—
as impertinent as syphilis.

Never mind her apple-blossom airs,
her morals are as weak as sand.

A fine-boned monster, the wench plays monarch,
and she can, for she's a quean paraded in the sparkly stews
of the upper-crust,
who pretend they can down gallons of Champagne—
and never belch.

She be bold in silk and juicy in furs
(court her orifices, those honey aquifers).
She's particular in her pungency.

Or peculiar.

Insolently, relentlessly sweet—
this doxy cozies up
to the puissant, even myself,
and asks if she "might
do right"
by me—
under candles—or the moon.

Her *Candour* is not dour, not unaffecting
(even if affected).

I know that, a-bed, she's a flood of tricks—
as ambidextrous and as oratorical
as a fellatrix,
but more categorical
meritoriously,
meretricious....

Her body covers her lover
as if she's a swarm of bees,
sucking honey and stinging—
if one writhes too much—

and the after-smell is part-baby
and part-cadaver,
a scent of milk plus formaldehyde.

She sighs—
and it's a lesson in *Law* and *Metrics*.

She is certainly more evolved than—
is an advancement upon—
Venus,
And all males are vicious in her compare.

(*Beauty* is selfish, not only difficult,*
for it credits that it's a law unto itself.)

Where other ladies clop, Angel glides.
Where other ladies clamber, she ascends.

Gold is, to her, as ordinary as air:
She receives it as she receives sunlight—
as a given, not a gift.

---

* Cf. Beardsley.

To treat her well is not to accede to *Prostitution*,
but is an obligation,
as it is to travel to the Continent to view
Da Vinci's *Mona Lisa*,
which is yet less perfect than Angel Colley,
that coal-scuttle Pomona.

She is the Beloved—
who mustn't be outlived
by any lover,
necessarily pitiful,
whereas she's *Beauty* made extra beautiful.

Indeed, Colley can't be outlived!
Without her, every garden is rot
and every kiss is scum.
Perfume goes up in smoke.

Unstabled *Radiance*, that's her!

To take the alphabet and boil it down,
so that it's only moans and yelps,
consonants that murmur, whisper, and howl
into vowels,
or vowels that buckle into consonants,
truckling,
is what happens when she deigns to buck—
with such infuriating, irritating *Succulence*,
Truculence....

Her petulant swain—
Jacko Wentworth—
is a gigolo
with an igloo heart.

But I take her—sidelong, headlong;

Her colour—at our crux and *Crisis*—
is a black candle waxing white flame....

—*Prince Edward Augustus* (1799)*

[Dartmouth (Nova Scotia) 27–28 *octobre* mmxi
& Paris (France) 14–15 *juillet* mmxii]

———————————

* Cf. Page 298 of the *Bankruptcy* ruling of the Milanese court.

A Portrait of Alexander Ochterloney

I.

The superintendent of the Maroons,
Ochterloney stabs salted pork with silver forks,
gobbles down dark, rum-sodden macaroons.

Got lotsa £ outta Jamaica
to put 800 coloured, guerilla goons
(sorta like gorillas)
on 5000 Preston acres.

But Ochterloney taketh care of *Business*
by constructin a *seraglio*
outta the Maroon maidens—
yippie-yi-yo!

Ochterloney swears (his verbiage smears):
"Wealth is rum, a roof, a woman:
Nothin chilly but drink, and nothin
painful but *History*. Bring on liqueurs!"

Dude is sunlit *Depravity*,
gilded shit;
his *Treasure* is the cavity
he carves out the colony's *Budget*.

His ample *Amplitude* maketh
Ochterloney as glutted as th'Atlantic.
He taketh salt cod and salt pork til his butt breaketh
wind, and he frigs wenches somethin frantic.

He seizes and frenches each slut; serene
he is, to stick a black ass raw in bed—
"like you'd stick a head in a guillotine."
and then he does Greek (which gals dread).

Ochterloney goes diggin into the earth,
so he comes up with friggin worms;
his boot-heels click and clack his hobnail *Worth*,
clobberin slobberin Negresses
(bedroom empresses)
til mutual sweat curls their hot-comb perms.

(Every worthy poet confirms!)

II. A Sea Chanty

Ochterloney's silver cometh in coins;
his gold comes in vaults.
So warm and white are his wife's loins,
I tilt her tits to somersaults—

to get some milk shake, whenever I thrust
her white-ass down, and shove
my regal rod deep til my nut gets bust
and froth up her darling snatch with *Love*.

That woman with a rump as skinny
as a snake and flanks so blanching,
I smear with sweat until she's spinny,
then seed with mead unstanching.

She's a fine lady, milky, and doth wash
in French soap; I split apart her legs
and smack between her thighs as we clash,
while Ochterloney's fertilizin dark gals' eggs.

He wolfs down pies, scarfs down cakes,
takes beer and rum and wine in barrels;
he has roast pork, lotsa Trini roast bakes;*
chews on bacon and swigs down sorrels.

He swallows plates of perch and pots of port;
butter, milk, and fat, so he's as plump
as the gross worm that he doth chomp for sport
at the butt of a tequila pump

or bottle, when he ain't swillin mead, that melted
honey, or fuckin a filly, sable and svelte.
To his wife's bung-hole, I'm buckled and belted,
but her *con* gets also banged as insult.

—*Prince Edward Augustus* (1799)

[Wolfville & Dartmouth (Nova Scotia) 4 *février* mmxii]

---

* Trinidadian English: Salt cod.

An Analysis of Lady Wentworth

The Governor's boutique *Ugliness*,
his baroque *Ugliness*,
mirrors his revolting *Gaudiness*.
His balls and soirées and levées
parade much black-hearted gilt,
much sordid *Glitz*.

In sum, he is such gold-leaf shit.
You could say he's stuffy with *Vanity*
and stuffed up with *Stupidity*
and super-impervious to *Virtue*.

But Lady Wentworth has delicate ankles,
if also sassy *Vulgarity* in dress.

She's mistress of the vinegary *double-entendre*,
suiting her chirpy *Menace*,
her zing and zip.

To enter into Government House
is to smell a rat
and bed the girl,
that picturesque prostitute.

All about her is settee and divan
and ottoman and chaise longue:
Fuck-furniture!

Like all preeminent queans, shady ladies,
she keeps herself immaculately pale—
wedding-cake-white—
a fountain of shimmer:

How I love to spread-eagle
and crackle her chalk self!

But *monsieur le gouverneur*
is a disposable bastard,
a frothing fuddy duddy,
who is rightfully bamboozled and cuckolded,
on oodles of occasions,
by a vivid woman.

Lady Wentworth—
La dama blanca*
with the *oracabessa***—
is a wave of gold,
moving wherever she waves,
thus cleansing the unhappy tarnish
that is her husband.

Yes, she is implacably beautiful,
unrelentingly sinful,
wafting the perfume of the sea.

Ah! To fall in her as moonlight falls on us!

—*William Colley of East Preston*

[**Waterloo (Ontario) 19** *juin* **mmxi**]

---

* Spanish: The white woman.
** Corrupted Spanish: Golden head.

Lady Wentworth Considers Love *(1799)*

I.

Monsieur's monstrous *Lechery*
churns my guts;
retch I, wretched.

When my carriage fords mud-stew streets,
I can sniff my lord's half-breeds—
the char and phosphorous spew
of his salvos of *Adultery*—
the cockeyed *Debacle*
that is each crude "dropping":
his bastards denied dignified births.

Jealousy? Vengeance?

I buy a stocky, rock-necked buck;
claim "Caliban" as my *caliph*.

Let him thrust down the *Lust* that bothers my belly.

Let angular iron perforate
my silken perforation....

(This despoiling wreath
is my thighs' oily heart.)

II.

Gov'nor Wentworth dolls me in mink.
I prefer *Nudity*; it suits *Debauchery*.

I need one heck of a lecher—
a warlock that can do *Witchcraft*;

I want *coitus* that is *Statecraft*:
I hate the waste that's posthumous *Beauty*.

III.

Any squeaky-clean lad's a dud.
I like a black who's fun to foop!

Let us swim—
crotch to snout.

Lying upon him, nailed to him,
I'm a replica messiah.

My dribbling pelvis baptizes him—
even as I'm baptized.

When we twine, *zebra*
rhymes with *Scotia*.

[**Dartmouth & Enfield (Nova Scotia)** 5 *février* **mmxi**]

Eyeing Lady Wentworth's Rival

Either a full-dress Venus
or a Botticelli-bronzen nude,
she be the Governor's lover.

Usually, when he's 'wifed'—
one hears the mumbles
and rumbles of a stable.

Her skin has snap and sparkle,
and probable, milky give,
whenever she's manned.

Often her lover's this smooth Negro—
as efficient as a horse.

She issues from a Caribbean cellar
as a Chigress,*
who has a mare's guts—
readily randy,
bandy-legged,
and never as dingy as a pudding.

In the Guv'nor's brackish bed,
he soils incomparable sable gals,
frisks those risqué demoiselles.

Black like me.

—William Colley of East Preston

[Ottawa (Ontario) & Hull-Gatineau (Québec)
11 *juin* MM & 11]

---

* Caribbean English: Half-Chinese Negress.

Abraham of the Seminoles: A History

I.

"Black Steel," the seminal Seminole,
light gone gritty—

swishing through pine branches,
sloshing through beach froth—

knifing from coastal Carolina,
insurgent through Georgia,

hefting a rifle like a black icicle,
come the juju guerrilla,

scrabbling outta debris of shacks,
run-down huts,

to sniper pale interlopers,
dyin to snatch up Florida,

put russet skin in graves,
put licorice skin in chains.

II.

Abraham—"Black Seminole"—Chief,
prosecutin the Second Seminole War—

1835–42—
rampage outta Georgia rice swamp,

into malarial Florida—
jungle cemetery—

Spaniards schemed to fortress
(to flout *Yanqui* imperialists,

gunning for Mexico and further south).
Borne was he from Gullah ex-slaves,

spliced with Redskin renegades,
who slipped overseers,

patrollers, masters,
the serial sprigs of whip marks,

and so donned liquid-quick boots
to high-step through pudding-thick swamp,

labyrinth of trees and rice,
and plant mini republics—

thatched-roof Gullah homes
upheld by corn, rice, fish,

tasty critters, and a civics
of callaloo and mash-up:

Gullahs garb like Seminoles;
field hollers turn to yodelling;

Seminoles sample Gullah song
and banjo striking

and gumbo—rice, fish, snake,
jumbled possum, corn, tobacco.

III.

Black Seminoles had smart brawn,
knew how to tug rice

outta gator water;
knew how to keep niggers and injuns

safe from claws of Anglo-Saxon Axis,
and taught *Offense*:

how to be as possessive as a tick
of swamp acres;

how to navigate in galoshes,
sneak up on a snow-skin,

axe him down to a pink pulp,
a ruddy core;

how to be as intangible as smoke,
but as disfiguring as gators;

how to leave the foe in sunlight
that's totally maggots.

IV.

Thus, Gullahs & Seminoles eloped, whelped chillun,
all cross northern Florida,

their edenic Canaan,
swept it free of yinkyank sadists,

who dubbed the Original Floridians
"Seminoles,"

a word conjured outta *cimarrón*—
Spanish declaring "untamed."

The Free Gullahs became Negro Seminoles,
primed to kill-for-keeps to safekeep their *Liberty*!

V.

Gen'ral Andy Jackson thrust the Yank frontier south,
1818, into Florida,

sparking cannon-*versus*-arrow *War.*
Black-and-Red Seminoles sally—uniform—*versus* uniformed whites:

See black, auburn backs
backed up against ocean waves,

rolling like logs, incessant....
Driven ever further south,

compelled by genocidal rifle and shot,
the Seminoles recluse in extra-dismal swamp.

Prez Jackson detests this "Indian and Negro War,"
so a *Truce* (not *Peace*)

is fixed up, but crumbles in 1835.
Once Seminole War the Second outbreaks,

1,500 Yank troops perish over six years,
cut down by "Rather-see-my-grave-than-live-a-slave"

Seminoles, relishing dying, fighting, rather than ever being
bullwhipped again.

Gen'ral Jesup warned the War Department:
"This Negro War saps, bleeds,

the entire soldiery of The Republic:
we cannot take Sambo Injuns alive,

for they will not be captives,
and if they could be sent as slaves

to Georgia or the Carolinas, would prove
inevitably an army of Nat Turners."

VI.

Encircled, then conceding *Capture*,
the Seminoles got slogged to "Indian Territory,"

the yet-unconquered West,
where they were made thralls

to slaveholding Creeks.
By 1850, the Red-and-Black folks,

slipped chains, exited to Texas
and North Mexico, to regain *Libertad*,

republican and green-thumbed,
agrarian and green-laurelled.

Come 1855, Texas Rangers maraud into
Mexico to shoot-down or shackle Seminoles,

but are shot to pieces,
so the "bandits" vamoose;

but, shaken, the Red Seminoles
relocate to Oklahoma,

while the Black Seminoles
stick to Mexico—

still speaking Gullah,
still seasoning rice with okra.

VII.

"Black Steel" Abraham liked a pint
and then to piss it all out,

don a fur hat,
go into the fens,

to sluice white troops pus and bile,
so they'd drown in scum;

or jam a blade into bemedalled ribs,
or ram an axe into skulls,

or fire his rifle and tear off pink lips,
so faces melted, slurping their own gore.

He'd even stick his gun barrel
in his own stinking shit,

to infect every whiteface he shot
with wasting disease, if not outright death.

He torched every European cart and wagon;
he poured his slop pail into their booze barrels;

he'd turn a company mess
into a pig sty.

The sable, copper guerrilla was a bog devil,
a nasty, dreadful will-o-wisp,

a marathon pond runner,
swishing through weedy slush.

He was a black mambo water moccasin
assassin with steel-blade fangs,

venom like frost in his veins,
and sneaky as a virus.

Abe is amazing because the swamp
is a maze,

and slain whites show off
fluorescent guts

or wear green, slimy panties,
or have tongues like dead socks.

Those pestered by pestilence (gnawing like vermin)
cry like bugs:

They have to use sinister fabric—
torn pieces of Old Glory—

as bandages.
"Father Abraham" is like "General Moses,"

a dervish in buckskin.
"Black Steel"—Souanaffe Tustenukke—

renders Americans *Terrorism*
for *Terrorism*....

[Hull/Gatineau (Québec) 22 *février* mmxv]

A Treatise on African Theology

By William Stairs[*]

Th'Afro'd god's portly, jolly–
scabby, flabby, crabby, gabby–
a cross twixt Uncle Tom and Santa,
pleased-to-tears with his jokes—
a crapulent crop—
conveys a blackness one may extrapolate
from pungent black ink itself,
an exponentially multiplying blackness,
because th'African deity
loveth *Geometry*—
the curves and angles of that darkly signifying skin
(plangently, not tangentially, black).

Venom-tongued, this god,
when not jetting immedicable poison,
ejaculates ebony giggles,
and blesses Oriental *Devilry*
like that of Cleopatra—
panting and gasping
as she dug needles into her slavegirls' dugs,
thus rendering *Torture*
an occasion for tantalizing *Metaphysics*.

The black god espouses
talky, gustatory spleen,
and riles up easy,

---

[*] William G. Stairs teamed with Stanley on his second, disastrous Congo expedition. The Nova Scotian (British) imperialist likely raped African women, but definitely murdered African men. See *African Exploits: The Diaries of William Stairs, 1887–1892*, edited by Hon. Roy MacLaren.

so his reputation is nasty,
and he applauds *Treachery*
as others clap for dirty jokes.

He weareth a waspish aspect,
shows an aspish posture,
assassinates saints sassily,
purples night with wine, dyes sunlight with blood,
and prefers midwives be pallbearers.

His Africa is a *rue Morgue* province,
a dung empire,
a backward El Dorado
(where gold is just tarted-up lead),
a scalding, mosquito'd miasma.

As crooked as a labyrinth,
this god will maul any brain, spoil any spine,
slather angels in dung,
guffaw through crows' caws,
and liquidate villages with laughing *Slaughter*.

He is so brutish, so abominably unclean,
that rankest muck is whitewash to his ilk.

This god adores odious, injurious tricks,
accepts no temperance in such "entertainment."

His chuckles quake his Buddha belly—
that jug of Bordeaux and *boudin*—
and his big mouth, liver-lipped,
shines with blood like red piss.

His glance drills one like lightning.
His eyes are incinerating torches.
His damned face—murky caramel—hosts flies.
His squawk—not *Speech*—celebrates
Damnation as if it's funky, a gag.

Not a cherub, a butcher,
and no better than an enraged dog,
this concocted exotic,
as atavistic as an anthropologist,
situates *Genius* in the gut.
His Gospel is plagues.

Carnivorous, but addicted to *Coprophagy*,
this kaffir deity,
titan of *Turpitude*,
grants Africa's humongous flies
molasses-sweet massacres.

(African politics is parody—
Comedy blacked up, tricked out, as *Tragedy*,
or *Atavistic Theology*).

This Ethiope god?

Imagine a toga'd goat (goateed too),
or a creature as nude as a newborn—
or a corpse—
a sable type of Priapus,
with a nappy, dissipated pate.
Consider him an "it"—
so awfully a superior fraud,
a cartoon nemesis,
a sooty idol,
with a gristle tongue—
grisly, drooling.

This mixed-up monster,
crafty artifact,
maggot mascot,
is plump, plum-coloured,
and statue-sterile.

Call him—"It"—a *papier-mâché* fetish,
a pastoral, "palm-wine drunkard,"*
but brutal,
with a pitchfork temperament.

A Muse for indecipherable jumble,
his worshippers mumble.

They believe his breath giveth life even to dust,
and so endorse *coitus* as a festive ooze.

So they regale themselves with frolics,
forego fabrics,
help themselves to songs,
notations of kisses,
and their music assumes thunder's rhythm.

All their scriptures (so to speak)—
reek of *Sex*,
stink with it,
and, in their worship, they writhe like obscene snakes.

(Their songs are uncouth versions of *Priapeia*,
those filthy Latin poems picturing the male organ
as a big stick.)

Hearing their polymorphous mouths jabber,
I plunge to my wits' end.
They don't cogitate, they cavort.

The charcoal theologians are just glorified
(peacock feathered) *maquereaux*,
stewards of bawdy chapel or pub.
For them, their dicey deity
is profitably lenient,
allowing them the gleanings of all surplus *Scarcity*—

---

* Amos Tutuola, *The Palm-Wine Drinkard*.

manure windfalls,
gold strikes,
a daily gallon of palm wine.

The mahogany-coloured warlocks vaunt
a *Chieftaincy* based on *Forage*:
their god struts—like a cock—in snakeskin,
claws eyes with blisters,
pecks bodies with sores,
chews up bowels with rheums....

Th'Ethiope *philosophes* know
their god's peoples, lazy,
are late to plant, late to harvest,
slave themselves to grog,
"grass" (screw) at will,
scoff at civil scruples,
think songs cancel curses,
dance, and cut hogs' throats
(to quaff the steamy blood)
in asinine *Republicanism*.

Still, they pen and fold the ruminants—
the remnants of uncooked birds—
with each animal's *Extinction*,
and eventual rendering
as a fugitive perfume
to pleasure their buck-toothed god's flared nostrils.

(Ethiopian aroma
combines chocolate and coffee.)

We Europeans expunge an olfactory *Faith*,
a heresy that fuses two unlikely things—
kitchen (okay) and bedroom (blessing),
that locates *Good* in the gut,
that sanctifies *Sex*.

Indeed, "A-Freak-an" *Theology*
proclaims our Bible a libel,
unless we decide their "god"
is kin to brother-slaying Cain;
alcoholic, daughter-tupping Lot;
dandy, roué David (poet);
wrathful, homicidal Moses;
duplicitous, tricky Joseph;
sex-idolizing Solomon;
peeping, backbiting Ham;
and Greco-Roman abortionists.

But let us see ourselves aright:
Our *Deus* is Sade?

(Each father's *Sin* becomes each child's *Sorrow*,
and their works never scale from *Craft* to *Art*.)

The natives' prayers sound like tempests,
I mean, the growls and howls of beasts.
Their equal, in imagery, is stained glass,
streaked by pigeon guano and gull crud.

Those dialects of cries, groans—
Africa slutting, demoralizing, English
(the mouth is an irregular crevice),
vent perfect pollution:
prayers that are hissing cyphers
and song that spreads like an epidemic,
crazing or collapsing soldiers,
and poisoning lethally our lethal *White Rule*.

The onyx ogres blab a detestable babble,
to praise (or abuse) a deity
whose highest skills
are *Devouring* and *Defecation*,
and whose epic *Lassitude*
encrusts him (it) in dust.

Here in Congo, meaty tongues uplift in shrieks,
so sweaty, off-colour and off-kilter faces
salute their "Xango" (or whatever),
his landscape of pyres,
excrement-dirtied martyrs,
while dull flames palsy
the palsying darkness.

(This catastrophic *Race* okays
the *Death Sentence* that is every birth.)

Survey their Zombie shuffle
about their desultory campfires
and their dull idol;
watch Golliwog loins lurch,
jigaboo faces strike quirky poses,
tarbaby bodies go rubbery....
Each believer accepts a seizure,
scolds the stars in animal tongues,
until the dance breaks up,
shatters,
and pairs commit male-female *Malefaction*.

Here in Africa, the Congo,
"Christian" church-going is impossible:
Black breasts and buttocks won't fix as immobile,
deny *Love*'s pliable *Frenzy*.

But black is not only a colour;
it is arresting, but not chaste.

Deeper than dark is black,
and pulsing,
amorous, violent.

Seduced by Satan in these tropics,
we white men stake—rake—sable pelts;

thus, our only *Salvation*
is to hatchet black men's heads,
plant them on picket fence posts
about our encampments—

missionary, educational,

civilizing.

Wm G. Stairs—
A "King Congo" Haligonian—
1890

[Halifax (Nova Scotia) **8** *avril* **2008**]

SKETCH OF LIFE OF REV. RICHARD PRESTON, D.D.

1816 to 1832

Pertinent Personages of this Passage...

Johnn Burton (Forerunner to Preston)

Septimus Clarke (Secretary to Preston)

Rita Cunard (English Lover of Preston)

Lord Dalhousie (Governor of Nova Scotia, 1816–1820)

Thomas Chandler Haliburton (Antichrist)

Pearl Olivier (Africadian Historian)

Richard Preston (Founder of the Africadian Baptist Association)

From the Loyalists to John Burton*

Twelve-hundred yelled, "Damn thee well / Go to Hell,
Halifax!" And the flowers of the Black
Citoyens, nevermore to live like slaves,
Keelhauled Atlantic waves to reach Freetown
Beach, Sierra Leone, though 65
Cadavers plumped up sharks. How apt our song,
"Many Thousands Gone": En route to Canaan....

Next, 600 Maroons banded—stranded—
In Scotia, as Jamaican guerillas,
In 1796. They condemned
The cold, the Caucasians, the crops, the chills,
And petitioned to be *"viraged"* also
To Sierra Leone. 1800
Witnessed their odyssey to Africa,
Though they left behind Governor Wentworth's
Brown papooses—the Colley clan (so-dubbed),
And pickneys Ochterloney—*Bastard!*—sired.

The Coloured folk remaining had no choice
But to squat on scraggly lots—either swamp
Or stony, skinflint-tight, miserable,
Good for nothing, and so the people—blamed—
For not being able to farm, got scolded
As being "Good for nothin but *Slavery*":
Neither agricultural (pastoral)
Nor permitted to fish, they became "fools,"
"Ragamuffins," "pickaninnies," and "thieves";
They were "welfare cases" and "mental cases,"
"Basket cases" and "criminal cases";
They had "cotton-pickin" hands and "wooly

---

* Cf. Oliver, *History of the Colored Baptists of Nova Scotia.*

Noggins," "black asses," "flat feet," and "big lips";
They had no letters but the crude, wooden
X's punched atop anonymous graves,
Soon to become—blight-poxed—potato fields!

     Worse: The outsized Loyalist Exodus
Of 1792, the Maroon
Defection of 1800, exposed
The Baptist Church to *Depopulation*!
Congregations, from kneeling, stood—and sailed,
Trekking to the Boston States, refusing
To starve in [God-damned] "Nova Scarcity."

     Enter John Burton, once an Anglican,
But Baptist turned, and then the sole Baptist
In Halifax, 1794.
English exile, he started baptizin
Converts at the harbour, and was able
To materialize a Baptist church
The next year: By 1795.

     Burton dunked Negroes—freely, equally—
As he splashed down Caucasians. Soon, his church
Swelled with Coloureds and all down-dashed "white trash"
(Drunks, sluts, the poor, Jack Tars, robbers, and thieves,
Recidivists, pickpockets, "mongoloids"),
Who believed that belief in *Redemption*
Would redeem em from all circumstances
(Unto the scarlet squeak or screech or squeal
Of a bloodied martyr's bloody last breath).

     Once the Black Refugees dunked anchor,
Exited 1812-War Man-o-Wars,
"Father Burton" (the moniker bestowed
By Black Baptists), roved among the exiles
From the "Hateful States," to preach and christen
And baptize and marry and to bury.
He solicited governmental *Aid*,

Given with slurs, curses; twas begrudging,
Judgmental, curmudgeonly, embittered,
Intermittent, stingy, crabby, and foul.

       Father Burton witnessed Father Preston
Hunker in Halifax, and fast enough
Assemble Africadian Baptists
Into congregations segregated
From white folks by white choice. So, Burton's church
Died out. It seems that Preston's Cornwallis
Street Baptist Church had hollowed out Burton's,
So Preston's emerged—like a butterfly
Flitting out a split-apart chrysalis
(A metaphor for Burton's "mother" church).

       The collage or mosaic poetics
Of his preaching—his thinking never
Ever denied that Black Loyalists could
Be declared "the crème-de-la-*Résistance*"
To *White Supremacy*. Nevertheless,
"The chemistry of April—snow transformed
To chlorophyll—does suit ye castaways—
Ex-slave Refugees—who've leagued in churches
Of your own design; who could be Midas
Many times over if boulders and swamps
Could be as negotiable as gardens
And orchards!" That sermon was plain, simple.
Yet, if *Love* is crossed-wires—*Electrocution*—
A shock, so could Burton electrify—
Frankenstein-piece-together—broken souls,
The shabby, ramshackle, shambling Xns,
And re-animate em as African
Baptists, bracing em with every embrace....

       Every Burton sermon seemed translation
Of *Inspiration*—transmuted, unmuted
Language, a distillation of *Debate*.
He'd warn would-be Believers, "God loves you,

Your being, but loathes your behaviour!" Every
Sermon was *librissimi*, arousing
Black-bottom congregants' reciprocal
Vocals, chaotic melisma, shouts, howls,
Hollers, as he'd inveigh against oily
Politicos, their greasy, lubricious
Latin. "Heart-attack telegrams," he'd voice,
To condemn the "lethal architecture"
That's courts and legislatures, capable
Of succumbing to *Corruption*, that *Rot*,
And crumbling accordingly. For Burton,
The Xn is rock, but the core's magma,
And that fire is what charges the whole corps.
(In contrast, *Baptism* necessitates
Suicidal rain, depth-diving waterfalls,
Fountaining jets. The feast table is dressed
With Danish blue cheese, mackerel, olives,
Brown bread, Macedonian feta cheese,
Pears, peaches, plums, milk, coffee, tea, or iced
Water, and meat can be chicken, turkey.)

—*Pearl Olivier, Historian*

[Halifax (Nova Scotia) 11 *décembre* mmxix]

*The Arrival of Richard Preston**

Came two-thousand and twenty-six exiles—
"Black Refugees," to "New Darkness" (*Nova
Scotia*—Englished outta Latinized Greek),
Between 1812 and 1815.
"War booty," they were, Brit troop-seized from fields
To deprive Yank foes of butchers and cooks,
To starve Uncle Sam into kowtowing
To John Bull. Landed in N.S., the Black
Refugees—pitiful poor—learned to fear
Ice and frost and blizzard, not only God.
Granted land that sprouts only stubble, thorns,
And burrs, and never grain nor grape nor meal,
They succumbed—by scores—to numbing, Arctic
Degrees, either starving or freezing, but
Dying of one or the other or both.
And having no store or stock of summer greens
Or root cellars, the heavy snows heaved sums
Into summide, summary graves, sunken
Under blanking out shrouds, pale erasures....

They'd held true Vice-Admiral Alex Cochrane
Who'd pledged that, accepting British transport,
The now ex-slaves would be a free people
In British realms, where "due *Encouragement*"
Would allot em plots that'd let em flourish
And nourish righteously body and soul.
But, no. The "Promised Land" was mist-on-strand
Of marsh or stone, a discouraging *Waste*....

---

* Cf. Oliver, *History of the Colored Baptists of Nova Scotia*.

One Refugee mama bawled bitterly,
Howled incessantly, to see once more
Her son, she'd abandoned in Virginia
When quitting *Slavery*. Could *Reunion*
Of mom-and-child be effected, ever,
Especially in Nova Scotia? Well,
God overlooks zero to satisfy
The heart! So, by 1816, with blacks
Docking in droves (most with souls bedraggled
Like their shoe soles) in Halifax, scrounging
A nook or niche for a chapel or shack
At Bedford Basin or in Micmac woods,
One singular ex-slave, Preston, ship-stalled
In Halifax, to search for his mother,
Had measured miniscule Nova Scotia
As "Canada," not yet realizing
That Nova Scotia is but an atom
In the galaxy that is Canada.
Yet, needing to commence his quest, Preston
Selected cheek-by-jowl Preston village,
Echoing poetically his surname.

After his dreary, weary, wracking trek
To Preston, Richard made tracks for shelter
As darkness locked down clocks at eve. Chancing
To clunk-clunk a modest door, Preston heard
A shuffling step, saw a curtain shifting,
A woman peeped his way. The door got cleft,
But she dreaded letting a lad, solo,
Bunk—or hunker—in her solitary
Estate, and the lady implored Preston
To forage elsewhere his pillow
And tea, porridge and heat. Yet, as the youth,
Turned away, turned away toward the night,
Discouraged, with no entourage but stars,
His scarred visage flared in the lamplight
The chatelaine suspended. She gasped, asked,
"Speak your surname." "Preston," he told. "The same

Title as this township," and a shriek hurled
From the madame! She beheld now her son,
Returned to her—as she had prayed—and on
His "Canada" debut—in Halifax!
Unquestionably a miracle'd dawned!
Unquestionably God-spawned! Two kin fawned.
Boundless now was *Faith*—refreshed—found: *Baptist*!

—*Pearl Olivier, Historian*

[London—LHR (UK) & Oslo (NO)
17 *décembre* mmxix]

What the Refugees Thought and/or Think*

The ex-slaves and Black Refugees pictured
Canada an Asgard of beaver, bear,
Bull-moose, salmon, trout, mackerel, 10 percent-
Alcohol beer (*svartekunst***), or Dixie @
Xmas, just slightly chilled, with plenty snow
To give Santa traction to toss off gifts.
They dubbed Canada "Bermuda"—a grove
Of frosty palms—whose icicles drip vodka.
(The *svartekunst* distills tar, but tastes as strong
As licorice.) Corinthians 13
Proves *Love's* roadmap through bog and bush and brush,
Muskeg and scrag. The exiled Black Yankees
Quiver restless Afros as each preacher
Emotes, quoting black letters or red,
Swishing befitting *Haberdashery*—
Black robe, black cape, a black-saddled sable,
Black boots—stirrups stirring the giddyup,
While the white collar gleams—pristine against
Black, polished skin, and drops starshine on black
Manes of black-hide horses. The ex-Dixie
Ex-slaves hypothesized that Canada
Duplicates Utopia so that pine trees
Aspire here to be palms. How could they know
Canaan's a place where buffalo—hooves rushed,
Stampeded, over cliffs—end as snapped legs,
Smashed skulls, smucked bones, at the hard-ass bottom?
They did invent their preachers as mechanics,
Geared to repair tear-warped theologies,
Or hiccough-dented, or sob-rusted-out

---

* Cf. Oliver, *History of the Colored Baptists of Nova Scotia*.
** Norwegian: Dark Arts. The ale tastes of coffee, chocolate, licorice, and blackberries.

Tinny prayers (the sound of bards holding down
Public office, always commandeering
The guillotine, always first to demand
Excommunication of their rivals,
Only to feel their own necks truncated).
Thus, the exiles sought to avoid the loud,
Drivelling, snivelling queue to Purgatory,
And *Go* directly to pastures and shacks
Where the sun flaunts the shade of ripe gamboge
And Hebrew characters shadow every
English letter, and iced Champagne disguised
As glacier water courses and nurses
The gut and pulse, and where swans are groupies
And winds cancel the sulphurous speeches
Of pamphleteers, irregardless of their
Irreligious or irrelevant screeds,
Paragraph after paragraph, driving
Their foul brimstone back at em, whiff on whiff.
Where else would *Salvation*'s thrill not recede,
Not evaporate, but Nova Scotia?
Where else, after nightfall, would spouses, wed,
Not blush to be naked? Where else is bread
Or manna potage? Where else can you draw
Pen-knife and carve out your name in a book?
Where else is *Realism* so uplifting?
Where else is *Capital* pure maple syrup?
Where else does the King castigate slavers
By setting fire to their soles, while razors
Flog their whimpering, sopping faces?
To where else could Black Refugees seek homes,
And not look back, save with Osborne's* *Outrage*?

—*Pearl Olivier, Historian*

[Oslo (NO) 18 *décembre* mmxix]

---

* Or Oswald's. Cf. King Lear.

Richard Preston, "Apostle to the African Race," Lands in Nova Scotia (1816)

I.

The late war—
1812–15—

a bio out of *Butchery*—

let me slip chains
for the sea,

to make waves....

(The Atlantic equals a liquid Caesar—
a fluid imperialism.)

II.

Arrived, I hear the xenophobes proclaim,
"*Our* Nova Scotia
is not your Nova Scotia."

I agree:

Ma *Nofaskosha*
ain't yo "Novice Scotia."*

---

* Cf. Kerouac, *Mexico City Blues*.

III.

In Haligonian streets,
possibilities get priced in pounds;
doubts in dollars;

but for Coloureds?
A buck, a pound:
Either sum counts for nothin.

IV.

The Loyalists who boss this colony
look dirty as a dung heap.

Each political preacher
stews in a toilet.

The common cur here
got more fleas than hair.

(*Paradise* is always an illusion—
except for its ruins.)

V.

The Gov'nor carpets his way
with coinage—
minces as he mints—
pausing his coach
only for his predictable
public *Urination*
from his mouth.

(He's proof that colonists reside
in a *Scotia* less *nova* than said.)

Always intoxicated tight to the tips
of his teeth

(he swallows *Happiness*
with his Guinness),

his glossy pallor,

his *Truth* all froth and fog,

befit a bureaucrat
whose pitch-black heart
pumps golden piss
out his latrine-style mouth.

The puffed up, pudding gut—
the urinal priest—
is no misanthrope:
Nope: He's an *anthropophaginian*—
if sporting tassels and spieling Latin.

VI.

History is built on shit,
but bad poets cover up this fact,
pretending that our foundations
are marble or gold.

Luckily, just as *Scripture* says,
Filth shows up.

[Halifax (Nova Scotia) 24 *septembre* mmxi]

The Recent Transit Through Washington, D.C. (1816)

Everybody's a fugitive in that city—
so clanging be the alarms,
clamour of sirens, chimes;
with cops eyeing sharpshooters on roofs;
constant loom threats bulls-eyein the Prez'dent.

Nervous city, galling city:
White marble sluicing blood.

Editorials holler *War!*
versus England or Spain
(either target's sport for *Profiteering*).

Pages, imprinted, can be like mud:
downsucking each forward plod.

Cloudy is the tap water;
malaria rises, insurgent, out the miasma
that's the Potomac.

Congress? So many bow-tied mannequins
lying straight out their lungs.
An injurious winter freezes their postures—
prostrate, supine, crucified.

(Lookit! Washington, a king minus a crown,
was an inhuman monarch,
odious as the crowned skulls of Europe.)

I seened the white derelicts lickin caviar
outta dumpsters;
the pig-faced whores, civil as devils,
cocksuckin makin em hoarse;
the homeless waifs bedding down on cardboard
outside the burnt-shell
of the Brit-torched Congress.

Gunshots outnumber flu shots, natch.

Guns are more plentiful—and beloved—
than be the Bible.

(Even priests brandish outlandish cannons here!)

White-marble "chocolate city"—
centre of orgies of centaurs and nuns—
bulls and bitches:
Snuffling and scuffling in bed,
each midnight;

Here *Faith* is always goin down-grade,
for *Evil* can't be rinsed away,
unlike watercolours.

Here *Cannibalism* is synonymous with *Candour.*

Here the murders of "niggers" just vanish.

I see my bushman's blood gush red
into black type—

my cast(e)—
my ruthless dye....

My problem is, I recall the phantom slaves—
that touch of smoke upon the Potomac,
that historians paper over with gilt.
My brittle treble
troubles the resonant glaze of ink.

But ya need dark-yellow tequila
and a brazen, brass trumpet
to wipe away piss-yellow journalism.

(*Civilization* is exacting,
but America is only merely playacting
at *Civility*.)

[Washington (District of Columbia)
31 *décembre* mm
& Berlin (Germany) 8 & 9 *mars* mmxiii
& Tropea (Italia) 6 *juin* mmxviii]

Preston Remembers

"Massa's beard was both napkin and toilet.
No virgin, wife, or mother, could be safe
From his tapping, or milking, or drilling....
And so my mama—with my aid—crept off,
And I did not expect to view her next
Until both of us havened in Heaven.

"Betwixt Nova Scotia and Virginia,
Every inch of Atlantic was hostile—
Brit battleships—sails white and cannons black—
Were spewing shot, flames, and raiding parties
(Marines). The waves drove haywire with *Havoc*,
So scum included scalps, the briny spume
Looked pink Himalay'n-salted, due to blood....

"The ship upon which my bow and keel dipped,
Skippered me away from *Slavehood*. Angel-sped,
I got spirited away, exiting
The "Hateful States," like a newborn ent'ring
Either the world or the haven of saved
Souls—the Church. Honest as nothing else is—
Is the Freed Believer, and, as such,
I crossed frost-crusted Atlantic, wave-blistered pools,
My prayers drowning—marinated—in tears,
Or wallowing in tea, until timber
And canvas swum upon the pale, soft foam,
Arrowing from our bow, so pointedly
Curvaceous, and we thus trajectory'd
Into Halifax harbour. I shouted–
Being delivered unto *Liberty*!

"Yet I was as skinny as a kitten,
When the Atlantic resolved to dissolve
Into the harbour opening. Disembarked,

I yearned for meal, a fire, a bed, a roof,
Then seek a wage on the morrow. Hearing
Of Preston, a village with my own surname,
I loped, lanky, the ten miles (o'er three hours),
Out to the Coloured principality.
Its echo of my name was, I trusted,
Coincidence—Illusion—and I could
Expect no *Miracle*. Still, alluring,
Was the locale, and I was curious
To take up residence, if lodging was—
If food and drink were, if church and work were—
Available, with no puttering bout,
No mouldering, no tear-sopping boozing,
No dissolution, no worry for meat,
No shuddering at sight of whips (their sheer,
Slashing, scalding, searing, hot *Agony*)....

     "Arriving at night,* it was so dark, I
Knew clearly that few would let a stranger
Broach their thresholds. My rap clapped many doors,
Then hush would mute voices within, candles
Would snuff, and inhabitants act asleep;
Or a rude snort would ask *Expenditure*
I couldn't satisfy, or grumps, grunts, dog growls,
Would warn me, "Trespassing ends at the grave."
However, just as I planned to shiver
Away the night in grass and dew or frost,
I tapped one last door, and a lady came
To inspect this petitioner, but quick
To say she had no room. I thought of X—
His parents, shelterless at Bethlehem,
His birth in a barn, and I dredged the *Grace*
To thank her for her trouble, and I turned
Away, to hide my heated tears, as night's
Foreboding chill seemed suddenly deathly
Colder. But, as I lurched to leave, the dame's
Lantern swung high enough that she could eye

---

* Cf. Christopher Levenson.

The whip scar scoring my face, and she cried,
"Praise God! My son, Richard!" And I turned back,
My tears—now scalding hot like a fireplace
Joyous with roasting meat or steaming stew—
And we—mother and child—held *Reunion*
Miraculous—on my first day ashore
In Nova Scotia.

       "But hadn't I had
Miracles already? To slip the yoke
Of *Sin* and *Slavery*, to kick aside
Shackle and fetter, to escape by wood
And wind cross water, to toss in timbers—
A vessel—to reach a subtle landing,
Withdrawn from Virginia, liberated!

       "Yet, how could I expect to be valiant
Enough to become a gala hero
To Scotians, to be a retro Xian—
Like Greeks and Hebrews and Romans? Or treat
Disciples to milk and honey, no rum,
No madeira, no sherry? Or afford
Th'Africadians a secretariat
(with Mr. Septimus Clarke as First Clerk)
For our own Church, after I docked, quitting
That big ocean—that frieze fluting and splaying
Light—while the boat skimmed disembodied foam
(And gales hammered gulls down into the surf
The brusque, husky waves, so their wings caught, dragged,
As if their feathers were lichened with spume,
Until they could wrench free—by inches—up
Out the liquid brambles), after I passed
The exams of the West London Baptists
And could voyage home from England to N.S.—
With my Divinity Degree—to preach
And muster and baptize and birth a church?"

[Oslo (NO) 18 *décembre* mmxix]

A Chronicle of the Lord's First Africadian Miracle Affecting Richard Preston

Funny thing: When I landed here,
a year and a half back,
I was homeless.
But I told folks my surname;
they directed me out
to a site of *Desolation* plus beautifying—
where the settlers call their rudimentary gardens
and huts—
my family name, "Preston."
Coincidence? No: *Miracle*!

I set knuckles to crude, flimsy doors,
boards and nails hardly able to block a breeze,
but no one would requisition a room.
I thought I'd bed down under the stars,
under a pine,
beside wispy flames warring with wind,
when I come to the last house in the last of the light.
Rattled the door as my fist thudded.
Old, grey woman loomed and beamed a lamp:
She eyed me; said, she, too, had no bed.
A tear started as I started away.
Then, she said. "Wait!"
She fingered the starry scar on my cheek:

Asked, "You know the Bull Styron plantation?"

I told about Tidewater and my sold-off mama,
and we both fell to our knees, weeping,
for we knew, instantly, that she was my mom
and I was her son.

[Cambridge (Massachusetts) cf. "Settling Africville"
mmxiii-mmxiv]

*What Preston Found**

Disbarked Preston to discover Scotians—
Africadians—huddled in Halifax
(And on outskirts @ Campbell Road), Preston,
Dartmouth, Cow Bay, Porter's Lake, Windsor Plains,
Refugee Hill (Northwest Arm, Halifax),
Shubenacadie, Cobequid Road, Beech Hill,
Fletcher's Lake, Prospect Road, Guysborough Road,
And Musquodoboit Road. Among far-flung
Redoubts—white villages, waysides, and towns
(Bossed by Yankee farmers, ex-Dixiecrats,
South Shore German fishers, the Brit Army-
Naval aristocracy pulling rank
In Halifax), Father Burton knelt, prayed,
Preaching and baptizing, but already
Recognized Preston as a radiant
Believer, and charismatic in stance,
And catalyzing in his eloquence
(No equal—and no equivocation).
And so Burton mentored Preston to plant
Grass-roots churches—a right-on-time preacher!

   Smallpox was pandemic among Preston
Negroes, but the legislature coughed up
500 £ to urge solitary,
Midnight, hurried burials, wherever
Trenches could be carved out, a corpse flopped down,
The shallow rent back-stopped by shale and topped
By soil: The disposable sick: Potted.

   Yet, Governor Dalhousie had lauded
(1817) every Preston "shade
Or darky" as exhibiting "the deft

---

* Cf. Oliver, *History of the Colored Baptists of Nova Scotia.*

Industry of macabre, gigantic ants,
In shouldering boulders, clutching fencing,
Hefting, heaving, hoeing, sowing, planting;
Then mushrooming huts, architecting homes,
Where *Nature* should be insurmountable—
Being marshy swamp and/or recalcitrant stone—
And white settlers profiteering, gouging,
Overcharging for everything, cheating,
Because the blacks' digits are their audits—
Their fingers are their sole calculators—
And *'Debt'* is an invisible abyss."

      One dauntless Refugee was Septimus—
"Seventh Son"—Clarke, who ploughed well 10 acres—
But feeble topsoil got exhausted fast.
Clarke petitioned the governors for more
Acres—Two hundred fifty—and secured
100. But sheer *Survival* required
100 acres, let alone *Profit*
Or *Surfeit*. Legislators already
Knew Negro *Self-Sufficiency* could not
Be gained unless each family could farm
100 acres. So the barren lands
Allotted were intended to coerce
The Blacks to either quit Nova Scotia
Or stay and starve, thus taking the worse jobs
For the least income, or having to bow
And scrape for hand-outs, or become almost
Again slaves, to sweat lakes for meagre coin.
Indeed, gove'nors refused the Refugees
Proper lands: Their options? Serve, slave, or starve.
Or accept swift transport to Trinidad.

      But the Scotians hunkered down on their plots,
No matter the *Destitution*, because
For most, they'd never owned anything prior;
And so, bad land was still *some* real-estate,
And so once solitary refugees

Became—now—black neighbours, eager to build
Huts, houses, outhouses, shacks and chapels,
And to huddle and cuddle together,
Liberated from *Slavery*, landed—
With property to call their own, even
Their own children (*theirs*—at last), and they could
Dream now of shared community, a shared
Faith. They were becoming—yes—a people:
The Coloured Baptists! Th'Africadians!

—*Pearl Olivier, Historian*

[Oslo (NO) 18 *décembre* mmxix]

Lord Dalhousie Surveys "Africadia" (1819)

2,000 Negroes in Boston;
1,700 Negroes in Halifax.

Only New England States harbouring
more Negroes than Nova Scotia
are Massachusetts and Connecticut.

The reason?

Nova Scotia's coast hosts
Africans, Americans, Europeans;

and New Scotland ships
shingles, staves, and slaves—

and salt cod
(slave staple)—

to the Caribee

to purchase sugar, salt, molasses,
and rum
and fresh ("seasoned") slaves.

★

We auction niggers on Black Rock Beach
in Halifax,
right beside barrels of brandy.

We dole out whippings—
"wet jobs"—
and grog.

★

Got no use for free blackamoors—
they scat about,
tomcat about,
cut throats by night,
spendthrift and/or snooze by day,
layabout,
straining the Treasury's *Charity*.

Worse, the Dixie escapees
run disloyal to masters
and dissident to monks,
and seem a brood of seditious,
whiny brats.

No wonder the Refugee Negroes
exercise purely the right
to starve!

What "Promised Land" springs up
on shale, granite, gypsum, and spruce—
unless one ploughs up stones,
fells pines, maples,
and sets to planting, seeding?

"Yep" (as Yankees say),
it be as hard to digest the kaffirs
as it is hard to digest coal.

An accursed, demonic lot!

Mice chewed up their first, stubbled crops.

They ganged together in caves
and/or shacks,
never proof'd gainst th'elements,
and minus foundations, cellars,
and/or constructed of green branches,
and/or wood maliciously capable
of *Rot*.

They got no wool, no cotton,
and no weavers;
they're bootless, coatless, *sans culottes*,
gloveless, and shoeless.

Maybe mindless
and maybe headless?

Definitely penniless and toothless.

Bare-arsed and bare-headed!

(A naked nigger sugared with snow?
A joke-worthy spectacle!)

They're denuded of wood and stripped of fuel.
Their lands are swamp or stone.

When they don't have potatoes,
they have mosquitoes;
when they don't have ale,
they have ailments

(cholera, grippe, malaria, polio, typhoid,
consumption, belly-gripes, palsy)

enough to exhaust any medical library!

No matter what,
they all got Bibles!

But that blessin does em no good;
is mo a *blessant*....

★

Lookit! Their cannibalistic cabal extolls
sanguinary visions of Christ—
dreams of Jesus splashin His blood
all o'er *Hell* and *Creation*!

★

Gotta pack em all off to Sierra Leone—
or Trinidad!

ASAP!

They're waspish, "yep,"
but they ain't WASPs!

[Florianópolis (Brazil) 19 *juillet* mmxii]

I. The Records of Richard Preston

I.

Halifax—this Venetian backwater—
shrinks from the *al fresco* sea,
openness.

An *Inferno* of rum and opium,
it yields only bones of light,
broken on pebbles,
tangled in seaweed,
mangled in breakers.

White gulls screech grey ruin
over the foam-scourged beach,
the *Waste*.

Provincial is Halifax,
and its Baptists mere backwash
(hogwash)
of London's ocean-striding Believers.

(Each colony is the Empire's cradle and grave:
Shakespeare fathers Shakespeare the slave.)

II.

Flinching at sight of Africans
darkening their walnut or cedar pews,
our local, blanching Baptists
dangle before us a Dante Christ—
sallow, yellow, sickly,
in Rembrandt-sombre shadow.

(This sun-blackened Jesus
dies like Beowulf-butchered Grendel.)

These Jimmy-crack-corn-and-I-don't-care nihilists,
Negrophobes and antichrists,
want no truck with Black Refugee idealists,
yet reject any Negro-nursed-up church,
and so yell involuntarily convoluted objections.
They prefer us pickaninnying Caucasian cotton,
to look away, look away, look away,
to bullwhip land,
somewhere over a red, white, and blue,
star-spangled rainbow,
but not to look to X,
not to exercise the hard muscle of *Faith*.

They want to corner off blackness,
head it off,
rope it in,
nail it down,
shut it up,
white it out.

In Nova Scotia,
Theology furnishes theatre.

Here, then, not only is every black—
if Nova Scotian—
an American,
he or she constitutes, *by birth*, the Devil's Party.

Hence, the Haligonian Baptists—
icy in blood,
sulphurous in heart,
eager to play white-face gods in *noir* robes,
carp at us more than they harp.

Sometimes silver-tongued, brown-nosing blackguards,
but often green-eyed, yellow-bellied, purple-faced, raging,
they don a pristine, black-framed whiteness,
claim,
"Adamo ed Eva perdettero il paradiso
*Per aver voluto sapere troppo."**

They pour cold water on our baptisms,
try to stifle our worship,
because we are not eunuchs
or anus-souled Believers.

In our Black-Arts services,
a tambourine bleats like a heart.
"Pass Me Not" starts up.
Mournful trumpets
and brash, brash trombones
promise a Heaven that's nigh—
as if we're on the brink—
ebony us—
of cerulean blue.

And why not?

Against our epoch of *Erasure*,
we raise a song.

[Nantes (France) 26–28 *janvier*
& 4 *février* mmix]

---

* "Adam and Eve lost Paradise / Because they wanted to know too much." *Lo Strano Vizio della Signora Wardh*.

Preston Considers The Black (War of 1812) Refugees

For too many, *Hunger* pressures head,
oppresses heart, suppresses haunch....
The background sniffles?
Echo flu, allergies, TB, pneumonia.
Laughter—giggles even—are funeral *Etiquette*,
for we're grateful that the dead
can abandon *Grief* for *Joy*,
can escape constricting tears
for unrestricted *Song.*

They don't expect any passerby
to go out-of-pocket
to benefit their soup bowls and water glasses;
yet, too many go bony to the gallows,
get well-strangled because so skinny.

Their *Emergency Month*? December!
Children greet no glittery prizes.

Shinier still is coal—
as precious as sunlight.

[Pointe-de-l'Église (Nouvelle-Écosse) 21 *août* mmxxi]

Dalhousie Condemns Preston's Black Refugee Congregants

Preston's voice rollicks shivery with rhythm.
So un-Scottish a New Scottish man:
He cometh to Nova Scotia
to speak back to Bluenosers;
to make history,
and not to study it!

But his watery itinerary—
fugitive voyage to these shores—
is an experiment in *Mischief*,
if he plumb won't understand
Immigration is class warfare:
It's an assault upon the *primo*-landed,
who must be uprooted and robbed
to make way for the *arrivistes*;
or th'already settled must oppress
th'incoming settlers,
render em slaves, servants, serfs.

Check the Original People here
in what they called Megumaage,
in a city they called Chebucto:
the Mi'kmaw—
or "Indians"—
prove perishable
and are already massively obediently dead,
and our scientists intrigue to dig up their graves
and raid their tents,
ship th'artifacts to the British Museum.
And we nab and sack their land,
by treaty synonymous with *Theft*,
and we scalp em if they protest,
axing out their brains if they sob too much.

Now, Preston runs a considerable congregation
of Coloured people.
But we whites won't let his black pioneers muck up
our cemeteries' white bones.

As His Majesty's Governor of Nova Scotia,
I, th'Earl of Dalhousie,
propose we tame Negroes by *Culture*—
Agriculture, silviculture, pisciculture ...

I'll have em eat cold, sparklin snow,
gnaw no grits or greens,
chew no bread or beans,
if they won't break backs
turfin up gypsum
or spadin turds on fields.

If the Black Refugees won't take
the work we have to give,
let em starve
til crows chow down on their bony hides!

Th'outcrops they do work
yield dust and thistles,
inedible mosquitoes, inevitable maggots.
Don't the blackies fail to set roots in slime?

Preston and his ilk think they're as clever as fungi,
as surreptitious as mushrooms,
to cling to this land where they've no roots.

A governor—like me—must be like Confucius:
Put stock in potatoes (not *Poetry*);
balance books even if bellies get upset.
(Anyway, stomach cramps make for dinky coffins.)

Too, I know sailors and slaves make slippery citizens—
unruly as air-strangled cod.
But the noose is an itchy necklace,
and the gallows sits next the auction block
smack dab on the Halifax docks.

[Cambridge (Massachusetts) cf. "Settling Africville"
mmxiii-mmxiv]

The Poetics

I come from pork-and-beans *Gentility*.
Unmentionable roots.
(No perfume of cash!)

My colour is as "coolie" as a copper penny.
A poet's *Complexion*.

I sound to you like a sour preacher,
but my word's as serviceable as gold—
the right sort of coin—
or boisterous poison
or quicksilver—
to upset and sicken
the astringently genteel,
whose evident *Plenty*
renders em as fragile as infants.

To be exact is to be indelicate.
I need to sound crude, yet elegant,
with the discipline of Elder Lightfoot,
Br'er Michaux—
the Negro as Confucius—
who extolls *Salvation*, soulful,
but delivers to mere *hoi polloi* profound positives too:

"Exalt *Splendour*,
but buy land.

"Homestead in *Paradise* later,
camp out in the library now."

That's Gospel for our frontier *Struggle*,
and one I preach—boot-sole earthy, gritty,
bringin dat extraordinary *Freshness*
(no highfalutin thesaurus)—
a tongue epitomizin the lash—
even reachin cross multicoloured seas
(in imperial atlases)
to be *Exacting*.

Can't be no prophet if speech is blurry!
Can't make no bogus assertion!
Nor be as snotty as Coleridge,
as snivelling as Hank Pye!

My sermons must be as definite, pungent,
as unignorable, as stinking pig shit.

Damnation ain't superficial:
The *Law* is oral first,
and then it's ink and iron and fire—
I mean:
Splintery words that bite like fangs.

The wise cuss as they gush their passions!

I must be as radical as Sade.
Vinegar can split stone.

—*Richard Preston*

[Helsinki—Vantaa Airport (Finland) 22/11/12]

Fragmentary

Greyed folks say when David George,
o' South Carolina,
preached in Nova Scotia,
after Washington's *Revolution*,
he got along so far as to set up a church
with a piano in it,
before a pale mob,
outraged
he could baptise a white lady,
broke up the meetin house,
torched every wooden stick,
so what was left of the piano
gave out smoky music, burnt melodies.
what some of us now call "Blues."

(I think that hurt piano still tears up, sobs—
smoke snarled in its lungs.)

[Cambridge (Massachusetts) ?? mmxiv]

Theological

The pews of black churches face
a hanging, blanching "Saviour,"
a dangling, pallid weakling, sort of....

Can't blame any worshipper from wondering,
at eyeing such a fop,
"Will it preach?"

Better to get to the roots,
to find God therein,
in the sap, what nurtures.

Each leaf manufactures light
into sugar:
That's just like *The Bible*!

A human *being*
is only as human
as he/she is humane in the doing.

Our *Religion* tides outta
watery *Cataclysm*—
the fearsome exodus from Africa.

So we baptize the whole body,
call down the *Spirit* thus,
so water turns amniotic fluid—

liquid lightning and sugar,
a satin *Translation*,
galvanizing the body,

so each limb branches up
to light,
while the saints gather bout,

shoutin,
gettin *Happy*,
conjuring *Divinity* outta song.

—*Richard Preston*

[**Nantes (France) 8** *février* **mmix**]

Preston Plays Odysseus

I stroll, survey,
the shattered silver of the strand.
The clattering, rattling pebbles
glisten as if live particles of the moon.

I hear the tide's raucous monologue—
or dialogue;
its almost intolerable *Exuberance*,
or verbose, profuse *Jeremiad*!

Slavery has fashioned me a man of waves
and tides.

We have known such ominous wanderings,
then the silent scream of brands gone cold,
the stamp of some other mortal's *Ownership*,
that priced us as we howled.

(We blacks washed up as scruffy flotsam;
got beached on sand, shells, seaweed,
hissing with surf,
but grating where pebbles begin.)

I like the brine of a brisk breeze—
and ships as shapely as a Catholic cathedral,
but as precision-honed as a Baptist chapel—
the cunning bosom
breasting surf.

Even if the moonlight be dirty,
the surf is weeping snow
that scours even viscous *Ugliness*.

I like each wave's snowy *Effrontery*—
despite the night's concentrated *Gloom,*
or the blank *Grief* that's *History*—

despite *Estrangement* from Africa—
a continental ocean away—

[YHZ—Stanfield International Airport
(Enfield, Nova Scotia) 14 *mai* mmxii]

To England?

That metallic plain of water hides—
shy of its oily veneer—
seaweed tendrils that grapple skeletons—
residue of violent imperatives.

Nova Scotia is shit and whores and dogs—
a governor whose mouth is mud and scotch.
But, *Antiquity*—Rome, London, etc.—
is also garbage.

It's a bumpy existence here.
Just touch and go.
No gross of food to top a pot.

It's hard work to not see *The Bible*
as a digest of ink and sobs—
the visions of wino ecclesiastics—
and the *Law* itself as worn-out measures.

Halifax boasts so many meticulous lunatics!
So, why shouldn't I try the hoodoo sea—
spell my name in accents of waves,
the sunlit, sun-spanked bubbles a-frothing.

If I go by rough reckoning—
mid brisk, salted down breezes—
to London's conveniences,
am I not salvaged by the flood of winds?

There are so many snakes in the world.
But even more are in the earth—
especially in Nova Scotia.
And *Treason* is a labyrinth.

[Napoli (Italia) 25 *février* mmxii]

Weighing Off

I away to a tax regime bristling with guns!*
To Georgian England, pseudo-Victorian England!

(England's an island of grass that's also real blades—
steel blades—
and lead shot and iron cannon—
arsenal of an arse-hole Empire.)

Do I leave off the insular odours—
of mackerel and rum?

Will I arrive arrogantly shabby
or demonstrate practiced *Charm*?
Get cast as a raffish (oafish) derelict
or seem an iffy opportunist?

Another Negro hustler off the piers
dotting banjo-and-fiddle Nova Scotia:
That's me?
Low-rent muscle?

(Do Londoners believe
Blackamoors must be treated as raw, dark materials
to be finessed as white men see fit?

Do they pretend to befriend "niggers,"
but break their word easy as they break wind.
Are they a pack of white-lie liars?)

For some Anglos, non-Anglican Xianity
is the posture of apes,
the profession of flamboyant crooks,
yacking a rummy parlance,
acting irredeemably "comical" in the pulpit,
treating *Salvation* as a circus act.

---

* Taxes are minuses, never a surplus!

Do I frown like clowns—
like stock-in-trade laughing-stocks?

True: I arrive with no convincing title,
simply "Mr." Richard Preston—
an ex-slave's invented surname,
an ex-slave's borrowed surname,
and proclaimed a "dubious disciple,
a misfit and a mountebank,"
by Halifaxian, albescent Baptists,
who deem me not meriting the good hemp
necessary for hanging.

London is likely as agog with rumour
about my *Provenance*—
what I countenance—
as is all of Nova Scotia province.

Am I washed-up, evidently pathetic?

Naw: I make *Truth* as elegant as undiluted ink
is black!

(Thus, I ply my Aussie *Kookaburra* pen—
"perfect in action"—
to ink "India" onto Mississippi-cotton sheets.
and in ink light enough to seem pencil....)

I'll land as a full-dress expatriate.
I'll not blubber or spit out *Bafflegab*.
Nor bluster nor act a lickspittle.

I'd like the Princess to eat from my hand—
to treasure tobacco—
to loiter and ruminate
and chew and spit tobacco—
that I represent as an ex-Virginny.

I should be no mutton-chop labourer,
a crafty zero,
fattened on animal fragments,
lotsa left-over liquor,
or "Nova Scotian cake"
that is rum,
omitting flour, eggs, sugar.

Nor chow down on sweet fat
and salty grease—
the derassifyin* spoils
of bad-for-you *Poverty*.

I may rely on my intuitive *Gravitas*.

I've already booted through dirt, dust, bones—
Virginia to Maryland, Chesapeake Bay,
Washington, District of *Corruption*,
to come onto, to come ashore at,
Halifax, New Scotland,
to bad meat and good wine;
to poor soil and excellent sluts;
to stinky swamps and husky mosquitoes....

Landin in Nova Scotia, we had to say,
"Someone drank up all the wine
and ate up all the salt ham,
and left us neither dram nor morsel."

So, why do the whites oppose me so much?
They vaunt a Scottish-besotted New Scotland.

Beware politicians' fish-lipped mouths!

[**Malaga (Spain) 11/10/12**]

---

* Neologism of Tyrone "Rex" Mendes. Means: Tasty.

The Yarmouth Herald *Chronicle of a Melancholy Wreck*

That January, Friday, resistless *Gale*—
part-blizzard and part-tsunami—
brutal—
made futile the striving of the *Lizzie Chute*
to shoot past Chegoggin Point—
that boulder-studded harbour.

Rock-wracked, the schooner smacked
against a billion barnacles.
Who lived? Nil.

(When the ship bellied and bottomed,
but floated slivers and splinters,
onlookers heard a blood-freezing cry.)

Messrs. Chute and Donne of Bear River
were owners,
speculating on molasses bound for Antigua,
to ferry back barrels of Scotian Gold rum.

The schooner was brand-new—
and tonnage a hefty 162;
but the smashing of the dashing vessel
took down cap'n and crew.

(P.S. Among whom was a
Coloured quartet
also dunked in the drink,
thus baptized unto Eternity.)

---

* Cf. Robart-Johnson, *Africa's Children: A History of Blacks in Yarmouth, Nova Scotia.*

Insured for a measly $2000,
the melancholy vessel dispersed
only a portion of damaged rigging.
Its molasses is now saltwater.

And at mermaid breasts, skull-heads nurse.

[Tropea (Italia) *Juneteenth* mmxxii]

To Worship

Why must I needs demand a warship
to savour a right to equal *Worship*?

The paleface Baptists' *Amercement*[*]
against African hue—
their disqualification of our *Salvation*—
is unsanctioned biblically.

How dast they solidify their *Arrogance* and *Scorn*—
into a staged, tyrannical passion play,
wherein they forcibly part
Black Xian from white Believer—
though both have hope of Heaven
only through *Intercession*
of the crucified Saviour's purifying *Blood*?

Would they frisk us of—confiscate—our crucifixes—
as if our *Piety* were mendacious?

So why offer em a single "bravo"
for their misfortunate, grieffull^{**} *Theology*?

We Africans are unambiguous runagates,^{***} anyway,
for we've abandoned whip-in-fist tyrants—
explicit sodomites and tacit antichrists—
who so diabolically and immitigably
nursed vicious pollutions and sanguinary tortures
unisonously upon sire and dame,
lad and gal,
pickaninny and brat.

---

* Penalty.
** Cf. Robert Browning, *The Ring and the Book*.
*** Cf. Robert Hayden, "Runagate Runagate."

We did not answer Southern sadists and vampires
with *Cachinnation.**
Nor shall we primp and coo in pews
where we are prisoners of Dixie-style *Contempt*,
"Great White North"-style.

They make *their* Church
not God's Church,
our penitentiary!
Yet, the Coloured Baptists' anthem is,
"Before I'll be a slave,
I'll be buried in my grave,
And go home to my Lord and be free...."

Thus, I will to London to win—
the papers and the paper—
the documents and the script—
the ordination and the dollars—
to construct an Africadian Baptist Church.

These now are my ABCs.

"Confer a passage in the Canticles"!**

[Tropea (Italia) 22 *juin* 22]

---

* Guffawing.
** Cf. Browning, *The Ring and the Book*.

The Yarmouth Herald *Announcement of Double Drownings*

Not long ago, Chuck Clemence,
while chucking timber down the falls
at the East Branch of the Tusket River,
skipped his footing, slipped
(like a backslider)
into busy, pushy flood—
the punishingly "waterlogged" river—
the lopped trees bashing and crashing
furiously atop the rapids—
clipping, clashing, dipping, squashing—
so his ground-down, surf-pounded body got grappled
days later
at the falls' foot—
in a hole 25-feet deep—
where he was planted like an Atwood post.

*

A coloured lad—Virgil—
in the employ of Shakespeare and Company—
yesterday took his horse to a pond to gulp.
The animal ventured deeper than it ought to've
in the glass-smooth water,
and slipped its footing.
Virgil then sprang from his cart
to straddle the steed's spine,
and wrangle the creature to firm ground.
But the equine—panicked—whinnied—plunged,

---

* Cf. Robart-Johnson, *Africa's Children: A History of Blacks in Yarmouth, Nova Scotia*.

rolled over and got entangled,
and both horse and jockey,
inextricably
muddied—ephemerally—
the dark, murky fathoms
of their undistilled *Disaster*.

Grappling hooks salvaged a saddle, a cap....

[Tropea (Italia) 14 *juin* mmxxii]

Farewell to Nova Scotia

Nova Scotia—
North Atlantic Kingdom—
refuge of blizzard
and gluts and dregs of rain.

When there's sun, it's oily—
the tint and texture of sunflower oil:
Mist gauzes light.

The sun's only ever
a strained, painful glimmer!
(Dimmer and dimmer.)

So many Africans are gathered here:
Charcoal skins awaiting snowy graves.

★

When my ship embarks, I spy only
foggy timber, fog-hidden rocks,
fog-shrouded icebergs.
Clouds dim and damp the day.

I make for London to win the right
to build honest Baptist churches
in this spruce and birch-bark lair—

in the name of our at-first, mangered Messiah
(and then double-crossed Saviour)—
the caterwauling babe in the Bethlehem crib,
born while glittering starlight
swished and snowed.

So, farewell to Nova Scotia,
the salt-white clouds
or salt-tanged mists,
the nattering or roaring rain,

and this marketplace of slaves,

plus fishing hooks, anchors, grapples,
shark spears, whale harpoons.

Where Africans hunker in huts—
amid scraggly, unruly, tufted up meadows
and motley pines.

We gotta plant potatoes under a fungus of fog
or plough up stones
under chill, cruel rain—
almost miserable as snow,
more *mucilage* than mist.

Gotta cringe and bend and scrape—
to slave like trolls;
to slog through leech-rich swamps
and mud-gob glens
and mushroom-littered patches
or bramble, thorns, burrs.

"Nova Scarcity" got the substance
of a shark-chewed-up gull!

I say again,
"Farewell"—
penitentiary peninsula!

★

See the drool of spray at the bow!
Our belching sails refute hissing waves—
teeter-totter waves—
the glistening pallor of the white caps!

The ship is a tease of timbers!

Upon the mid-Atlantic,
spray becomes a landed rain,
tumbling, pooling, flooding—
gust after gust—

so each sailor's crying, blue-faced cold,
or green-faced nauseous,
snivelling,
fearing to disappear
into the gale's slobber:

The clobber of that wailing wet!

Amid slosh and screams!

The ocean is thrashed to a maddened *Sensibility*:
We float upon *Bedlam*.

Far-off thunder thudding:
Each cold riff of howl—
howl upon galloping thunder—
each wailing, incoherent *Obscenity*
of whitewash, impacting,
delivers harsh, death-bed *Clarity*.

To face elemental *Ire*, ruthless—
a muzzy, muddled sky—
and ramshackle crackling of waves—
and pray to behold
the starry sludge of eve—

proves that godless *Life*
equals consummate *Misery*.

Even the pilot stumbles
on this askew sea,
the demented dents and indents
of vast, corrugated inundation—

a mile-high, next a mile-deep,
this slate-grey, or marble-coloured,
tombstone-like,
tottering, toppling water,
a million sloppy pyramids!

Ship quakes over shaking fathoms—
foam and froth that's ceaseless *Epilepsy*.

We waddle in serious troughs,
then execute a gutsy shimmy
between two contending winds—

as gingerly as the moon slides tides about—

until we can finally waggle—
finagle—
free of the tempest,
and love each merely sticky comber,

coddling,

as we skid across the last, sentimental,
nautical miles,
to make a harbour—English—

pooling white swans of ships.

★

Let us give our mundane thanks
for the undeniable *Nirvana*
that is our sodden-ass'd *Survival*.

We'll welcome London's slimy sunlight:
To have our pipes toy with smoke;
to endure even the thorny texts
and prickly textures of *Theology*—

rather than the hapless struggle
through delirous, murderous water;
the cholicky *Decrepitude*
(moral *Turpitude*)
of a sea-sick ocean!

★

I'll mind my p's and q's—
dot my i's and cross my t's—
do whatever it takes—
by any means necessary—
to acquire the wherewithal
to erect my Africadian Baptist Church
(my ABC's).

Let the London Baptists show cold *Disbelief*,
eye me as a colourful scoundrel,
or scorn me with harrumphing giggles:

I'd rather enjoy their *Hate*
than suffer Nova Scarcity's
weeping crocodile eyes
in blanching faces—

the fronts for wormwood hearts!

★

I know that X's gilt cradle
is stabled amid pine and spruce
and gleams amid a green-gold-maple dusk:

He hath brought me over jolting waves
to the Thames' shivering tides—
the priceless silver of imperial rain—
and across inky mire—

to become acquainted with sunny poets—
illuminated dispositions—
London's mortal stars—

(all of whom okay liver-shrinking drink)

and *Liberty* renowned
and renowned liberties.

And so:
"Farewell to Nova Scotia"—
disjunct Dystopia!

Until....

—*Richard Preston*, 1823

[**Pordenone (Italia) 21/9/12**]

Passage (Suppressed Text)

★

The ship splays, fucks, the waves,
and is fucked, bucking, in turn.
Each spray hits us, slaps us—
irritating ejaculate.

The water is as restless and constant as breath—
or these words,
jetting free like rain.

(But my words won't rinse away
in rain and flood).

The wind has more power than an army,
and can sink us in seas so high,
stars get mistaken for seashells.

Storms ruin us.
We must beware of *Passion*—
tumults of *Feeling*,
for such is just as productive
of destructive *Waste*.

Anxious in my exile,
in desolate blizzard—
icicles even weighting my eyelashes—
honey mead is no more than silted tears,
I see.
The sea is a million African graves.

I want Hyde Park to be
L'Angolo dei poeti—
The Poets' Corner—
where every lunatic of ink—
pages soggy with verses
more ink than words—
is as conspicuous as lightning.

★

The ship skids through gauzy mist.
ahead is cool, green grass,
and fog tossed up and torn apart
by eructating smokestacks,

and scotch everywhere there are Scots,
plus stew and/or fish-n-chips in kitchens,
silver polish on the good tableware.

★

I do carry the spirit of Nova Scotia:
Those particular degrees of *Intensity*.

After all, *Lying* and *Arrogance*
and *Fraud* compose Europe,
peddling poems of *Romance*,
but murdering, nonstop,

with *Impunity*!

Thanks to the bullet-buying moolah
got from peddling black-skinned souls.

—*Preston*

[From a Train Seat, Mannheim—Berlin (Germany)
4 *mai* mmxi
& Malaga (Spain) 11 *octobre* mmxii]

In England!

I.

I've jaunted to London, then,
to bring home my Church,
i.e., the papers that say London says
I've *Authority* to preach,
countermanding the pallid Haligonians
who burlesque African spirituals,
sneering, we're "loud-mouth organs."

I have gumption and backbone
to brave the Atlantic—
an ocean that chomps on ships
and wind that stomps em down—
to cross green sea, a bump-crosshatched sea,
unmeasured *Emptiness*,
storm-beset pinnacles,
and skirt sea-buffeted rocks,
to locate a river as bright as light:
The Thames.

II.

A dazzling Mariner—
Pericles—
or/and a son of Yemanja,*
I jostled blue-green churn,
passed over the dead, spilled down vessels beneath
the rolling, unscrolling water.
The sun squatted, bloodied the sea,
or was wetted by it.
My journey unscrolled in sympathy with Jonah's.

---

* In Brazilian *Candomblé*, Yemanja is the Queen of the Ocean, the patron deity of the fishermen and the survivors of shipwrecks.

I reversed, single-handedly,
the *Race's*
chaotic *Diaspora*,
fording water
as affirmative as *terra firma*,

to England—
a no-sun, no-nonsense country,
as trim as a coffin.

III.

London:
the pleasure of Olde Lucre, yes,
but also frozen aristocrats
spewing hellish values.

Functionaries flush toilets.
The Empire creaks on.

Each mongrel newspaper jets
Mongoloid journalism—
here a "nigger,"
there a "kaffir."
They don't mince ink.

Gleaming like bandits' knives,
rain perforates everything.

Grey and piss-yellow mists,
miserable, poisonous weather,
the always rapping rain.

Brown puddles brim at curbs.

Scotch mist, English fog, Welsh rain:
the seaweed wind is sweet sometimes,
but never edible, never nourishing.

Pigeons applaud royally
each commanding statue,
bestowing a white laurel
or a white medal.

Monuments gather *guano*,
then dust or rain-beads,
suddenly statuesque—
a quotation, a patina, an echo.

Yet, eras are not carved in stone;
they vanish into ossuaries.

I move among turbid, acrid apartments,
dingy, mangy rooms,
rubbish reeking of coal dust,
dead rats,
mouldered news,
smouldering cabbage....

Bent, old men—
some grey veterans—
spit tobacco against the Crown,
their quiet grousing.

(Civilizations rise with shopkeeping,
collapse with begging.)

Churches, as richly empty
as a bankrupt Treasury,
echo with the dried-leaf noises
of scraping chairs,
shuffling shoes.

From each colonized ghetto—
suturing Indian-ink oceans,
bawling passages—
arrive Africans and Asians
to a Parisian *pissoir*-stench—
yellow journalism, white lies,
and black comedy.

Thanks to the refined *Tyranny*
of the Anglo-Saxon *Imperium*,
tea-coloured or sugar-coloured
or coffee-coloured Negroes and Asians
unfurl a pedagogical English,
while chasing long-legged, snow-pale chits
who label us
"jabbering jigaboos,"
as they flutter their dirt-streaked skirts.

(As promiscuous as war wounds,
Porn's as plentiful as small beer.)

Among the City's gargoyled banks,
London harlots—
Cockney, self-conscious whores—
model themselves by strutting
beside banked, spindly, sidewalk fires.

After radiant fathoms of sloggering seas,
deliciously gleaming waters,
I take as quarters
random, run-down, waterfront rooms.

I wallow in textbook ugliness—
the black, industrial gutters,
hear bastard, red-light-district moaning,
tend rags of flames.

London is coal-black,
dingy-yellow,
a factory, wage-slave hell.

The air's polluted prematurely with *fin-de-siecle* airs—
the putrid, acidic smog.

IV.

Thieves pry open St. Paul's
and tear down from its crucifix
an eight-foot-tall statue of X.
No overzealous *Faith* inspires this theft.
Rather, the criminal "liberators"
mistake the Saviour's green plaster
for salvageable, sellable copper.

Lo! *Capitalism* cankers cathedrals!

V.

The Nova Scotian Africadian Bible
is pages as innocent as clouds,
but as each page is lifted,
the dazzle isn't sunlight,
but lightning,
amid the clapping darkness of ink.

Each poetry-inked sheet
is awash with light—
spiritual codes of fire.

My Reference Bible connects
the Whole Word—
both Testaments
and all the prophecies.

How can I glance askance at God?

VI.

Here I meet masters of *Blarney*,
chitchat ejaculators,
Jabberwocky and flim-flam artists,
all Bible-banging preachers,
articulators of gilded bilge.

I listen sharply.
Then, my questions
—a grappling hook—
shred a moron's sermons.

To Hell with every sugar'd Bible!

The Gospel needs me
to cast its hard figures in searing speech.

I'll hold nothin back,
bring everything to light.

Wrath unmasks *Love.*

VII.

An ex-pugilist preacher with a shaky jaw,
Brother Jason Heaney insists,
"We must not love the present world,"*
i.e., *samsara.***
Though a purist, he mixes folk figures
with his Latin grammar, Greek rigour.

---

* C.I. Scofield.
** Vietnamese: The perishable world.

On Easter, I heard him sermonize
to this effect:
"The lynched Lord
forsook the grave,
ascended the air—
treading down clouds—
like a spectacular Daedalus,
even strutted through solid walls!

"Coffin'd flowers burst open
at the command of the Christ-like sun;
Lazarus-mimicking perfumes arise!

Here's the conflicting vision:
Dew—or ash?
What's your choice?"

The swooning is rich;
the harvest of sinners—
and donations—
estimable.

Heaney tutors,
"Worms, not worries, dizzy the dead.
And there's nothing to be done for it,
but to sing of Heaven
and praise our Lord.
Our duty is to orate *Paradise*.

"We must hang out nooses
to scare off debt exploiters
and flesh profiteers;
open to liars the hidden hellfire.

"The Imperial bards clamour
in iambs and pentameter,
but the true poets," says Heaney,
"sun themselves in pubs—

not to imbibe 'suds,'
but to hear sinners' spontaneous confessions
in authentic, inimitable—
but inspirational—words."

And so he goes into the stews and taverns,
or stands at their blazing thresholds,
yells,
"Gentlemen, if you don't smoke in brothels,
why should you object that we smoke you out?"

Heaney teaches well:
"Remember, Richard,
lamplight travels through the dark—
like a sermon,
indoctrinating all who desire to see.

"The culture gives off light, eh?
Great ideas, aye?
Well, they are gathered, dry on parchment,
then torched.

"Ignore vain *Philosophy*,
inane politics.

"To speak unexpectedly
from an unorthodox perspective,
is *Poetry*,
what Christ spoke."

VIII.

In that Whore House Parliament,
every seat is leather—as in a hearse.

Leaflets blow with leaves along a gutter.
Beetles clash over dung: Civil war.

Tories sortie from one flaming city
to the next, never finding water.

Even when rejuvenated, post-election,
carcasses still prop up the Commons:

Wolves, mackerel, foxes, warthogs,
bears, rats, pigs, mice, bitches,

Tenniel-drawn figures, pawns
in a contrary chess game, gritty.

The chamber stinks of politicians;
the air is hot, hellish, rancid with farts.

An azure Tory,
not a true-blue or royal-purple one,

hiccoughs of cigars and absinthe,
lobbies to cancel the Corn Laws,

while Bobby Southey, poet-mandarin,
stoops in back rooms,

scribbling hymns for *imperium in imperio*
(the government within the government),

where Scotch flames high in glasses,
and the poor are brought low.

How much oinking, snarling, growling,
braying, neighing, giggling, and howling?

(Every politician is oceanic—
wishy-washy,
affluent,
fluent with effluent,
hot and cold,

wet and dry
[in *Temperance*],
intemperate in war,
fluxing one way then back,
depending on season,
depending on the hour:
He is malleable
and unstable
like a ballet—
or tides.)

History is as transparent
as water at twilight,

its image, lying, murky,
laying open to disturbance.

But *History* remembers
nothing forgotten.

Summer brilliance—lightning—
darkens the Parliament.

IX.

Boss Shakespeare done
dub me an "Ethiope"—
washed up in London,
I'm shit outta *Hope*.

If I have a head for Shakespeare,
I've a shaky hand for a spear.

No: My "I" is a spear
hurled nicely by Shakespeare—
to transfix this African,
whose English is his crucifixion.

What if Cleopatra castrates Antony
to bed down with Caliban,
Juliet goes ape with Othello,
Aaron's codpiece eclipses Lady Macbeth's sheathe,
and Sycorax, dame of Sodom and Gomorrah,
straddles and coaxes a cucumber into Queen Tamora's *queynte?*

X.

At the Heartbreak Variety Store, I can purchase
Irish Lace / Scottish Woollens / Chinese Silks /
Newfoundland Cod / Nova Scotian Rum.*

XI.

Turmoil: The Thames;
Peace: The Thames.
Piece by piece,
river froth ends as flowers.

Upon shimmering fool's gold, melted down,
to a paraphernalia of white foam and waves,

I'll turn about Gibraltar—
Arabic for *Jabal Tariq*

(Tariq's Mountain),
then land in Septimania—

Languedoc in southern France,
where Muslims once bossed from Narbonne.

Let the tide-entangled, not reef-embrangled, vessel
hurtle me to *Raunch*-besotted Rome—

---

* Cf. Anna Minerva Henderson, "Corner Store."

like a Baptist hymn
across the rich wine

(brine)
of sea—

to anchor in a port of slime and miasma
despite sonnets of pollen Maytime recites,

despite grottoes of flower-unfolded air.
It be a terrain of worm-drilled coffins.

But *Time* withers all to bones,
ridiculous under dirt.

[Ottawa (Ontario) 25 *janvier* mmix
& Nantes (France) 26–28 *janvier*
& 4 *février* mmix]

On Viewing Depictions of
The Crucifixion in The National Gallery

What no artist ever gets right
is the inevitable plum colour
of the prickles and bruises
X's briary halo inflicts;
nor do they mix a tint suitable
for God's uninhabitable *Complexion*
while the morose vagabond—
the too-mortal, divine Monarch—
the King of the Jews—
is being systematically martyred—
spike by spike and spear by spear.

Intriguingly, not one artist balks
at depicting the grisly *Butchery*,
for God looks best in Gothic circumstances,
the *giallo*-yellow schtick,
the *film-noir* pall,
and the macabre is synonymous
with mediaeval evils—
inquisitional tortures and massacres.

Anyway, the rent—or vent—in X's hide
features a hellish haemorrhage,
no matter how one angles it
(as either colourist or pictorialist).

Apparently, English artists believe
that all any Crucifixion depiction requires
is a crucifix and a peasant slurping ale.

Then, again, the sublunary, Brit kings
influence portraitists badly,
for each one's a carny talent,
each beds a harem of rats
(from Henry VIII to Edward VIII),
and are skilful at achieving divorce
via beheading the discard.

Ultimately, an art gallery satisfies
parasites only—
the leeching appetites of blood-sucking eyes,
those visions that gorge on *Gore*—
the ruddy flood that flushes,
that permeates and saturates....

But X's *Purity* in our world
is as frail as rainwater
sluicing down a gutter en route to a sewer.

All these canvases I canvass?
The parading of a dead populace—
each corpse'd personage,
each personable cadaver,
and so a spectacle of spectres—
subjects of miserable *Slaughter*—
until the subjugated—
an Easter-corrupted, bloody April X—
is overkill,
suiting our cannibal *Compassion*
for raw meat.

Now, here's The Crucifixion set
amid unexpected English scenery,
a village feast on complacent greenery,
and yet a completely chilling canvas:
To spy our Lad bolted to a cross,
lanced between the ribs,
while glib onlookers dance....

It's a story best drowned—
lost—
in booze,
as occurred after The Last Supper.

—*Richard Preston*

[Niagara Falls (New York)
25 *avril* / *Nisan* **mmxix]**

On The Crucifixion

Jesus is easily amiable to the Xian,
yet not homicidally biased *versus* unbelievers,
for He accepted to be billboard garbage
alongside a thug and a thief....

(A trio of thin carcasses
got hauled off three crosses.)

Stones may tumble off any pinnacle,
But nary did Jesus slump pon His crucifix.
Rather, a jagged gleam of slicking sun
nagged down from clouds
to lick at wounds (now scars),
so that *Illumination*
dressed gouges in a gummy glow—
Light affixed to every pore of His body,
while the ignorant looked on,
snarling in their ale,
mumbling in their cups.

Blood ticked into—
tickled—
linen loincloths.

A thumbtacked coffin-top—
a shroud—
tacked down, clamped down, all.

But One was a heretic to *Death*!

And the sky is—in its *Rectitude*—
as shameless as God.

—*Preston*

[**Port Credit (Ontario)** *27 Nisan/April* **mmxx**]

The Diaries of Richard & Rita

Persons of the Dialogue:

Richard Preston & Rita Cunard

Situation: In London, England, in 1823, to acquire ordination as a Baptist evangelical from the West London Baptist Association, Preston encounters the courtesan—nay, *geisha*—Rita Cunard, at a theatre. Soon, minister *et* magdalena are lovers.

I: Richard

London's Baptists laden me with gold—
leaf, letter, wafer, and chain—
trust me to forego plebeian temptings,
yet eye me, too, with smiling *Suspicion*:
Who's to say I ain't merely a *dormant* barbarian?

Their sanctimony is barbarous.
When I look out over a rally—
torches bright as pears—
and, feeling the *karma* spell of beaten tambourines,
and the *frisson* of believers' open-jawed moans,
see the lean flames of female forms,
bewitching,
being such focussed *Illumination* that incinerates the heart,

I spy receptive ovals—
faces, mouths, eyes—
and I can imagine, too easily,
abysses within pantaloons,
wispy or crispy hairs announcing
each glad, intaking sex
(haloing it, as it were),
and, elsewise, there's no image of *Good* in our drama.

I can—and do—stroll past *prima facie* harlots,
ignore *Coquetry* in either ragged or powdered form,
but there is no final refuge from *Beauty*
(or *aesthetic Biology*, if you prefer),
but *Death* or *Disintegration*,
and God hath wrought a good, if troubled, *Creation*.

i.

My carnal larynx is at fault.
Every gold-leaf gold-letter Sunday, I speak
raptures, with volume, energy, style,
and some Xian ladies shiver pleasingly.

My *schtick* is *Kitsch*:
I'm either a true preacher
or a bumptious, rambunctious *poseur*.

I ain't the latter!

ii.

I saw Rita C_____,
a woman as pretty as a proverb,
centred at the frontal oval of the crowd,
and, from my podium,
our eyes staged intercourse so hot,
the real Believers vanished,
even as they fainted, swooned, in their *Faith*.

Later, with candlelight gilding her chamber,
I gallivanted among her guiltless silks,
Rose-and-fell obscenely virile, non-stop,
a rampant, private, *in camera* superman.

If my soul is stone,
her body is an ocean.

Our lewd duel
steeps me deep in individualist *Lust*.

iii.

I can't cogitate. I can't pray.
All's in vain.

(Amid a hurricane,
what good's a weathervane?)

I look outside:
Mill smoke, too white, blacks out the moon.

London's red-brick houses, row upon row,
black and dismal, slime with soot the primal snow.

Paradise—even paradise—
spawns parasites as much as pilgrims.
I know which I am.
I write, yearning, to her:

"I speak these words with volume, energy:
My every breath awaits, hotly, your reply."

[Paris (France) **25** *mai* **mmviii**]

On Meeting Rita

A strange, wan, thin, phthisic Madonna—
inmate-mannequin of a house of windows
and drawing-room curtains of slushy scarlet,
the ladies all open secrets to dawdling gents—

gawkers, ogling, but falling back when she exited—
heels striking lightning off cobblestones,
the London smoke swaddling her silk, leather,
linen. Who'd not want to fall—unholy—

but wholly twixt her knees, whether on carpet
or in tall grass, rank, where vipers lurk,
that sometimes blazingly verdant grass,
swooping hind her la-di-da dollhouse doors.

I espied her, fantastically, at a Baptist tent.
Her smile was bagged light, ragged lightning.
Could she ever desire, really, the wreckers
to flock and knock down her boudoir—

to let a Church interrupt—with *Piety*—
a space let for pleasurable *Impropriety*?
If *yes*, how could lamps douse *Loneliness*
with *Lust*, with partial but impartial light?

Decamped for our different, shallow homes
one day we all must be, always at least one day too soon,
and then her woodsmoke smell and sparking heels
will be meaningless perfume, then light gone dark.

To love, lovers are daily survivors, nightly
strivers. My cash for her wasn't *Contraband*:
Love, without *Lust*, is mere *Affection*.
We were affable, cordial,

then beastly, animal,
yet always in saintly *Communion*?

[Roma (Italia) 27 *juin* mmxviii
& Ottawa (Ontario) 14 *septembre* mcmxciii]

Rita's Recollection

Come-by-chance, by the mist-scrimmed Thames,
I spied the (not quite) Right Reverend Richard!
His lantern's shadow slapped black against the fog.
How else was I to pick my way to my rooms?

Our boots skittered over the cobblestones, striking
sparks, as parley sparked, unparliamentary,
and his lantern served as my stark moon.
Weren't we *ukiyo-e?*

Ambulatory via a smoky labyrinth—
the lantern bright like *neve, luna, fiori*—
we passed a flock of black barges
as black as Preston's ink got from purified coal.

And his light uncontaminated....

[Roma (Italia) 29 *juin* mmxviii
& Ottawa (Ontario) 7 *février* mcmxciv]

---

* Cf. *Cold Mountain: 100 Poems by the T'ang Poet Han-Shan* (trans. Burton Watson).
** Japanese: Spectres of the Floating World?
*** Italian: Snow, moon, blossoms.

Intermission Admission

I step into dusk-muscled wind.
English *filles* dance Slavic *mazurkas*.

There's candle light and wood panelling.
Chess thrills of *Repartee*.

Her hair's so red, it's blinding—
a flare of *Genius*.

Rita's papery—no, silk—flesh,
a joyous likeness is her body to silk.

"If *Beauty* is illegal,
then thou art guilty."

A sunburned, soap-scented girl,
she arias like a little bird.

Rita—she is:
a Madonna out of nowhere.

All blue-black at sunset now,
night ripples, cascades, like ink.

She glows like any silver thing
as a slight rain dusts us off.

Now, she coils like a cobra in the lamplight.
Black, knee-high stockings, a white chemise.

She is up for "comforting,"
and lies down.

Rita is as delicate
as a glass kite

tethered aloft
by burnt thread.

The bed holds her
like a bottle holds fine wine.

"Holding you is like holding wind,"
she says, "that shifts direction constantly."

That lune-miel *Madonna*
Glows as silver as a mirror.
Her eyes seem to outshine the night—
I can recognize no Error.

Perhaps the dawn will
be warmer than this night's stars—
if she wakes with me.

★

Too soon anyway we are worm-corrupted corpses,
and the walls of our graves
lick black with flames
(*Infamy*),
or we are mutilated quickly—
reft of coins and jewellery,
proving our survivors' gilded *Ingratitude*.

I adore her slippery, shimmying fingers—
an ounce of sunshine—
citrus
(Moroccan cyprus wood)—
the pink enterprise of *Coitus*—
unto our dying breathing.

Immortal *Beauty* reminds us
of our fatal lives.

[Ottawa (Ontario) 25 *janvier* mmix
& Nantes (France) 26–28 *janvier* mmix
& Helsinki (Finland) 21/11/12]

Reverie

Rita's a girl who gives as much shade
and fruit as a tree,
once I lounge neath her limbs,
or curl about her trunk.

Her good business is bare—
not barren;
the bare-ass lovely
is secret *Succulence*
to which I'm privy.

We're sloppy saints a-bed,
sassily riled up,
nervously giggling,

and rejecting any scrawny living!

[Oslo (NO) 20 *décembre* mmxix]

Reverie (II)

i.

Her gleaming *Nudity*, the sassy masterpiece—
"mistress-piece"—
light talcuming milkily each silky breast—
equals nothing misshapen, malformed, unbeautiful.

(If she could be ugly, then *Beauty* itself would be ugly—
or all *Ugliness* beautified!)

She beatifies the dusk, beautifies the dawn.
Her fresh, succulent curves feed me *Loveliness*
in eyefuls, mouthfuls, handfuls.

What is lovely if not *Loveliness?*

Yep: A kept woman equals an unkempt bed!
There's a glory of snow
impressed by my sullen, leaden *Mystery*—
nay, my ebony weight
borne up by her uncreased body—
cream-leased—
the dram upon dram, pound upon pound,
of white....

ii.

This flamboyant dawn, sunlight diamonds
our sweat,
and we are lunatic bullfighter (*moi*)
and lyrical ballerina (*elle*)
as we tarantella-tryst
in serpentine angles, tangles,

and so I get a kink in my tongue,
a crimp in my neck.

iii.

Thus we are brutish angels,
bestial saints,
in cahoots until the celestial *Climax*.

And then let us swizzle in our mouths—
guzzle in our mouths—
Masi Serego Alighieri Possessioni (Bianco),
so effortless to drink,
come all the way from Veneto, Italia.

[Georgian Bluffs (Ontario) 24 *août* mmxx]

Journal Entry A: Loving Rita

London is this domino* night—
black in light,
but white with snow—

and this naked white woman,
in our *camera obscura*,
falling.

Was a drizzle of snow all dusk—
a gold whisk of flames
hissing from fireplace wood,

while our kissing proved good
for bad behaviour,
Fornication—
while embers looked painfully rusty.

(Aglow, in this domesticated *Warmth*,
this furnished *Illumination*,
Rita is a blonde-embossed redhead,
and her naughty nightie
is instantly for nought,
for, unknotted,
it's not on, anymore!)

Was a stagnant, violet dusk,
a coldness that secreted—
within walls and doors and beds—
slippery *Warmth*.

---

* Cf. Fleming, *Thunderball*.

Rita stripped conch-pink-white
before an aquarium'd octopus of flames;
soon got wrought
soothing *Exhaustion*.

(Her beauty sponges perfume out the air!)

Rita could be Carmen or Carmilla or Camille—
any one of that corps of tarts—
theatrical.

No, she is of an understated elite—
the delicious matron—
skin as silky as a schoolmarm's rump!

In this bogus hotel—
a Great Brit brothel—
this obscene pantheon—
this untidy Parthenon—

Rita reciprocates kiss for kiss,
amid lanterned sighs;

and milk gets mixed with madeira—
a holy meal
(or malignant diet)—

and *Amnesia*'s as good as *Salvation;*
for *Forgiveness* follows *Fornication*
so closely,
that both endeavours are re-engaged
again and again—
without *Renege*

(or any other potential *Negligence*).

Again, Rita is undulant—
while vermin scurry, slither—
all rats and roaches,
as cosmopolitan as the cosmos....

But my black, arched figure
traces the upturned North Star.

[Rönnäs (Finland) 30 *juin* mmxiii]

II: Rita

i.

Once I was ... a Utopian vulture,
a happy, ivory, oily harpy,
eager to claw, rip, and guttle
every minimally bestial male *Anatomy*—
all fat and gristle and meat—
that dared offer up his penetrating *Compliment*,
or to relish flesh, our feminine array.
Never could I trust their vows.

Now, brazen hypocrites perched upright in church,
who lust to prey as badly as they pray,*
damn and condemn me as a "bawd,"
molest *Love* unto *Malevolence*.

(Each "scrubbed and saintly visage" masks
an unsavoury, unchaste churchgoer.)

Their sun hunkers overhead like some gargoyle.

ii.

I'm a woman and would be loved,
and, if not embraced, respected,
for I know too well the truth
about purported purveyors
(really perverts)
of *The Truth*,
who plead to their (our) thorn-crowned God,

---

* Prey.

for a season of *Sin* in one séance, one sitting,
to romp and riot
in that comedic, coital, civil war
before—God forbid—they needs endure
a good dose of burning and incineration.

iii.

I ponder my fond
preacher-pastor-fondler,
Preston,
his unexpected blackness—
as black as burnt-up bone—
his sparkling playacting in his sermons,

and then (finally) our wine-drowned vision,
our wine-tasting sighs,
and then the delirious plunge,
his rooting for truffles....

I love that Preston drinks like a poet,
does not whimper regrets over wine or rum,
truncates our floral words
to explore my—ahem—actual "flower"....

Reproach him for his "weakness"?
Spurn him for his manly (ungodly) "lust"?

I don't; I can't:
We fuck
to uproot our sepulchres.
(Why the mental lament?)

What I know is—
We rehearse *Eros* unto the hearse.

iv.

Let the good reverend minister unto me,
make free with me,
make sport with me,
enjoy my "allurements galore"
(sinister only in their end).

Our bleeding births foretell our tearful deaths.
Loathsome clay *is* all we are (or mud).

True, true, true: All too true.

But every galaxy is a cyclone of fire.

[Ville de Québec (Québec) 28 *mai* mmviii]

III: Richard

The concert featured yellow hands
seducing a sombre ebony guitar.

Red wine steeled my nerve, so unused to wine.
A gentleman accosted me: "So you're *the* Negro divine?"

"Noooo." I stretched the vowel as I did the truth:
"I'm only one of them."

I set down my wine glass hurriedly,
but glugged it anew when I saw her.

In the theatre's foyer, I gulped sour wine:
I yearned to jail her in a warm cell—my arms.

(Lovers use the cold as ruse, excuse—
for public hugs.

For a heart gone rusty, cold,
every embrace is a dream.)

Leaving the comedy, we laugh in unison.
Her copper hair daubs night's palette.

I signal a hack; it clatters cobbled alleys.
The direction is her address, Cockney.

Pale apple blossoms sob,
mob white as blowing snow.

Like fluorescent lanterns, petals fall,
fade to black against the damp stones.

According to my theological heart
and the fixed slant of the silvery moon,

this lady is like light that rekindles light.
All our light is natural (and she shimmers white).

In her chamber, a jug blossoms an orange-red rose.
Its waxy, forest-green leaves freshen moonlight.

Now a candle bronzes the room,
burns away night.

The flower envelopes her in perfume.
The light laminates her in a thrilling shine.

She plunks on her bed; I watch the magic
of her foot, nodding, shoe half-off, insouciant.

She decants thimbles of raspberry liqueur.
Next, this lady-of-*Value* kicks free her shoes.

I ask for a kiss, and, coy, she refuses:
She teases me about the size of "Africans."

But she's already removed her shoes,
and now her glasses.

I kiss her; we kiss:
Teeth click in the clinch.

Wholesome cavity—her mouth!
Breathy curves—her body!

Now, furious come our kisses,
and we manoeuvre from our stays.

Liberating *Satisfaction* be
our animal *Nudity*.

Our sweat is rain, a silver honey—
bonbons, truffles, of kisses—

Unimpeachably beautiful, intensely feminine,
Rita opens slowly, limb by limb,

so intrinsically luscious—
a milk-and-sugar commodity....

We mingle odours.
Her perfume storms the pillow.

I see my blackness heightened
where it touches and breaches her moon-white skin.

I love her with a shouting strength.
Each tries to outsing, outlove, the other.

She is undone—and, yes, done, again, again,
and I prove a proper charlatan Puritan,

convincingly "clean," yet sweaty,
"preaching" in an about-to-cry voice.

Ebony clasps a lily casket
(that cold ignition of light).

We church together a raw *Good*,
unto the raw birth of stars.

An eye-blasting *Illumination*, truly,
or *Annihilation*,

      and yet....

[Helsinki (Finland) 9 *mai* mmviii
& Frankfurt (Germany) 9 *mai* mmviii
& Paris (France) 20–21 *mai* mmviii]

Journal Entry B: Loving Rita

Femininity purrs;
Masculinity preens.

Undercurrent of alcohol.
A good quota of booze....

(Nothing is more intimidating
than *Intimacy*.)

We stutter *Scripture*—
rewritten as *Rapture*.

Her copper-coloured hair—
Pre-Raphaelite—
sets fire to her creamy, ivory skin.

I gotta shout in my shimmying *Vernacular*!

(To commingle wherever I snatch glimpse
of her impish, simpering flesh, singling
out that pouting mouth, not ever a-whimper.

I gotta harangue the hussy,
grip her like scorpion or octopus,
tumble her in her sumptuous, no-fuss bed,

where I show the weirdness of a horse—

cantering, neighing, whinnying, snorting, ramping—
sweaty flanks driving, plunging home,
delivering a lesson in lyric poetry.

Amen!

Lo! The bedroom looms best for face-to-face,
toe-to-toe, back-to-back, hand-to-hand tussles!)

[Vancouver (British Columbia) 9 *avril* / *Nisan* mmxi
& Enfield (Nova Scotia) 26 *mars* mmxii
& Helsinki (Finland) 19 *novembre* mmxii]

IV: Rita

i.

So many preachers are just
unjust, Sunday-morning wolves
baaing like sheep.
And all men credit the ideal of the harem—
the harmless idyll—
where they can play inconstant flies
at a dung-orgy.
They go to it, they sport, they groan, climax;
then, as contradictory as a teeter-totter,
they sit and judge some tattered ex-virgin.
For them, women are either stained glass
or stained sheets.
These mountebank gents—
all high-collar and top-hat *Dignity*—
preach the nothingness of *Lust*,
the nullity of flesh,
the futility of generation.
But they prey on cherubic angels,
pollute virtual madonnas,
until backstreet butchers carve,
from saintly, innocent bellies,
bloody, illicit spawn.

ii.

And what of Preston?
Am I for him a floating dream
of white woman flesh?

Or are we two flames burning as one?

[Prague (Czech Republic) *6 juillet* mmviii
& Marburg (Germany) *8 juillet* mmviii]

V: Richard

i.

Ly Lady is the Louvre:
Parian-marble body, Egyptian-copper hair,

diamond-shape silk nipples, turquoise eyes,
coral lips, Cockney accent....

ii.

Our hearts, bodies, union like ball and chain;
we aspire to a tense brink.

Ours is a bony, gritty *Love*.
We gallop like triumphant horses.

Our tender catastrophe felt,
the sheets boast a glittering honour.

So happy, so happy, I almost feel
God is someone else's problem.

iii.

It's much too hot for the foolishness of clothes!
And there's beauty in disrobing,
letting hands speak the vocabulary of flesh.

Our shoes are off, my pants undone (done in),
our legs thrown together.

Off comes her blouse—
already as transparent as dew,
and I eye the extraordinary curving
of her slender, splendid torso....

Irritating perfumes,
mechanical cloying:
Both figure the repertoire of the courtesan.
But not her, oh white *Elegance*,
recumbent, pliant, like snow.

iv.

Do I exalt *Whiteness?*
Does *Whiteness* equal, for me, ostentatious *Purity*,
a hieratic *Nudity?*

Well, Othello did not view his bride
as fragile tinfoil—
but as a woman!

True: An *aurora borealis*, white, ethereal, waving,
is her body—
an Asgard of nakedness,
dressed, ornamented, by only her gilded talk.

No hampered sweetness,
no uneasy Mardi Gras,
only infinite indulgence
is she:
see the filigree of down that leads my eye
from navel to sex:
That fine hair is (saith the *Kama Sutra*) *rumauli*....

v.

Around our planet,
everywhere, black lads drill the holes
of little white girls.
Their fucking is a mutual, scarecrow *Crucifixion*—
pure dirty moans and groaning deeds.
Their sweat is a laurel of thorns;
each kiss is sharp steel—
enough to stab spikes through limbs to straight wood
(in their case, a bed).
These "saints" sport thorn tiaras on their brows
and nail punctures on their backs.
(But these piebald pairs ain't saints.)

vi.

I wager that,
to be intelligent *and* corrupt
is *Damnation*.

Sometimes, the sunlight, sifting twixt Venetian slats
(slits),
squirms, worm-like, over our flesh.

Even so, a sunflower,
complimenting our union, arches—
frozen meteor—from a vase.

vii.

Her pale hands pour out red wine
that scorches my throat,
then nestles like lava in my gut.

viii.

Oh God, Arbiter of *Love*,
I go to *Infamy*;
she goes into my poems.

The stars? They shine like fire!

[Stratford (Ontario) 7 *juin* mmviii
& Montréal (Québec) 27 *juin* mmviii
& Brno (Czech Republic) 2 & 4 *juillet* mmviii]

Journal Entry C: Loving Rita

Amid a nightmare of rain,
I realize the dream of lightning....

There's no teapot breeze:
It's a tempest wind!
The rain is blinding, dazzling, brilliant.

There's so much rain,
I should desire to be a fish—
to exchange nose and mouth for gills.

But her kiss is oxygen and medicine.
It's a resurrection!

She resembles a lighthouse amid a storming sea.

The rain pools *Pleasure*—
so long as she stays.

One seeps
and the other steeps.

She is a woman more necessary than water—
and as satisfying—
and as flawless as the scent of fresh water.

Then the lightning struck—
white, gold, purple, green,
as our eyes traced its shape—
a spectrum of hectic surges—

in basic black India ink raven-dark wildness,
and I feel a poet deluded with *Illumination*!

I want us to be as festive as a beehive:
I want to graze skin as divine as pollen.

(If she is overdeveloped Venus,
I cannot be underdeveloped Eros!)

[Enfield (Nova Scotia) 26 *mars* mmxii]

VI: Rita

i.

One school of opinion insists
we play Sambo and Salomé—
a bull-and-pussy tale;
hence, our tearful *Excellence*
is just homely *Poesy*;
our monumental *Harmony*
is just a decadent *Liaison*.

Our mismatched similarities agree—
the battlefield of the bed
pacifies the battlefield of books.

Ecstasy demands *Complicity*—
that we agree to give and take our pleasures,
so a scirocco undulates over a glacier,
so that, in successful *Conjunction*,
tensions dissolve,
contradictions melt away,
and over-brimming *Happiness* floods us.

ii.

Civilization imprisons human animals,
even Preston and I, tamping down instincts,
but there is nobility, and, above all, *Joy*,
in eating, drinking, fucking.

Innocence is a luxury.
Beauty is what one feels.

Lewd joy is *Love.*
All else is ruins and sludge.

He speaketh a courtly *lingua franca,*
enough to ope wide my jade-sapphire eyes.

Let's carouse, ruckus,
leave wilting to the dead.

Despite my savage hunger,
I await, patiently, the delicious giving way—
the simplicity of union....

When I see my man again, I'll ask,
"Where was you
when you wasn't
where you was?"

[Brno & Prague (Czech Republic)
4 *juillet* mmviii
& Roma (Italia) 29 *août* mmviii]

VII: Richard

i.

Africa's distinct *Diaspora*
makes every slave
a perpetual migrant,
his or her *Citizenship*
constantly perishing, vanishing,
into a white *Lacuna*.

Our mixed blood is spilled;
our spilled blood is mixed.

Human skin merchants
pimp pickney gals, market Negroes,
pretend to be as white and as refined
as the sugar and cotton
that black folks tend and harvest.
Certes, these paleface black-profiteers
are as black as their slaves,
even blacker,
even if they deposit their charcoal hearts
in marble tombs.
Their blue-blood accent
issues from blood-dripping jaws.
They are as violent as *History*,
and their nubile *apsarases*★—
bodies as lifelike as mannequins—
are only ranks of whip-striped courtesans,
pox-tattooed whores,
all perennially foaming pus.

★ Hindi: Nude dancers.

The British monarchs swallow gold, shit corpses,
but play connoisseurs of *Humanity* in *noir*,
wresting tea from India—
and gold from Africa—
to stage an empire of fog and rum,
mist-freighted wind,
ocean-flogged shores,
the stench of fevers,
so England, this rainy asylum,
is just a kingdom of tarts and tars and rats,
cat-and-dog weather, a fog-cancelled sun,
wind dumping down dirt, disease, and dust.

Her "lost," disgraced daughters,
and we blacks, the damaged lot,
all are spawn of slavers' water-borne
orgies and holocausts,
fathoms-deep Hell,
a satanist's Atlantis,
unfathomable.

ii.

So what is my London baptism,
if not a swank *Victimization*?

The Thames, this stockpiled rainwater,
this fen of urine and feces,
swells with bacteria,
even when sunlight gilds its ripples.

(Upon this sickly brown mess
impinges no disinfecting sea.)

Around Nelson's memorial column,
I run the gamut of pigeons—
their rabid hovering and squawking cooing,
the white hash they make of every bronze,
and then encounter the grime and tears of flocks
of Empire's dark, shabby bastards,
gathered raggedly here—
like the lepers who mobbed X,
begging His instant cures.

iii.

London's dark, white streets
run empty and cold like prophets' graves.
The City is dirty workers and muddy booze,
but the true *Corruption* begins on high.
Note the ooze of filth out *Royalty's*
white fundaments,
the seat—theirs—of Empire
(a sewer).
Count the assorted purveyors—
x number of sluts,
particularly vehement drunkards,
and you cannot claim London ain't
a citadel of asses meriting assassination....

(The British Museum sells
postcard watercolour massacres.)

iv.

I float here—
a kidnapped, bleached, well-polished "African"
(a faceless Ethiope,
passing as a grinning "Negro,"
happy-go-lucky)—

to carve out a home of *Liberty*,
not here,
but back in a Halifax of fists,
a Nova Scotia of phthisis.
Now, I have no cabin but the road—
or a ship's cabin.

Am I only an indiscriminate Romantic,
a pastoral pictorialist,
adrift from improbable Nova Scotia,
a Moor unmoored,
drifting from city to city,
from jail cell to pulpit,
on the corpse-strewn, sun-sloshed sea
(between the unbound sea and the unjambed sky—
two sheets, interchangeable),
an ocean as omnipresent as *Death*,
and, at times, take mustard-pungent rum
until I can camp in a swampy margin,
i.e., drown unto *le petit mort*.

So I have nursed a love affair:
Warped in some eyes, maybe,
but it ain't;
it's just not *ordinary* in any sense of the word.

v.

Rita is multifaceted, but wholly brilliant
as a diamond,
as authentic as stainless steel.
Her beauty excommunicates—
and salvages—
her beholder, her vassal.

She is a white-canvas beaut
needing always my black-ink pen.

Under almost edible sunlight—
honey—
the shade of her golden thinness,
we melt together on hidden grass,
and tip our berry bucket by accident
(our feet tilt against it),
as we embrace each other's shadows....

vi.

Every church is a virile brothel:
the urge to ministry
compels the arrangement of a harem,
a "Ladies Auxiliary,"
or some other lacy, perfumed sorority,
that may kneel to pray or....

No milquetoast Negro—
his melanin pure aqua—
I do my sacred duty:
Let us pitch and rock and sink.

vii.

Overpowering the Thames' stink,
an Atlantic breeze lifts her perfume to me—
a cinnamon-and-rose scent
gracing a salt-sea aroma.

Oh God, how I love her—
her history, imperialist, sexual—
also her auburn hair,
her eyes blue-green, a grotto
taken from Italy and set in a Nordic face.

And, as I preach to her,
she converts *me.*

[Grottammare (Italia) 3–4 *septembre* mmviii]

Journal Entry D: Loving Rita

Here is my mellifluous handwriting,
but she delivers dirty, galvanizing speech,
bellowing tropes that are sport,
if also ulcerous talk.

Next, I clamber the lattice of *Coitus*—
the latticework of *Coitus*—
dovetail upon dovetail,
so that Rita is my palimpsest
and I am hers.

We are two debauched worthies,
I suppose;
and *Lechery* is first *Appetite*,
then *Art*,
the rough equivalent of *Worship*.

The belly woos us first,
then the loins,
then the heart
(if at all).

If I were Adam and she my Eve,
I'd stroke her breast—
even before she'd offer the aphrodisiac—
and apocalyptic—apple.

We spit out sonnets—
all slobber and whines—
not one jot like Southey's
(save as *Blasphemy*—
the cacophony
that's Southey*).

[Helsinki (Finland) 19 & 20 *novembre* mmxii]

---

* A rusty trumpet of Empire....

VIII: Rita

i.

Pastors, those thin-lipped primitives,
gripe about trivial things.
They brandish, black, best-selling (unread) Bibles,
deliver whitewashing smiles,
then direct nations—
glittering congregations—
down dead-ends to darkness,
brutal morgues—
War, Starvation, Slavery....

(And their pamphlets look best orange—
ablaze—
yielding real light, useful light,
warmth in a hearth or a stove.
Burning, singed (though unsung),
these meagre encyclopaedias
look and smell like Seville oranges.
Used for kindling,
these texts spice up *Truths*
they otherwise fail to smoke out.)

Spurn their chatter!
I'd rather cry carnal hoarseness,
offer up zoo-born chuckles,
while convulsive thunder shakes my loins,
a man's hot tentacle hooked therein.

ii.

Cities raise scaffolds and gallows;
clergy raise Hell and dollars.
So what if I raise my skirts?
I raise *Hope* too.
(Others raise children.)

iii.

It all comes screaming back in dreams:
The cream of his moans, his gasps.

Preston should die like a king:
Encunted until overthrown!

iv.

I ogle him among a cabal of bluestockings—
more rum in his blood than "Negro."
At their tea parties
(boasting a posse of prurient intellects),
the pale belles hold up monocles
to inspect Richard's lips
and focus there
their lust for his kisses—
pantaloon-removers—
and/or wine akin to absinthe—
for each "lady" is a camouflaged copulatrix;
suspecting that Dicky's manhood
is as upright as his conduct.

[Charlottetown (Prince Edward Island)
23–24 *juillet* mmviii
& Roma (Italia) 27 *juin* mmxviii]

IX: Richard

To kiss completely her body;
to arrest her with silk;
to mouth and tongue each inch;
so she is utterly a-melt and buttery;
to produce moans in *Poetry*;
to ply honey where it smokes;
to douse Champagne on welcoming passages....

I am not the *vir bonus*—
good person—
Scripture orders:

I treasure my Church—my wife—
and pleasure my Muse.

As if I'm a new-convert Mormon—
or an out-of-place Mohammedan—

or Br'er Augustine before sainthood—
or *homo sapiens* as a Black Baptist bonobo....

[Montréal (Québec) 1 *juillet* mmviii
& Brno (Czech Republic) 2 *juillet* mmviii
& Grottammare (Italy) 6 *septembre* mmviii]

X: Rita

You admire my "Babylonian brightness,"
once I've discarded "shameless" lingerie—
tender *Splendour*—
shamelessly,
go naked as mist,
shake bum-bum,
and you plaster your lips on me,
and my kiss goes straight down your throat;
so we—ebony and ivory—
form a piano marriage:

My unbound hair
and your unchaste heart....

Preston! This night makes a bed
of wind and longing;
moonlight dresses our sheets.
As midnight turns up blue,
let us stage a wedding
of my flesh
and yours in fresh
bedding,
and groan and grind
til our thighs—
fulfilled—
sweatily sunder....

True: The skin can burn coldly;
flesh can run cold to the touch.
Love can be as one-sided as murder.

But let *Love* make us reckless—
so you are angel-sinewy and I am angel-dewy,
as we tumble and fumble
unto finale.

Love that never wanes, never pretends.

[**Nantes (France)** 5 *octobre* **mmviii**]

XI: Rita

i.

My little clock imprisons *Time*.
Old wine, old waltzes, old flowers, old news,
pass away;
new weather, new *Love*, new kisses, new news,
arrive.

If Richard gifts me kisses,
I'll take less wine.

He craves inexhaustible *Tenderness*,
twilight-blush rosé,
all the spicy intertwisting of *Love*,
and grunting over *Speech*.

(Words only block *Touch*.)

I feel his Bible-thumping heart....

ii.

I am a *hetaira*, a whore, but hieratic, priestly—
an apostle of *l'amour*, a pontiff of *Coitus*,

half-in, half-out, of clothes—
unto the vaginal *Transudation*....

Most intellectuals' talents
consist of chin-chin and chitchat.
Sparkling wine ends their symposia.

I prefer dirty talk*
to double talk,

but *double entendres*
to white lies.**

iii.

Is it right to low—
of *Love*—when I don't know
if your French tongue's just show?

iv.

Painted aristocrats looked down at us enviously
as we murmured, reminiscing about our *Bliss*....

We'd fornicated in his small, broken-down room
under a dove-coloured moon;

no more among the liquor'd lonesome,
he learnt that joint personalities harmonize.

The *demi-monde* denouement?
Nothin halfways ā'tall!

v.

Sometimes a pale gull,
mimicking fickle moonlight,
glimmers amid gloom.

---

* *Truth.*
** *Love's* glitter: Fool's gold?

vi.

We prosecute exquisite *Business*—
no cute give-and-take,

but *outré Exchange*.
Nothin cut-rate, but the acute *Bargain*.

Bitter plums go sweetly into our liquor.
(Ink a poem, drink down wine: Same thing.)

vii.

Let no one hack up or hash our *Love*!
Ours is a *smukke drøm.**

We should hold each other up—
just as the Cross grasped Christ—

or like some Christians
who grapple with the life-size crucifix.

viii.

Stars glitter like girls waiting—
in strung lassos of pearls—
for swains.

I unpin my hair;
it avalanches down
like an undammed ocean!

Preston's as sombre as red wine—
as brilliant as white wine—
and as composed as rosé.

---

* Danish: Beautiful dream.

His diary is bits and pieces of *Truth*,
a volatile Bible:
Black and white—a colour stalemate.

Not *Love* do tears drown.
Not *Love* does anyone denounce.
Not one loves tales that omit lovers.

Consolation is wine.
Salvation is wine and bread.
Ecstasy is wine and bread with the Beloved.

ix.

How white the moonlight
That night our lips first clutched tight—
like fused dynamite.

x.

Lacklustre white,
dubious black—

monotone black
versus monotonous white:

Clouds collect—
like poets in an anthology.

White cat
bounces 'top black rat.

xi.

The weight of moon—
thrown snow—

defies night
(*Gravity*, the grave).

Taking wine as easily as medicine,
taking rum as readily as *Gospel*,

Preston displays lucid, cleaned-up *Blackness*—
dark-purple elegance of a monarchist—

and sees me as touching as lightning
and surely as whitely dangerous.

But I "sinsist" (pun):
Pry open my *riemurasia!**

xii.

How do I dissect this ex-slave?
What can be dug up from his heart?

I don't mind labouring over him in our bed,
for he's uncommon,
the fireball of the pulpit!

And firewater lets him "speak in tongues."

(His beseechin preachin
gets even a guard dog yappin!)

And so I gussy up my "hussy" self—
to be as teasing
as is a curtain to a breeze.

Yes, the man can express a prayer
that knocks the devil on his ass!

---

* Finnish: Treasure chest of *Joy*, i.e., the vagina.

He don't need Ouija boards
or oracular cards.

He's no mere dabbler in *Rabble-Rousing*!
Nor does he voice callow insights.
He spits out each bloody spirited lyric.

Yes, his manners are operatic in *Conviction*
and dogmatic in *Charity*!

(When we push body against body,
Orgasm is the *coup d'état*—
that tit for tat!
His *Potency* is a sword.)

Swathed in pear-scented *Pears* soap,
I set going the "commotion"—
fucking under kerosene lamps
(rank *Illumination*—
as if fog-smeared—
suiting scruples sooty).

Oh, I lust for salt herring and dill pickles!
(Quirky, mischievous hashish—
and mescal, absinthe:
Neither is fake.)

Jesus steps also outta simple churches,
elementary churches,
lobbed or slapped together,
neither by nails nor glass,
but by *Freedom* that needs a temple.

Now, Preston's not the type to tumble
a lady
in any place shady—
as if a smutty dog.

Our lovemaking? Harmonious storms!
Argumentative rutting!

He votes for *Honesty*—
to have me exultantly horizontal.

The majestical flame in each lamp
tosses a lasso around each of us—
until the halo shrivels.

[Ottawa (Ontario) 24–25 *janvier* mmix
& Nantes (France) 26–28 *janvier*
& 3 *février* mmix
& London (Ontario) 1 *juin* mmxx]

XII: Rita (*après* Catullus)*

43.

That sable Adonis—
my beautiful male specimen
with the long, lean legs and high, tough ass,
plus pianist-slender fingers,
a preacher's bright, black-star eyes
and a capacious, yet firm mouth,
from which rude, randy, pillow-talk Gospel
gotta issue once the churchy sermonizin's done.

I think he's a new, natural king,
stepped fresh from the sun!

(No wonder London Baptists brand him "elegant"!
Why don't they statue Romantic he
alongside Byron, Keats, Shelley,
those radicals that other poets dream to be?)

48.

Richard,
could I kiss your mouth
like split peaches—
or watermelon—
or plums—
always and always,
so wealthy with *Wet*,
healthy with *Sweet*,
all luscious, plush, precious—
my kisses,
unto *Infinity*,
wouldn't be enough—

---

* Cf. *The Poems of Catullus* (trans. Peter Whigham).

even if heaped up like the *smörgåsbord*
of cherries, raspberries, pears, and apricots
tumbling out a Bastille Day horn-of-plenty—
cornucopia,
floribunda—
No!
There'd still not be enough—
never enough—
of my kissing
you, for me!

5.

Darling *hombre*,
love me so,
we'll cuss all the dull, dumb, stupid-assed,
pasty-faced, shrivelled up folks,
make em feel evilly foolish—
when ya go on and on
kissin me
all over;
I mean,
all over!

70.

Preston says he'd rather I be his bride
than he be a provincial apostle,
though Paul—Sainted—appeared
before him as a mini-sun
to commission his *Sanctification*.
But what a man tells a woman
as she parts her legs
should be written out
with lightning for ink
and wind for paper.

[Ottawa (Ontario) 20 *janvier* mcmxciv]

On the Continent

I.

The madame in the coach, her breasts
jouncing slightly as the horses bounced,
says she loves, *"France sud,"*
but especially *L'Espagne....*
I did mention X, His sacrifice,
but she preferred to deplore
the counterfeiting of currencies
(not counterfeit Xians—

such as "Dixiecrats").

II.

Alighting in Toulon, or Toulouse,
I saw a spiffy *gar*, quite officious,
and stooped over,
his top hat balanced upright on his skull.
Despite his league-wide, determined strides,
only after several seconds, did I realize
that the dandy bureaucrat,
that aristocratic mandarin character
was wholly teetotally drunk
and staggering amid the horse-hustle
and buggy-bustle
of that hole-hobbled, cobblestoned *rue*.

(Don't hypocrites also seem, initially,
Respectable?)

III.

In the Arles café, a woman asks,
once I order,
"Is that an accent
from the newest African colony?"
I answer, *en français*,
"Yes: Nova Scotia."
Eavesdropping, the patrons giggled.
But I did—and do—possess that vision:
To see a Nova Scotia of Africans and Métis,
a New Scotland of Thiopians and Mi'kmaq,
where saints are born of common labourers
and murmured or shouted blues—
melismatic, mournful—
become gospel, spirituals,
a salt-spray testament!

IV. À Saint-Tropez

Down topsy-turvy streets to the Mediterranean
coloured blue-black-grey—
indigo-slime, twitchy white sleaze—
due to indecisive, topsy-turvy weather,
but also splashes of lemon-marinated light,
I overhear an ice cream seller
tell a vanilla-tint blonde,
"Your hair was spun by Rumpelstiltskin
and dyed indelibly gold by the sun."

V.

And I cry with my lungs torn outta Windsor Plains!
She is light, light, light, so fine.
Rita's profile—as she walked away?
Gold!
She smiled when I said I liked
the Rev. Al Green.

VI.

The garden was thoroughly wild roses—
mauve, magenta, pink, blush—
where I told her clearly—
did finally speaketh, I to her—
my abundant feelings, *Love*,
amid the savage, uncultivated *floribunda*!

VII. À Paris

À Notre-Dame, I enter the cathedral,
and I spy an African, "Quasimodo,"
who oversees the pilgrims,
with absolute mansuetude,*
Gentility, in directing them to regard gargoyles,
anti-seraphic in visage,
whose credible, architected *Faith*,
is to veer *Evil* from the accommodated worshippers.
He and I lock pupils—
a colonized African and a once-enslaved African—
he in Europe and I in North America—
and our ebon-mahogany eyes inquire,
"Cousin, what commerce do we have?"
What can I say?
Our genealogies, once smoothly aligned,
are reconfigured—disfigured—
by European signatures on sales' certificates,
and our unknown parents maligned.
Purged have we been of histories—
smitten so efficiently—
that my *Faith* replaces ancestral glories,
X-cancelled presciently.
Our joint regard is welcoming, yet wary—

---

* Gentleness.

in case either denies our continent:
To pose as a *nigger* in the dictionary,
rather than as a confidante of the Covenant.

[Toulon (France) 19 *mai* mcmxcvi
& Saint-Tropez (France) 19 *mai* mcmxcvi
& Durham (North Carolina) 1 *juin* mcmxcvi
& Ottawa (Ontario) 1 *juin* mcmxcvi
& Tropea (Italia) 23 *juin* mmxxii]

Approaching Caravaggio

I boat to Roma—to boot
the papal peninsula,
where *Sin* is Catholic (universal)—
enthroned:
Thus, churches flourish ornament,
flush with statues
(an ambush of *Fragrance* and icons);
so the spirit is cushioned
on plush luxuries,
and dissuaded from the permanent pleasures
of *Salvation* unto *Eternity*.

Here I am a Moor:
As a "Moor," I moor in Roma—
itself so "noirish," Moorish—
Decadence so Babylonian—
as to be iconic
(the *Theology* moronic).

The *Art* guidebook instructs:
Holiness resides even in a murderer's *Art* ....

Here I am more a Negro than a Baptist—
but I hie to Santa Maria del Popolo
in the Eternal City.

Thread I through beggarly throngs—
pickpockets and cripples—
jongleurs and deviant saints
still vicious in their Civics—
the cavalcade
of marble idols and gilded devils—
rot-faced lepers and Sodom's *Quintessence*—

the whole abominable *Plague*
of charming charlatans—
charismatic antichrists—
beautiful she-wolves—
disgraceful *Ordure, Trash* blown everywhichway:
And this be the *narrow* road to the Church!

I expect to view, *via* the killer's eye
and homicidal hand—
The Conversion of Saint Paul—
that Ganymede splayed, supine,
beneath his steed's upraised fore right-hoof,
set to crush the saint's ribcage
(perhaps to plump up a blood baptism;
and, helpless where he lay—
God-stricken for his *Persecution* of the Faithful—
the prospective prophet can only look on—
horrified—paralyzed—
by the *Violence* of *Sanctification.*

I must also eye in opposing parallel
the murderer's masterpiece,
Crucifixion of St. Peter—
that saint nailed to an upside-down cross—
his left hand clasping sympathetically about
the prostrating spike
goring his palm—
already trickling a surplus of rose madder
(tint derived from J.M.W. Turner
and the Moors)....
Pete's rock-steady head is turned toward
his stretched-out hand and its rosy penetration,
and away from his assassins
(including the burly hefter of the Cross,
tugging the sudden Rack bottoms up,
a shadowy, crinkle-haired potential Moor);
so that the Caucasian criminal—
Caravaggio—

communicates the *canard*
that Beelzebub is black,
that the antichristian is African.

And yet there are Ethiopes
throughout the Bible!
And the Coptic Church be as old
as Hebrew itself.

Now, here I am, but I cannot enter.
I will not enter!
A horse-drawn hearse faces me!
Its open rear faces the church front,
from which edifice issues
white-robed *squadristi*,
a pallbearing sextet shouldering
(or holding)
a mahogany casket
as their dozen feet
caterpillar down a dozen church steps.

The *Faith* is as much imprisoned in a church
as the now-deceased priest (whose rites I observe)
is incarcerated in his coffin—
regardless of the incense that puffs—wafts—
his *Egress*—
his outward going—
and no matter the harpist and violinist
who serenade—musicalize—his mute *Eulogy*.

—*Richard Preston*

[Tropea (Italia) 21 *juin* mmxxii]

To Rita

Expectantly, I travel;
ecstatically, I arrive:

unhesitant to kiss,
unhappy to stop kissing,

unless there's more touching,
unless there's much undressing,

and unrehearsed
our undulations

undertaken—

until all morals
undo.

[Helsinki (Finland) 10 *août* mmxii]

At Dover Beach

Sea-broth—froth—rattles the grating pebbles:
Surf, batters hard, then shatters—splats against
Rocks, then recoils, the pounding resounding,
Redounding and skittering and scattering

The tittering pebbles. Winds' currents thrash
Trees, crash branches, splash down leaves. Spray bombs scrag
And crag and cliff. Clouds clot, then vaporize,
Disintegrating post-squalls, to let frost

Stars gleam between lighthouse beams, scissoring
A sky mirroring the sea's streams of glint.
Come new-mint constellations, arisen,
Blizzarding, streaking our seeking eyes. Milk

Silk is vapid fog vaunted next. Us, agog,
Should lounge in the wet grass, scrounging kisses,
And sound, then founder, flounder in moist sand,
Cloistering our limbs, quite enwombing us,

As we twine and twin, with gulls' howls searing
Our ears—jug-jug, glug-glug—while we're coupling,
Supple, surging, urgent. Then, to emerge—
Sweat-sodden, becalmed, while channel combers

Come back, gloomy, their froth glomming pebbles,
While viscous waves, vicious, wangle, wrangle,
Our two-forms-engraved sand, so the strand caves
Versus the tide, also breaking open shells

And vipering through urchins' singular skulls,
And raking serpentine swipes cross ships' hulls,
And docks. We'll walk beside rocks that waves stalk,
Roil, and then uncoil. If we'd tour Dover

As lovers, would any tears sully coupling—
Our bully-pulpit wedding—mid supple
Sand, bedding down in gully or grotto?
Let's fuss like Sisyphus, swig out bottles,

Adjacent unchaste loins until falling
Dew-drops should summon stalls, the chill crawling
Our nakedness like tarantulas, raining,
And biting and burning where mandibles

Prove *Lust*. The moisture'd be our *mucilage*
(No *Persiflage*), joining our groins, while dawn
Tides sloppily mop, in their webbing ebb,
Our nudes—fluid atop pebbles: Rebs at stop.

[Roma (Italia) 28 *juin* mmxviii
& Ottawa (Ontario) 20 *novembre* mcmxciii]

Envoy (for Rita)

i.

Dante's Beatrice, Da Vinci's *madonne*:
Thou art each masterpiece doubled in one;
A *Beauty* sassily superior
To each fragile or fault-finding mirror.
But Dante's and Da Vinci's dames—abstract—
Model *Beauty* unfleshly, *sans* defect.
Nor sneer you at the shadowed *demi-monde*
Where preachers pontificate on sins spawned,
Jetting purple prose, scarlet similes,
Blue-pencilled, blank verse, yellow-sheet decrees,
Or proverbs—black-and-white *Wit* from a tome,
Biblical, yet not *Truth's Epitome*.
Thou art Psyche and Venus—Queen *d'Amour*,
Blithe, gaudy, glittering, blinding *Glamour*!
Never extinguished—nor extinct cosmos—
The ashen, post-holocaust of *Eros*—
We'll never contemplate or entertain—
So long as, solo, twain we remain.

ii.

She is no Mauregato woman
(a virgin booted as booty to a Moor),

the white *femme*—dame—lady—
her valentine heart so hugely red—
trails an air-borne coffee scent,
so reminiscent of Chianti wine.

(Who could back us,
if not Bacchus?)

[Durham (North Carolina) 13 *août* mcmxcviii
& Roma (Italia) 27 *juin* mmxviii]

Rita* Answers

*L*ove has no comparable *Supremacy*.
Its sting apes that of wasps, and its stabbings
Equal assassins' knives. I loved our bed—
The marshy reek of my silk sheets—when you
Made *Climax* seem anarchist *Upheaval*.

Perchance it is, here in Saint John, where blacks
Still chink gleaming chains, that thou, sweet swain, seem
Uncouth Caliban, not dark Priapus,
Making love while gulls glide o'er buckling waves.
I never saw *Race*, just my parallel.

[Saint John (New Brunswick) 5 *novembre* mmxv]

---

* For MWP.

Departure

The moon winters in the black tropics
where Rita hurries past—
her face white as a torchlight's flash.
And shadows gird the scene.

She herself flickers while sunning my sheets,
Making a quadruped bridge for passage
(Kneeling); we jiggle like train cars, coupling.

"A boat does fit in the water: But water
Doesn't fit in the boat. God fits in us;
We don't fit in God. No other way does
The once dead tree—dead wood—be ready

To be dead ash, until ...." Sunlight bends back
Straight, firing from eyes, and, swinging purses,
Women push through each church's door.

[Oslo (NO) 20 *décembre* mmxix]

Last Meeting at Saint John

New Brunswick vanishes.... I traverse now
A blue *Peril*—foam-edged, V-formation,
Bow wash—water too heavy to be sky,
Too light to be land. Soon, in mists, a waste
Of fog, I disappear, tears obscuring
The shore. I voyage, stranded between two shores,
Where *Love* was sure, a mooring, where London
Was Rita—half-marble, half-milk—molten
Not frozen, and who steamered me homeward,
To the Saint John idyll, where black ladies
Act gourmets of harmonies, ushering
Me home to X, and my Coloured Baptists.

Now, Fundy gusts torment this sorry boat—
This schooner clipping white combers—sails full—
Introducing me to bluesy blank verse—
Dull clouds amid grey space, calving seagulls—
Who squawk, brazen as *Opinion*. I cry!
There's a lady, her red hair flogging
The fog, the bog of it, her lips purpling
Verses—our own—lifted from Solomon....

[The Bay of Fundy, 15 *juillet* mcmxciv
& FCO (Italia) 30 *juin* mmxviii]

Pertinent Personages Pursuant to the Previous Passage....

Thomas Chandler Haliburton (Antichrist)

Pearl Olivier (Africadian Historian)

Richard Preston (African Apostle)

Revanchisme

Saved, conscious, enlightened, I view Victoria properly
as exalted filth,
no more than a ghetto landlady.

What's her income the outcome of?
Where's it skimmed off like cream—
or, veritably, scum?

Her *Adultery*-born church be
honestly just whitewash hogwash.

Her religious ministers (priests, bishops)
are pigeons blacking out light.

(She herself is a pigeon, blacking out light;
but titters like a whorelet.)

Her imperial ministers (admirals, generals)
faces flush
like bloody matter in toilets.

Victoria's pulpits, political cabinets—
all those water-closets—
exchange vomit for diarrhea:

(Vomit of *Law*
leads to diarrhea of arrests,
dysentery of hangings.)

Prisons nullify schools
and sanctify poorhouses.

Nowhere—not here—is *Virtue*.
Nowhere—not here—is *Virtue*.

The Times complains, whines,
unless *War* rah-rah displaces corpse-still *Peace.*

Never discontinuous are those headlines
braying, yahooing, for *War*!

Newsprint? Unclean toilet paper,
used bandages,
unsanitary and unsacred, bloodshed-prone *Lying,*

& gusts of fetid whispers,

the screeling of a Napoleonic *Ideology*—
histrionic.

(No wonder Whitehall is all alarms!
Treasury coffers stuffed with coins
engender battlefields rebuffed by coffins.)

I gotta be a swashbuckling preacher—
in black robes—
garbed like a pirate,
and also sport an eye-patch,
essential for encounters
with eye-gashing God.

I look about and survey—
in this "Unreal City"—
stiff-lipped, mean-faced bankers,
Caucasian cannibals, pornocrats, abortionists—
primping panders, the buyers of virgins—
"cocksuckers"—the dandy pimps of the poor.

These are the identical fronts arrayed against me—
in a Nova Scotia that's British New Scotland—
typed faces that arraign and impugn me
in Haligonian, tart-and-tavern *"Christianity"*!

The white Halifax Baptists—sadists—
are ranked—banked—cranky against me.

But Africans—victims—are with me,
craving *Salvation, Liberty, Independence*!

—*Richard Preston*

[**Tropea (Italia)** *6 juin* **mmxviii**]

Thomas Chandler Haliburton Critiques
The Black Refugees

These provincial Negroes bathe in dirt.
Second-guessers, dead-enders,

they set up their books of "salt-spray" prayers
in stables.

(Each one's a horsefly that whinnies like a horse.
Each hoarse preacher stinks as nasty as *Incest*.)

Their towns are just bull-breeding grounds.
Bare-ass *Astrology* constitutes their embarrassed *Theology*.

Immaterial, yet as obscene as infant flies,
a defunct light

shrouds cracked crockery, tarnished cutlery,
Black Refugees whose graves are lifeless—

no flowers, no mourners.
Weeds are their *Luxury*.

They died nonchalantly, noncommittally.
They were very slow to dream.

Our complacent gentry let them starve.
Kaffirs are His Britannic Majesty's blackguard subjects.

In my own *History of Nova Scotia* (1829),
they constitute a chapter of garbage.

Grass rustles up their villages,
then turfs over their cemeteries.

Though giggles oscillate among em,
they marry their coffins.

Theirs is the country of Macbeth:
Cradles dressed in black crepe.

If they have a poet,
his hand is a claw in black toffee.

[Salamanca (Spain) 12 *décembre* mmx
& Cairo (Egypt) 15 & 18 *décembre* mmx]

Preston's Critique

I.

This unspoiled Nova Scotian spray?
The crescendo of *Provincialism!*

Do not allege
this colony is illuminated!
(Too many ungovernable Scotians!)

The sun doesn't care
where its light
falls;
so, it lolls and sprawls,
helter-skelter,
like carelessly sprinkled seeds.

No one's holy here!
The Governor's last breath was whiskey!

(He died off-key.)

II.

Should I lust for a bride—
white, pink-nippled,
a black-thatched sex?

Our baby would be a cross:
Race affixed.

Race afflicted!

The libertine only be liberated?

[Calgary (Alberta) 31 *mars* mmxi]

Haliburton's Anatomy of the Negro

I.

The Negro has a demonic composure.
The Negro is *aurum* and *argentums*.
Big butt and big head defines the Negro.
The Negro's ornery mind floats in paralyzing liquor.
The Negro is a SNAFU, a goof up.
The Negro is a lavatory and a *pissoir*.
The Negro is *Hesitation*.
The Negro is stifled *Purification*.
The Negro is a petrified Hell.

Is nothing but his penis—
the "terroristic" black phallus....

and he's objectively as dark as the Minotaur?
And he's an outright "public" poet?

Problem is—
Ethiopes love their undulant copulation
more than they love X.

II.

When th'Africans berth on our shores,
I see *Decay's* birth.

When I look at this lot of ex-slaves,
I see a lot of filthy slaves still.

Even if they soldier, battle by battle,
still, little by little,

they parade finally into the poorhouse,
with rusted weapons and rusty bandages.

And these folks just get fangs in their butts:
They're asinine about *Work* and *Wealth*!

No Negro be any good for Nova Scotia
than a spavined horse is for a farmer.

Blackies just raise thistles and thorns,
mosquitoes and maggots.

(Sometimes, a blacky steps off the auction block one day
and climbeth the gallows steps the next.)

III.

And I suspect that, just like the Loyalist "Nigrescences,"
the Refugees will petition to slip to Sierra Leone—
that mountain range that pierces clouds and soaks up rain—
to people that shore,
emerald as Madeira,
where the ocean arrives as an austere sparkle—
like furrows and furrows of diamonds....

The so-called Refugees display
unmitigated *Sloth*,
but blame our colonial authorities for their shitty crops.
To me, the fault ain't their bush-and-boulder properties,
but their lust to be back in Dixie,
where our sun-burned brethren go way too easy
on these soft-headed critters,
lettin em guttle watermelon, fried chicken, roast pork, the works!

IV.

Best prepare a homicidal *Theatre*.
Best, first, be—surreptitiously—belligerent;
pretend *"Normalcy."*

Gold demands harsh *Government*,
for our money supply isn't endless,
and our *Good Will*'s done run out.

[Cambridge (Massachusetts) cf. "Settling Africville"
mmxiii-mmxiv]

A Rejoinder to Haliburton

No, he is a Privy Council wit (twit)—
as deadpan as any civil servant—
but....

You can't say what I can say:
Haliburton's a Scotch-yellow, pudgy body.

As low-down as a rat-hole....

Excuse me for saying these words in church, but
his paunch pisses; his mouth shits.

We shouldn't badmouth. He isn't all dirty, I wager.

Shit is unsanitary, but he loves it.
He must:
he scrawls crap that crawls with fly larvae.

Haliburton suits this country of thorns
that's also sleet, or sleaze-greased streets.

It's always cold peas and cold potatoes,
and never grapes and never wine.

—*Richard Preston*

[Cambridge (Massachusetts) cf. "Settling Africville"
mmxiii-mmxiv]

Nat Turner Talks (1831)

Virginny's wig-and-silk "pharaohs"—
lashing us with cat-o-nine (Hydra) tails,

mix up *Democracy* and *Defecation*,

nixing the former
to fixate on the latter.

These florid gentlemen
waste oxygen.

They claim, *"Superiority"*?
Well, let's watch their blood flood out royal purple!

Leave off the chalk damsels!
Be stone-cold muscle,
disinterested in *Fornication*.
Just cut em!

Turn Tidewater Jerusalem
into a slough of dead pigs!

Grab meat cleavers and bombard necks;
lift up boots and stomp hard on newborns
or choke em with their umbilical cords,
while their mamas shit themselves weeping.

So many plantations, disciples!
Too many whippings to avenge!

Time to wield pitchforks as brute blades,
to pitch lily lads and ladies
putrid decapitations.

Gouge each body an extra loathsome anus.

[London (England) 23 & 24 *Nisan* / *April* mmxiii]

Notes on Ecclesiastical Presence!

By Richard Preston, Lic.

1831—Acadia College—Horton, Nova Scotia.

Epigraph?

*He disports himself amid his northern snows fashioning
his own brand of Christianity....*
      —Luís Vaz de Camões, *The Lusiads* (trans. William Atkinson).

★

I come ashore here to "Nova Scarcity."
Studyin on bein a minister—
Baptist—
Coloured Baptist—
to preach the Gospel frank,
my speech too sassy, pungent, for bleached pulpits.

But I say I follow X—
and God the Father—
for namin things as things is.

What brings out Believers
is when they hear
forked-tongues bein called forked-tongues,
cut-throats bein called cut-throats,
masters bein called torturers,
overseers bein called rapists.

My words are treasonous
wherever slaves can read
or hear.

Our patois injures schoolmarms' blackboards
and hurts reporters' spellings.
But that's cuz a black tongue
is too honest for whiteys' ears.

(Yet, Mansa Musa started Sankore University.*)

Had to get away
come that War of 1812,
when Yankee and John Bull got to shootin
or cuttin each other ...

So, the contest twixt "Man o' War"
and "Manifest Destiny"
freed me to slip away
and home to this homely redoubt—
where my mama awaited miraculously.

Yep, here rats squeak like seagulls
and seagulls squeal like rats.
Every summer feels like a steady winter—
with flowers of frost.
All our land grants be mosquito farms, really,
just swamps and stones.
Even if a crop appears,
mice bite it off at the roots.

To be continued....

[Cambridge (Massachusetts) cf. "Settling Africville"
mmxiii-mmxiv]

---

* The oldest existing, continually operating institution of higher learning in the world
is the University of Karueein (University of al-Qarawiyyin), founded in 859 CE in
Fez (Morocco) by Fatima bint Muhammad Al-Fihriya Al-Qurashiya. Aye, a woman
founded the first university.

Catechism

How to instigate *Conversion?*
How to jeopardize *Sin?*
How to rescue *Intelligence* boggled by gobbledygook
(manhandled, mishandled Scripture)?
How to spur on ardent *Altruism?*
How to forego being *Property, Cargo?*
How to forbid *Failure?*
How to salve *Agony* and salvage *Agape?*
How to preach the Bible and give no quarter?
How to expose frauds, imposters, antichrists?
How, alone, to storm Nova Scotia?
How to transform grievous *Deprivation*
into tables laden with trout, smelts, greens,
meat pies, shortbreads, stew, gravy, bread,
Windsor apples and Annapolis Valley pears?
How to use everyone good?
How to rise up out the grave of slavemasters' governments?

—*Richard Preston*

[London (Ontario) 1 *juin* mmxx]

SELECTIONS FROM THE AFROCENTRIC BIBLE:

PASSAGES CRUCIAL TO AFRICADIAN BAPTISM

OR *DECISIVE* FOR THE MISSIONARY LABOURS OF RICHARD PRESTON

Genesis X.

1. The generations of the daughters of Noah
(innumerable beauties)—
Shem, Ham, and Japheth—
they and sons—siblings—born post-diluvian.
All now are moving shadows in genealogies.*

2. By these were the isles of the Gentiles divided
in their lands;
everyone after his tongue, after their families,
in their nations,
all the colour of ebonized pearwood
or dusky or amber (Semitic)
or "red Negroes" with copper-coloured skin.

3. The sons of Ham, Cush, Phat, and Canaan
equal black, copper, gold, and ivory "Egyptians"
(Gypsies).

4. And the sons of Cush; Seba, Havilah, and Sabtah,
and Raamah, and Sabtechah;
and the sons of Raamah; Shebah and Dedan:
Be all Libyan (i.e. "black") in tint.

5. And Cush begat Nimrod:
A tough-as-nails personality,
a charismatic hunter,
he'd eat uncooked iguana,
but skin monkeys, scraping off the fur.

---

* "Unquestionably dark-complected.... Anthropology supports this conclusion." Cf.
McKissic (p. 39).

6.   He'd soak in saltwater,
glug black coffee,
and, merciless to mere farmers,
go out and plough under homesteads
and pave over graves
(after digging up the gold secured under headstones).

As cerebral as Cerberus (and just as doggèd),
Nimrod became a repugnant despot,
"the Maximum Leader of the Known World,"
and a political cancer:
Heaping up creepily mismatched corpses everywhere;
turning pianos into urinals;
commanding arbitrary police raids;
arranging heavy guns to batter down towers;
rendering adversaries as bodiless as fog
or as a set of terrain curiosities,
malicious stragglers—
castrated and/or decapitated.

7.   Nimrod's foes were left no drop of wine,
no grain of bread,
no splinter of kindling.

8.   A detestable libertine—
a being of ornate *Vivacity*—
sacking scullions incessantly,
the Sino-Negro Buddha—
fathered a polity of grasping and dirty slaves.

9.   Depicted always with a pistol in one hand,
riding crop in the other,
he was the prototype Richard III,
ruling a parliament of the damned.

10. Still, his Empire invented paper
and tamed horses;
created clocks and calendars;
forged iron and tempered steel;
launched a navy of sailing ships;
practiced embalming....

11. And his realm thudded down apples;
his soil fielded miles of beef, tankers of vodka,
skyscraper pyramids of potatoes.
(Even his butterflies were as hefty as cows!)

12. His docks dispatched oil, butter, olives,
indigo, cotton, coffee, tea, milk, sugar,
candles, vodka, vinegar, and wine.

13. Nimrod presided over a treasury expansive as Canada.

Such be the animal-tough sons of Noah—
down to the nethermost discard;
and by these were post-diluvian nations sired.

[Leamington (Ontario) 1–3 *novembre* mmxx]

Exodus XVIII.

1. Once the Midian priest, Jethro, appreciated
that Israel's God is pure *Beneficence*,
he welcomed the arrival of Zipporah,
wife to his son-in-law, Moses.

2. One of her sons was Gershom—
that alien in a strange land.

3. Jethro then camel-convoyed Zipporah and sons
and schlepped to parley with Moses,
housed amid mountain wilderness.

4. In that railway car at Compiègne, they kissed.
Venison, bread, coffee, honey, circulated.
The wine? *Casillero del Diablo*—
a savour of cassis, mocha, and dark chocolate.

5. Moses spread out maps and recited epic verses
to pinpoint how God had ended Israeli bondage.

6. Jethro had to jump up joyous, raucous!
Israel's God twas "The Real Thing"!

7. Clearly, Pharaoh was "history";
his army, cut out for marching,
not swimming,
had been clobbered by God's weaponized Red Sea.

8. Time for burnt offerings—
plus marshmallows seared black and crispy.
Plus a stevedore's supper of grog and mussels.

9.   Come dawn, Moses donned his judge robes.
Jethro now audited delivery of *Justice*:
To strip whores nude, but lace virgins in bridal gowns;
or grant blankets to the homeless,
banknotes to the hopeless.

10. Moses commented: "The people know
I'm aligned with God because my proposals
become prophetic
and my actions become *Law* and/or *History*.

11. "Furthermore, I decide disputes,
rewarding the righteous but wronged,
rebuking the questionable.
I be The Decider!"*

12. But Jethro saw that weighing sins and crimes
was too drastic a burden for one man.

13. Always supervening, convening, intervening?
Moses.

14. Not the best *Policy*, the proper *Realpolitik*—
although the man was turnip-tough, hard-boiled.

15. Jethro advised his son-in-law:
"You're gonna burn out, get tuckered out,
tryin to be judge, policy wonk, army general,
chief engineer, plus psychiatrist,
and theologian!

16. "Moses, implement a government:
Tax collectors, bankers, lawyers, and cops.

17. "Let these officials handle the majority
of minor *faux pas*,
while you hand the minority of major dilemmas to God.

---

* Cf. U.S. Prez #43.

18. "Simultaneously, have em pass down to the *Volk*,
the orders-in-council that God commits to thee.

19. "That's the right way to work *Church Government**
Let clerks settle petty matters,
while you dictate the Divine vision.

20. "Let Blake be your Machiavelli;
let Shelley be your Pound."

21. Thus, Moses set up poets as lawyers;
clergy as *sosha*** workers.

[**Leamington (Ontario) 4 & 5 *novembre* mmxx**]

---

* Cf. John Milton.
** Cf. Judith Thompson.

Isaiah XVIII.

1.   **W**oe to the wing-shadowed land
of Ethiopian rivers,
that nation of *Total War*,
embarking ambassadors in papyrus vessels
to clipper far-and-wide
a policy of bullish *Aggression*.

2.   No the rascals weren't above ambushing others!

3.   An erratic, violent *Civilization*—
their *Obstinancy* so *deus-ex-machina*-like—
still they could be scattered and scotched,
battered and botched,
and shrivelled to a nook,
a desert siding,
a dump,
not a garden—
but a cauldron of lava
and/or squadrons of worthless brambles.

4.   These ebony warriors, teak-sleek people,
gotta be warned,
God will trumpet thundering shock waves
and fire off laser-beam lightning—
incisive as X-ACTO blades.

5.   God can Krupp-pepper priests
with lead bling, an iron blitz.

6.   God can reduce kings to spectres
and princes to lunatics.*

---

* Cf. Hamlet.

7.   The awesome Ethiopes will fare awfully Gothic
and so clamour to Zion for *Succour,*
if they don't cease to study *War.*

[Leamington (Ontario) 6 & 7 *novembre* mmxx]

Zephaniah I.

1. Zephaniah, dude of Cush, caught the Spirit!
I now gotta prophesy!

2. God's gonna scorch all green to black,
blast all vegetation dust-brown!

3. Birds gonna drop like rocks out the sky,
thud down dead;
fish already half-maggot, half-bone, gonna roll—
flopping, gasping—onto beaches;
clerical stumbling-blocks and theological blockheads
gonna fall,
dashing open hard heads pon knife-sharp cliff edges.

4. Swords are gonna thin out army ranks;
jog ruddy streaks across bellies;
tug out bowels.

5. Plague's gonna strike down Judah,
strike down Jerusalem;
and every hall of idols
gonna crumble down to rubble.

6. Coffee-stained, coffee-tinted smoke
gonna waft from every Kindergarten—
as repetitive as a Warhol,
or a Xerox.

7. Let the Holy shout "Hosanna, Hallelujah,"
from every rooftop,
shuddering the stars!

8. Let *Dummkopfs* and evildoers alike
perish in flame and sulphur.

9.   Let kings toast to cinders
and their babes roast,
skewered on cannibals' swords.

10. Let royal heirs—gangwaying to crack safes,
axe open wine barrels,
tup the harem inmates—
well, let all their necks and cocks
be set to chopping blocks!

11. Let em be stinking carrion
amid dishevelled grass;
let em suffer ferocious impaling—
steel fanging into carotid and larynx.

12. God's gonna explode the dams about every city,
thus detergenting away human beings
like so many pollutants—
turds, gliding bacteria*—
crud—
reconstituted bile.

13. All ye *citoyens du* Magog (Québec) gonna howl
because merchants are sold as slaves
and bankers are tossed to grizzly bears
or flung into bullpens.

14. God's gonna commission 120 disciples
of Diogenes—
all gents with *Coleman* lanterns and *Eveready* torches—
to scour Jerusalem to find the virtuous few
and abolish the vicious.

15. The Sinful? Gonna be looted of all booty,
their homes deloused *via* TNT,
and their vineyards porcelain'd over into "pissoirs."

---

* Cf. Dr. Howard D. McCurdy's articles in *Bergey's Manual of Determinative Bacteriology.*

16. When the Grand Troubles commence,
monarchs and presidents gonna try to creep
neath boulders,
and so feel jealous toward ants.

17. That Final Day?
Rife with earthquakes, infernos, black skies,
suffocating and/or toxic air,
blood squalling down gutters.

18. Simple trumpets gonna prove ample
to tumble down towers!

19. Every euphoric trump?
Reduces a palace to a shit-hole,
the residential "president" offed
via shit-stuffed jaws.

20. Guv'nors and rock-stars are gonna stumble, blind.
But others will see their flesh turn to pus and dung;
and see blood piss out their asses.

21. Kings shall cripple and topple into graves;
or they shall wither—rot to dust—on their thrones;
leave behind one kilo of excrement each.

22. Name the weapon, name the treasure,
name the medicine,
that can remedy these things:
Zero!

23. Nor can torches heat up stars.

[**Point Pelee National Park (of Canada)**
@ Leamington (Ontario) 7 & 8 *novembre* mmxx]

Jeremiah XIII.

1.   The Lord commanded:
"Don a linen girdle to coddle thy genitals,
and don't launder it!"

2.   This I did.

3.   Secondly, to the Euphrates I went,
and there performed the order
to doff the girdle and secret it in a cleft
in riverbank rocks.

4.   The mangy, rank, acrid-stinking cloth—
as intimate as a urinal—
got stuffed into a rocky abscess.

5.   After 90 days,
God bade me to excavate the garment.

6.   *Done*!
But what I recovered was so bedraggled,
begrimed, and bug-chomped,
it could not have sheltered
even a mouse's minuscule prick.

7.   Moths had eaten;
spirited termites had bit and chewed;
rats had gnawed and pulped.

8.   Now God explained:
"The worthlessness of the loin-cloth?
Such will be the value of Judah
and Jerusalem!

9. "Refuseniks and hypocrites
who satisfy perversions
and invent idolatrous ideologies, etc.,
are gonna end as torn and tattered
as these here underpants.

10. "For as the girdle cleaves unto a man's loins,
so have Judah and Jerusalem affianced themselves
à Moi-Même,
in exchange for *Military Glory*, a plush *Treasury*,
and *Cultural Bragging Rights*.
So, they'd best heed My *Rage*!

11. "Jeremiah, warn those imbeciles
that I'm a-gonna overflow their wine bottles!
'They'll answer: Big effin deal!'

12. "So, tell em that I'm a-gonna nurse
their entire ruling-class on brain-dissolving wine!

13. "The result?
Fathers will slay sons and rape daughters;
sons will rape mothers—and daughters slay themselves
rather than mother their self-born siblings.
No *Pity*—no *Mercy*—
until all are dashed down dead.

14. "I'll disgrace em to their backbones
and backsides,
so their asses groan,
then dump a cargo of blood.

15. "Warn em, Jeremiah! Alarm em!
They best u-turn and humble down
befo I stumble em down hillsides and into fire
or befo I tumble down sun and stars
and sink Israel neath hurricanes of muck.

16. "And survivors of my *Wrath*?
Gonna be abject slaves!

17. "Jeremiah, caution the royals:
Repent thy wrongs—
lest thy crowns get recycled as fetters
and thy persons starve to dungeon'd bones.

18. "And southern cities gonna be toppled,
and the citizens chained.

19. "I'll let the northerners invade
and sack and havoc, riot and rob and rape,
so they guffaw, mocking,
'Where now are thy beautiful flocks,
thy *Ausgezeichnet** rieslings?'

20. "And when the Hebrews weep at these sorrows,
remind em that their iniquities have wrought
sabotage of *Virginity*,
abortions of children,
and existence restricted to sewers!

21. "There'll be the sinuous, facile,
chop-chop of blades!
Les filles de joie—scabrous and insolent—
will be pulverized, exacted,
just as a scalpel gouges out a *furunculus*.

22. "Ask all, 'Can Ethiopes change their skin?
Or a leopard its spots?
No?
Well, then how can the backsliding soldier forward
any *Virtue*?'

23. "I've no choice but to batter em to bone and gristle,
scatter em like dust.

---

* German: Excellent.

24. "Their skirts are gonna be lifted to their faces,
while foreign blades disembowel and castrate.

25. "Warn em, Jeremiah, this is the forecast!
Their adulteries, *al fresco* abominations
with their own offspring—
their oinking, broad-daylight orgies—
all will be repulsed as repulsive.

26. "Tell em, Jeremiah,
I'll cleanse em by scourge and by purge....

27. "Tremble their quills and quake their ink!"

[**Leamington (Ontario) 9/11/20**]

Revelation XXII.

[N ot to be Translated.]

PRESTON ORGANIZES THE AFRICADIAN BAPTIST ASSOCIATION OF NOVA SCOTIA

~

1832 to 1861

Pertinent Personages of this Passage...

Louisa Bailey (Poetess)

Septimus Clarke (Secretary to Preston)

Thomas Chandler Haliburton (Antichrist)

Randall (Randy) Day (A Natural Man—as in Ecclesiastes XII)

Kiss-She Fells (Theologian)

Joseph Howe (Politico/Journalist)

F.R. Langford (Hellfire Preacher! Hell, yes!)

Richard Preston (Founder of the Africadian Baptist Association)

Benson Smithers (Afrocentric Africadian Baptist Pastor)

Mona States (Africadian Baptist Believer)

James Thomas (Welsh Baptist Pastor)

Preamble*

In 1827, a Great Fever
Afflicted haven and hovel, scything
To earth—aged and infant, parent and child,
The strong, the sick: Just indiscriminate
Expiring! Or folks took scurvy or rickets,
Because "taters" were the sole food. *Hunger*
Was the new *Terrorism*! Or *Plague*—
The panic of chills, shakes.... The black folk howled!
Dependent on rum, grog, eggnog, and ale
And molasses; or chewed tea leaves to mute
Bellies groaning for bread and meat and milk.

Despite freezing, not one Africadian
Went stumbling back to Dixie, to kneel down
And beg an ex-master to whip or chain
Or rape em again, just so they could eat.
Instead, the Refugees held close to God,
And loved their land plots—as bare as they were.

In their pebbled demesne, those dismal plots,
Seldom massaged by silken rains, the blacks
Hammered up tumble-down dwellings, abodes
That looked bungled, then loped cross loam to lace
Vineyards on trellises, or plucked up
Berries, green things, hay, wheat, apples, and corn
Or pears, and poured down milk, and prayed for *Peace*—
That sons become fathers *not* pressganged tars,
While maples pushed syrup or rusting leaves.

---

* Cf. Oliver, *History of the Colored Baptists of Nova Scotia*.

Because Preston was a unique tribune—
And opposed by brainy theologians,
Pooh-poohing his African Baptist Church,
And scoffing at his name's lack of trailing
Letters, he voyaged to London, Great Britain,
Docked at Pall Mall, White Hall, to be ordained
By the West London Baptists—the primates
And popes and potentates of Baptism—
Second only to Saint John. By gaining
Their imprimatur, Preston thus became
The premier Baptist in Nova Scotia,
His "papers" superior to all others.

Preston didn't cakewalk down the gangplank
To Halifax. He stepped along the planked
Catwalk onto the dock, but just-in-time
To see timber lumber to Cornwallis
Street, where two-and-a-half dozen Baptists
Had dredged the £ to raise the maiden
"Black" Church, along with a letter pledging
300 £, thanks to Charles Carpenter,
Of Clarendon Square, London, to support
Th'erection. For that reason, ragpickers
Could worship alongside haberdashers....

As glacial as *Grief* wearing down to *Peace*—
Is the process of propping up a church:
So many words must be shed! In winter,
Steam rises from baptismal pools—scalding,
Smoking, like dry ice. Nigh irreligious.

—*Pearl Olivier, Historian*

[Oslo (NO) 18 *décembre* mmxix]

Port

A choice city for shitty coitus—
bacchanalia, *inter alia*:
"Chebucto."

Try Haligonian asses and Haligonian glasses—
ply lucid wine and loosened hair—
frantic by the frothing, brothy Atlantic.

I stake a wench—
tits of ideal ivory.
We trade dirty puns,
gulp murky port—
slurp muck of molasses and cream—
amid broken-down light,
a kerosene lamp, say.

To the pneumatic bed,
I take my fevered bone—
and, with smiling *Agility*,
defile my la-di-da nymph.

This tight-pussy, white hussy
curses with cursory groans,
while port limps from a bottle.
I swear we screw like *scarafaggi*.*

(O! I'm like a lewd cockroach
scuttlin o'er this pale Acropolis!)

Chips of flame chink the fireplace.
Unkirtled, my maid mimics curdled milk.

---

* Italian: Cockroaches.

Once she dons her silks, let her sulk!
I'll skulk "the whale road":
Hi, London! Ho, London!
Lo! Spray springs gainst boulders!

—*Joseph Howe*

[**Wolfville (Nova Scotia) 12** *mai* **12**]

The Death of Alexander Pushkin (1837)

The earnest chatter of treaties—
the patter of noble entreaties—
falter, fail, perish,
for I'm poised now to shoot
every bastard aristocrat on first whiff!

Spy the trifling whelp of a no-count Count:

Georges d'Anthès confiscates every spotlight,
preys on wives,
even hopes to drag mine from our bed
and bring her to heel,
kneeling before his erect form,
as if I, her husband, am already a corpse....

The cur believes he can sit in my chair—
beside my wife's bed—
or dine at my table in my absence—
or scheme to slip through a window
and dip into my wife
and then joke about it—
with flawless *Indecency*!

Well, I equal Othello in *Jealousy*
as well I do in *Complexion*;
but I best Othello in that my *Rage*
is not against my spouse,
but with he who'd dishonour her,
bruiting that she can be "screwed"
by brutish all and sundry.

I'll not let such guffaws haunt my skull.
Rather, I'd lop the walls of a body—
a man's chest—
and gut horses,
sooner than brood over slanders—
as empty-handed but as brutal as slaps.

I prefer my wife *Sacrosanct*—
not some white man's dame—
slagged by moral *Butchery*
and slogged through *Debauchery*.

My wife's *Shame* is my *Agony*,
which I cannot assuage,
unless d'Anthès feels lead
plunge through his lungs,
tear out his spine,
pin down his *Life* as he wriggles,
ever more slowly,
to *Stillness*.

I crave *Justice*—
which is a Negro's gold—
just as fat craves fat.

I have more love for a bitch
than a vixen who forges quarrels
via her lascivious coils—
wiles—
provoking the harrowing *Barbarity* of a duel.

So, I await my bullet's whetted cleaving
of d'Anthès—
slanderer, snitch, tattle-tale, liar—
and no wad of cash
or universe of vodka
(my *Rage* is as universal as vodka)
can win me to *Peace*!

Rather, let me see d'Anthès so mutilated
that he watches with me
while I sic a dog to gobble his genitals
and next devour his windpipe,*

and onlookers applaud,
and not one tear drop
burnishes his body turned carcass.

I must put down the unrelenting cretin
mercilessly.
Lookit! *Mercy* is what one shows horses,
not pigs.

[Tulum (Mexico) 1 *septembre* mmxv]

---

* Well, it's *perro come perro* (Spanish: "Dog eat dog"), eh?

Paulhan Preaches "Happiness in Slavery" (1838)*

Who dast scotch the *Beauty* and *Serenity* of *Servitude*?
Beige-dashed or tar-dark Bajan Negroes?

White Glenelg and his clan suffered black,
macabre, disgusting *Murder*,
not because they were savage sadists,
but because they were savagely beloved!

Emancipation of the Canadians** was
a "womanish sop"—
barren of iron *Direction* or *Provision*.

Freedom arrived on feverish,
wind-razoring wings—
inaccessible to mushroom-stunted, mushroom-fragile,
mushroom-dim Golliwogs.

Who thus dast blame Glenelg's (ex) slaves for chopping
he—his wedded wife—their progeny—
into white-and-red, blob-rich custard—
for the jigaboos were bereft of Glenelg's *Caritas*,
his love—
yes, his *Love*—
his liberating *Authenticity* of *Care*.

The news of their *Emancipation* was as repugnant to them
as is *Celibacy* and/or *Chastity*.

Glenelg's (ex) slaves preferred the gossamer spider-webs
of kindly *Tyranny*
to the surreally beautiful, open-air of *Liberty*:
They saw that light as too bright,
felt that atmosphere as too cold.

---

* Cf. *Histoire d'O*, writ in Roissy-en-France (France).
** Mississippi euphemism for *niggers*.

The Queen's sermon was not alert to facts
re: the Negroid;
Glenelg was not indulgent re: *Discipline.*

His commanded, sugarcane chores—
always undertaken in subdued wind,
or dawn breezes,
never slivers of rain—
were hardly onerous.

His *Generosity* was as immense as sunlight.
He was a love poet who loved *Nature*—
including his niggers.

Enslavement—for his pickaninnies—was *Happiness,*
apt glorying in the plantation's
Platonist order
(akin to Darcy's in *Pride and Prejudice*).

Due to their interfered-with *Pleasure,*
Glenelg's slaves—
his *liberated*, ex-slaves—
mashed and bashed his skull with a machete
in a shit-dull dusk.

One of his half-breed, scrofulous, mustard-tone,
retard bastards,
hacked Glenelg harmfully,
for his pappy had allowed him too much *Privilege.*
For this whelp, *Emancipation* meant release to *Regression.*

Glenelg was the once-lover of his assassin's mammy,
and so was extra-raunchy in his *Liberalism,*
while treating his slaves like royalty,
sporting toy crowns,
naming them as princes and ladies.

Glenelg's *Enlightened* acts authored his *Death Sentence!*

Maybe he'd've survived to see grandchildren if
he'd been an out-of-bounds Sade—
eager to dress his serfs in surfeits of blood,
and treat the insolent—
those as upstart as an itch—
to hemp-high-hanged necks.

(Indeed: Glenelg's stock was wily beggars,
lisping a Britannic-Dixie dialect
with a Bluenose slant—
all as villainous as Villon—
all deserving a Bosch-like Hell—
where all such cut-throat bastards broil.)

Now, lookit! His Roman-titled slaves—
Caesar, Augustus, Lavinia—
have set fire to his Rome.

Grotesquely, his whole spawn is now sun-blackened corpses—
their screams, piled up, are now eternal *Silence*.

Glenelg's slaves were bound to be irritated
once denied his white-gold *Munificence*,
his white-flag *Christianity*.

But Glenelg enjoyed overmuch
clandestine *Conjuncture* under stairs—
to feel a naughty trembling in his knees
in lewd crouching—
to spend in a Negress's upturned duff,
and milk his cream into chocolate pudding.

Glenelg loved too much to squander his filling
in every trifling éclair—
or in bottoms like mouldy, soft cheese.

Surely, *Civility* can't be maintained in the orchard
once *Barbarism* has triumphed in the bedroom!

But he was a sporty white—
more lewd than legislative—
liking the look of his johnson*
pricking a Negress's prominent prat,**
her soles pushed back—
pink—
to her head:
To stuff butter in her obscene clefts!

Misunderstanding undermines one's standing:
Slavery is *Utopia*—
a rough sketch of *Heaven*—
when slaves believe they're in *Hell*.

So, Glenelg's ameliorated execution of *Mastery*
led to all the white bodies
battened to—
or got of—
his white body,
being awakened in bull's-eye night
and butchered thoroughly,
while the placated ex-slaves,
satisfied that the tease of *Liberty* had been dispelled,
drank up all the broken-into wine—
pissed (urinated) into crystal goblets—
and went blissfully themselves to sleep.

The *Homicide* happened in August's green pall—
as red-bleeding Autumn crept nigh.

Glenelg took a knife in his groin,
a hatchet to his face,
splitting open his eye:
He died like a bewildered poet.

---

* African-American: Phallus.
** British English: Duff.

His whole nuclear family exploded
into ruddy pieces—

an uncontaminated-by-Christianity,
untouched-up *Butchery.*

Familial carcasses marinated in maggots.

Liberalism is a scripture fine for self-throat-cutting,
but not as *Insecticide.*

Better that whip marks crisscross black backs
than white babes end as fossilized as dead stars....

Eh?

[Roissy-en-France (France) 11 & 12 *juillet* mmxvi]

Preston Founds the African Slavery Abolitionist Society (ASAS) (1840)

"To preserve *Slavery* in one precinct—
and *Liberty* in another—
is like putting bandages on a dead dog....

"Free men who argue
'other men need chains'—
compose a symposium of cannibals
dining on corpses....

"The Senate has a graveyard reek:
Note the musty fragrance!
The Republic, allowing *Slavery*,
equals a formidable tomb.....

"To be human
is the *Labour* of a lifetime.
(No one 'kills' *Time*:
It kills you.)....

"There's no cheerful *Tragedy*
in *Slavery*!
Blood streams from every eye!
No percentage is a mirage!

"Look at the slavers' decaying churches:
Their incense smells of mould.
Our aborted generations
permit us vast scope for venom!

"Let no childish *Sin* persist unexcoriated.
(Lashing is the recommendation.)"

[David Hett Room, Government House,
Halifax (Nova Scotia) ii/II/11]

Haliburton Pens "The Black Brother" (1840)—I

His *Religion?*
Press *Opinion*
in a dog's voice:
Raw yelps and belching.

(His words cut fine—
when served with wine!
Add honey, whores,
his tongue adores!)

His true *Scripture?*
Luscious liquor!
Not sparkling blood
tapped from the Rood.

His "Gospel" brays
oinks like th'anus!
Putrid volumes—
no *Grace* perfumes.

Tar-dipped wolf—
Sodom itself—
his throat doth crow
heart of a sow!

Nymphs and satyrs
are his martyrs?
I'll bet he dies—
choked by his lies!

[David Hett Room, Government House,
Halifax (Nova Scotia) 3 *février* mmxi]

Haliburton Pens "The Black Brother" (1840)—II

Study Preston!

Mezzatesta![*]

A piddling poetaster,
hied home from London,
adept—
knowing, to preach is to hustle!

That showman disappoints:
He proves the poor are poor
at *Economics*
and even poorer
at saving.

He's either high-grade pork
or low-quality pork.
Can't decide.

Jet-black as coffee and shrill as a train whistle!
Exclusively brash,
his drivel is his embellishment!

The man's erratic chitchat
convinces darkies
they can screwdrive nails
and axe up water.

Totally a coal-scuttle Scotian—
his jungle *Heritage* screams in every word!

---

[*] Italian: Half a head.

His tongue is completely abusing
of English, of *Logic*.
His sermons sanctify tainted perspectives—
the monotony of vulgar, harmful *Doctrine*.

That fraud artist need be pilloried,
castrated, vilified,
not venerated!
Flogged—at least!

Cripes!

Why don't he wet his mouth with urine?
Chow down on some wholly unholy,
unwashed, unflinching,
exasperating, cock-lacerating, lil cat?

Let Mr. Man take a black hammer
to her white china pelvis?

That's what Rev. "Tricky Dick" Preston needs:
Tarts, rum, plus a good, hard whipping!

There's *Beauty* in *Sin*!

Consider Venice:
A city pirated from a marsh!

[Udine (Italia) 29 *avril* / *Nisan* mmxi]

II. The Records of Richard Preston

Bees breeze in.
Butterflies rise up.

I gallop cross Nova Scotia,
this unique

(one-horse) province,
where rain falls, Latinate,

half-new, half-Scottish;
and sidle through maple-mahogany,

elm-ebony, forest-sable midnights,
and wish I could moor

at a jasmine mine,
a jewel well—

here in *Nova Escócia,*[*]
among the WIN[**] tribe—

I mean, with a masterpiece of *Femininity*—
a lady with pekoe-coloured legs, wine-dark lips—

her chocolate velvet flesh
flowering in gold-cut shadows,

with eyes that steal away *Grief,*
with a kiss that plunders Paradise!

[Nantes (France) 8 *février* mmix]

---

[*] Portuguese: Nova Scotia.
[**] White, Indian, Negro. Cf. Estabrook and McDougle, *Mongrel Virginians.*

Preston Visits Windsor Plains
Africadian Baptist Church

I.

In the rose garden nigh the apple orchard,
the flowers seem ferocious, deformed porcupines,
bristling thorny spikes;
looming, threatening as cacti.

Turn the mind's eye *Nature*-ward,
and I spy vaginal openings—
exact in this whorish *Horticulture*—
but pouting, inviting....

To wander in this *hortus conclusus*,*
this *placuit oculis*,**
is to see women
as volcanic—if floral—inlets;
or as edenic apertures.

II.

(*War* is dust!
Renaissance is gold-leaf.

But guns turn a profit,
for guns seize others' profits.

Can savants end wars?

---

* Latin: Garden enclosed.
** Latin: Court.

Consider that Russian chevalier—
Mikhail Miloradovich,
would-be peacemaker:
His ultimately banged-up face,
kicked-in teeth,
stomped-on glasses,
knife-gouged-out heart.)

Geography pinches us;
History lynches us.

III.

Under the silver-stain moon,
I glimpse the spook of a Thomas-cat—
not a mere tomcat—
scatting about where men and maidens creep
to couple in bushes, thus scuppering beds.

Monotonous *Métissage?*
Unschooled white pimps
or well-schooled black whores:
Ugly bellies full of Creole bastards!

Even the roads are greasy!

(Stars are gone astray; the sky's gone askew!
The moon's a paltry gleam!)

We are as promiscuous as rats.
The powerful foam of conjoined thighs
leaves even dew *Lust*-coloured—
tint and texture of drool.

IV.

Hapless couples mash sex on sex
in honey mire, tirelessly;
skin sticking to skin, each connects—
like Punch-and-Judy puppets, but wirelessly,

covenanting, so the globe is
households of menstruating milkmaids,
a neighbourhood
of vipers—aristocrats decked out like gods,
with their wantons all fat with babes,

and where *Courtship* is browsing
in a sty, brown-nosing in dirt, mousing
for *(Sex)* slaves
and never, ever drowsing....

What are the odds?

V.

Let us have black soup
(coffee)
and *otello*—
bunches of bittersweet blue grapes.

Romance ain't hygienic.

[Budapest (Hungary) 18 *septembre* mmxi
& Wolfville (Nova Scotia) 4 *février* mmxii]

A Sermon on X

This man,
this human, humane, and humanizing God—
both Adonis and almighty—
in his abbreviated *Mortality*,
deviated out the penitentiary of flesh,
unpent the *Tyranny* of *History*,
the dogmas of *Statecraft*
(whips, chains, fetters, *gulag*)
the dictatorship of *Matter*
(*Birth, Decline, Death, Putridity*),
the Soul-*Censorship* the *cing* senses effect,
to assume presumptive *Power*—
preemptive *Power*—
and become the embodiment
of eternal, unalterable *Righteousness*.

This Kingfisher of men—
though tortured by taunts and thorns—
unhooked the shackles of his jailers,
surgeried the slashed gladiator's ear,
wished *Profit* upon those who gambled for his clothes
while stripping Him of all *Civil Rights*—
Human Rights—
and dined on bitter, half-penicillin'd bread
and salt tears and vinegar and salt blood,
to deliver to us poor, unconsciously soulless sinners
the solace of honey, wine, milk, bread, molasses, trout—
yet always oblivious He was and be
to our *Colour Consciousness* of blood—
the *Hatred* shed by an orator (Haliburton)
or broadcast by a writer (Haliburton),
and all the scum of *Darwinism* to come
(and here I prophesize).

Those who lust to prohibit us
do sin
(let's name it *Greed*);
and those greedy to travail us
(let's name it *Lust*);
all these miscreants and misanthropes
need heed
Lord X, who sayeth,
"My living waters of *Mercy*
gush forth only emancipating *Brilliance*—
Son-Light,
all healing and refreshing, redemptive and wholesome.
Get thee baptized!"

What *Freedom* be in this coagulated light,
this triangulated light!

Never the bright blackness of midnight snowfalls—
night-blackened light—
blotting out the moon!
Never the finesse—fineness—
of such black falling!
Never the bright page darkened
by black, shadowing words,
the dark lustre, rioting,
snowing evenly or raggedly—
blizzarding (*Blitzkrieg*-ing)—
bamboozling the eyes!
Never doth any such blinding
benight us!

Light differs from darkness, aye,
just as blackness nixes white.

X's *Sacrifice*, being wholesale, not piecemeal;
being full-scale, and nothing by halves
(or left half-done),
enlightens us
that we can depart from bad actors,
heathen ancestors,
and inaugurate a *Genealogy* of saints
and/or join a communion of saints,
my African brethren and Ethiope chillun of God!

—*Richard Preston*

[Roma (Italia) 26 *juin* mmxviii
& Halifax (Nova Scotia)
Liberation Sunday 15 *juin* mcmlxxxvi
& Halifax (Nova Scotia)
New Love Sunday 15 *mars* mcmlxxxvi]

Preston Forges Through Blizzard

Snow shakes—quakes—the town to flaky heaps;
blasts forth either cake or chowder to smatter
windows, too frail. Every shape cankers, hulks,
moulders, deforms, into some bulk—monstrous
as an amoeba. All assertions rise
blunted, rounded with *Abruptness*, the swerve
and curve of the blizzard as it seizes
every entrance, every portal, to mute—
stifle—muffle—silence X's Gospel—
or King Lear-like tirades.

(Snow satirizes* statues; so statesmen
resemble their ungodly doggerel—
blanching verse that's really gull guano,
plastering the ungainly regal and the Quasimodo-courtly.)

Here's a successful, whites-only Dixie
Gothicism—erasing everything
unlike itself. But I reject this pale
metaphor for Queen Vic's America!
Cold bites my bones and gnaws at my soul.
My mittens turn bricks; iced up, my scarf seems lead.
My great coat shivers; winter blanches my black steed!

I gotta cry to witness such *Beauty*,
so horrible, my tears lizard into icicles.
But *Faith* says one day blossoms'll detonate,
mushroom profusely, sugaring branches
throughout Annapolis's April realm.
(Snow ruffles; fog** smoothes.)

---

* *Satire* showcases the fake, the backward, the hypocritical.
** Romantic fog bests routine dust or abusive, invincible rain.

Every traveller is a shadow, unfazed,
passing through—even a passing phase
(or fashion), like gradations—striations—
infinite fluxing of ivory and foam,
or saturation on saturation
of chalk snow—democratic sepulchre....

[Roma (Italia) 29 *juin* mmxviii
& Ottawa (Ontario) 9 *mars* mcmxciv]

Haliburton Pens "The Black Brother" (1840)—III

I.

The varmint, scalawag, hoboes about,
dog-eared in collar,
flea-bitten.

The scent is gypsy, the stench is Negroid:
The black "brother" preacher, I say,
don't just master *Sin*,
he's a master of *Sin*.

Unflinching bitching in his dog-collar!

He is personal proof that coffee—
lacking cream—
is a black waste—
a black skeleton lacking "body."

His Baptist religion
is also as sexless as air.

Preston's not even a well-made shadow.

He's just meticulously and as mellifluously
as ominous as a murder of crows....

He be practically mud!
I can't believe Xians come steeped in mud!

Let him slap down slogans in ink—
the damned louse—
bastard So-and-So—
his sermons that toot and horn-blast!

I wish that anti-slavery types
were also anti-humbug,
anti-brouhaha,

as opposed to puffing out *Propaganda*
intended to inculcate—
in these assholes—
public *Panic*.

Wherever th'African Liberation League goes,
with its pamphlets,
there's the smell of paper burning,
of words smoking.

To hell with Preston!
To hell with th'Africadian Baptist Church!

II.

The Black Refugees *must* accept
interspersion of dung, vitriol, and pitch
in their sweaty labours,
for they are merely muscled larvae.

In summer, they eat worm-infested clover;
in winter, they eat cheese that's wormy.

Their houses boast *Necrophilia*,
Negrophilia, and sexual *Cannibalism*
(INCEST).

[Tropea (Italia) 8 *juin* mmxviii]

Longfellow Considers the Africadians (1847)

That negative *Nudity*—"blackface"—appalls—
like *Slavery*, Europe's savage visage,
disgracing every mirror.

Yet, the blackamoor *Theology*—
clamorous chitchat, venomous prophecies—
dredges the clandestine stench of dead rats.

Doth the Brit dominions pump out white devils?
(Well, the Law of Averages
presupposes the accurate positive.)

Yet, I've damned the Brits already
in my *Evangeline*, the tear-jerker,
a parade of Tennysonian *Schmaltz*,

the florid weeping for Frenchies put to rout,
dissolved into *Exile*,
resolved into martyrs

(through the breadth of my pages
that teardrops clout).
Nicely, blood drives a faucet of ink:

Thus, Negro *Slavery* could work a black *Tragedy*,
now that I've gussied up Acadian *Suffering*.
Yet, the Nova Scotian Negroes would crow

atop my corpse, cough up blood more poignant than ink,
roar out hymns drowning out the ocean;
still, they're no better than mud.

Poetry enacts a fantastic *Theology*,
wherein Milton's epic is just stitches and glue—
awesome verses from an awful brain,

puritanical when not satanical
(given his hero, a gutsy villain, with brio).
I doubt I can do the Scotians justice!

I know of their upholstery of bruises,
the scarlet aspic of whippings;
their reverent gaze upon Christ's corpse,

the bloodied Saviour. Their gaze never wavers.
What epic suits the North Atlantic's saints?
My pen feints,

caught between the tragic, the comic.

There is too much prosaic newsprint re: slaves' bios....

[Wolfville (Nova Scotia) 28 *août* mmxxi]

Of T. C. Haliburton ("Sam Slick")

That mean, fat, scrunched down, hunchbacked, petty scribe—
teeters, gyrates, about his canes—
two silver-knobbed, hazel sticks cut outta Hantsport forest
to summon Nova Scotia nostalgically
to the vein-gnarled, ink-douser's hands.

Now that he ticks and tocks and toes about
London, wheeling around the House of Commons
and reeling to pub after pub,
taking his "daily constitutionals" of nightly rounds
of scotch and whisky and rye,
and alerting the sundry duly sobre,
"Comforting is *Death!*,"
one reads the demise of the grey-wigged satirist—
as juvenile in *Thought* as Juvenal is not—
for S.S.'s ("Sam Slick's") attacked in *The Times*
for positing white proles as "niggers"
and smokestack-funded lords as "slave masters."

Now the Bluenose expatriate is execrable,
though he toadies and brown-noses
to British bluebloods, the Anglo-Saxon upper-crust,
for they read him rightly as a Yankee curmudgeon,
a Come-From-Away who can't get away
with cant anymore,
who scuttles over cobblestones—
a crab-like and crabby type,
shabby in his shambling,
and dotty and doddering,
whose draining powers allow only feeble-minded screeds,
produced *via* grimacing in mirrors,
while sweating from disembowelling cramps.

Haliburton's long believed discharge of ink equals
discharge of *Duty*,
but he grouses like the guards staffing Golgotha,
watching X bleed out his *Humanity*,
but, bored by imperial Rome's *Realpolitik*,
and wishing to profit by bidding on wine,
X's seamless robe, and half-globes of ready ass,
give way to sighs and moans of *Exhaustion*.
That's S.S.!
All exhaust; his witticisms now just Gothicism
rendered comic,
a lot of unfunny, *Rigoletto* giggling,
as if he's stabbed himself in his fat guts—
his harlequin motley—
his signature tracing a bad hand,
Penmanship proved fatal, toxic.

—*Septimus Clarke**

[Roma (Italia) 25 *juin* mmxviii
& Waterloo (ON) Holy Monday & Heroic Saturday
avril mcmlxxxiv]

----

* First clerk of the Africadian Baptist Association of Nova Scotia, as of 1853.

Haliburton Versus *the Africadian Baptist Association*

Do they give a shit-damn bout *Theology?*
Them demagogic devils?

The blacky Baptists wanna play the petty game
of Napoléon, exiled to Elba—
their prose so discoloured, so purple,
they tar themselves with ink;
they feather themselves with paper
as incomprehensible as confetti.

Sludge is their *Rhetoric;*
smudge are their sermons.

The Jim Crow minstrels—
purring poets and primping preachers—
insult Heaven!
Each is Dr. Worse and Worse—
demonic thingabobs—
hordes of porkers, oinking, trotting....

[YAM—Sault Ste. Marie (Ontario)
28 *juillet* mmxxi]

Septimus Clarke Scripts Church Minutes

I.

Light rains and light reigns.

Its downcome snares and rinses.

Where it lives—
or alights—
it arouses—

like *Love*.

Light executes a pitiless massage.
Animal flesh can't help but preen—

even if jealous gods take umbrage.

You even see light right here
in each wine-dipped line—
iridescent as surf.

(No *Opulence*
without *Turbulence*!)

We ain't piebald beings,
but incandescent—

and indecently so

(when naked).

My gold hand jets black ink
your white hand shadows.

II.

Next, a high-strung, discordant guitarist,
some star player who now plays out booze,

excites a twitchy guitar, an itchy guitar,
a touchy guitar, but also a catchy guitar,

his operatic *legerdemain* stringing along
a slapstick *Religiosity*, nervy, gutsy, hearty,

so everybody gotta stand up and croon
Preston's own hymn, "Where Do You Stand?"

—*Septimus Clarke*

[**Szentendre (Hungary)** 15 *septembre* **mmxi**
& **Nantes (France)** 14 *décembre* **mmviii**]

Where Do You Stand?

Moses had to take a stand.
Jesus had to take a stand.
I believe I'll take mine:
Precious Lord, take my hand....

God won't stand for the in-between.
God won't stand for the middle-of-the-road.
God won't stand for the Undecided.
God demands to know where you stand!

Even an itty baby chil
Gotta stand sometime!
I believe, I believe,
I'll now take mine.

—Richard Preston

[Nantes (France) 14 *décembre* mmviii]

Preston Establishes the
Africadian Baptist Association (1853)

On this pined peak, green-laurelled crag—Granville Mountain
(North Mountain range, Annapolis Valley)—
the consummate *Moment*
is palpably, inescapably *Now*:
To call forth intrepidly the congregations
so consentaneous* to our *Faith*
so as to annihilate the *Disenfranchisement*
of Coloured Baptists from X's whole table—
Last Supper and Tabernacle—
so that we fuse spontaneously
into the Africadian Baptist Association.

I hereby declare our deathless *Existence*
in determinable** words,
and now we shall gather the *Residue*
of Baptists
unto X's *Stewardship*.

This Church—our Church—is newborn,
yet has a weathered appearance
and ancient habits particular to our ex-enslaved selves.
Our finishing *Theology* has been decided by Word-o-Mouth
and by handed-down *Song*.
Homogeneity is thus impractical and impossible.
Variations and nuances of timbres and accents
brand our churches, each, with her own *Personality*,
as each is different from the other.
This is a merit, a blessing,
and our *Faith* can evolve mutually *via Praxis* and *Time*.

---

* Pertinent.
** Explicit.

True: It be probable and desirable that our Church lose
its initial, monochromatic aspect,
especially as we integrate and procreate with strangers,
who are welcome, but won't ever dilute
"Coloured folks'" *Baptism* rituals.

Dear God, preserve our Church—
even in its *Separate Development,*
and never expose us to the temptation of *Secularism.*
I pray that Thou will keep us eternally apart
from the easy-going sinfulness of "Babylon."

Then again, there is likely no great *Faith*
that ain't a test.

[Tropea (Italia) 24 & 25 *juin* mmxxii]

A *Preface to* Occasional Discourse on The Nigger Question *(1853)*

By Thomas Carlyle

I.

I blame ambrosial coffee, the allure of sugar,
the thirst for rum,

for our ruddy, wet-job *Sadism*
versus the blackskins:

Thus, their spirituals worry our banks
and harry our gunmen.

Their rabid, drooling jaws
gobble the language,
so our former English, now fangs,
gnaws and bites our ears.

But black, talky-talky *Jabberwocky*—
spiteful *contra* massas (us)—
is as misleading as cracked mirrors.

The whip is hot *Medicine,*
a searing *Surgery,*
planting welts on black backs
as parallel as waves,
so that the niggers slave,
compliant, productive,
earn their keep—

like white whelps in Manchester factories.

And the lash hits and hits and hits
until the ex-lazy-bones body falters,
drops like a crinkled, blood-red, autumn leaf.

II.

In the counterpoint of blooms and thorns,
that is master/boss *versus* worker/slave,
what are we
and what are they?

Our delivery of whippings suggests we're thorns,

but the blackies can't be blooms,
not unless they're blood-dark poppies....

III.

This 19th Century of *Loathing*—
empires smartly discharging cannons
and wrongly discharging slaves—

sees unchained blacks—
unleashed phalanxes
(iron-stern, lead-heavy *phalloi*)—
unconstrained—

set loose to become fodder
for unscrupulous capitalists,
or be used to minisculize wages
of hungry, po' white "chillun"—

so *"Emancipation"*
requires vivid bloodshed in obscure quarters
(West Indian),
too distant for *The* [London] *Times* to care,

but, soon, sunlight papers over shadows
and insect larvae scour blood stains.

Anyway, we trade colonies like skulls,
especially in Africa,
where folks regularly stagger headless.

IV.

Our centuries stumble from *War* to *War*,
forgetful that wars grant dubious *Immortality*—
at best—
unhappy poets drafting hateful books.

So, endless chatter, some of it *Poesy*,
answers "The Nigger Question."

[Annapolis Royal (Nova Scotia) 22 *mars* mmxiv]

Letter to the (Africadian Baptist) Messiah

I.

Tons upon tons of cold afflict us here—
Positive Nova Scotians of negative *Character.*

This province is nothing but a royal brothel.
(Bad, deficient, proves each female.)

The best of our lot are just mesmerizing scum
Dubbing this nauseating swamp "Elysium."

Incest thrives here—twixt cradle and gallows.
In white genesis,* stallions stab into sows.

Agony of *Desire* compels us to sin:
Pleasure plies its ominous *Religion.*

Hazy cheer is ours; *Redemption* is complex.
Our mission is *Salvation* (*via* intermissions of *Sex*).

Les putains de merde, O Nature Généreuse,
These unprecedented parasites leak glaucous mucus.

They live by joining in unhygienic contest;
Shit-soused, each *pute* imputes a putrid antichrist.

Their love has two faces: *Jouissance* and intense
Sorrow. They stroll bow-legged from séance to séance.

(Hear the whorehouse discourse of *salt, wet,* and *fish.*
All along the docks, one can smell burning fish.)

---

* Incest.

Glorious *Gynaecology* has come to this:
A goad in each cunt, a tongue in each anus.

II.

Not bland or blind or blond,
Thou art blunt Black Being from Beyond.

To forestall fault-finding Fires and Flood,
You accept *Agony* upon The Rood.

Smoke-laurelled heads and blood-lacquered hands
Prefer You dead as ghostly *Phosphorescence.*

The clergy are treasonous—as they are always:
Their sermons distill poison they deem delicious.

(Each preacher is as sincere as a courtesan—
Their façades mirror The Sphinx's insolence.

Prophet-frauds, those library libertines, compose
A *Codex Gigas*★ to damn all gullible Negroes.)

Entrusted with diamonds but encrusted with blood,
Governors erect rood after rood.

III.

In Golgotha, you meet antique, assassins' daggers,
The questioning eyeballs of dissatisfied beggars,

Unquestionable sluts, bankers clad in sobre black,
Cold soldiers whose whips burn up your turned back,

★ Latin: Devil's Bible.

A provisional deluge of curses, a draft of blood,
A blessing of vinegar, til *Sorrow* trickles into mud.

As violent as vultures gnawing a corpse,
Whips prey upon Thee so Thy spine warps.

Thy fine, dark face, unconquerable King,
Is laced with spittle during Thy ruddy scourging.

The epitome of *Pity*, and so pitiable—
Thou art hog-tied, hornswoggled, like any criminal.

(A glut of light in autumn copper and mauve
Flares: Halloween harvest brightens Xmas stove.

Dying is always in December;
Reviving is reserved for Easter.)

Should You return "too early," it will be too late:
Love, that whore, loves none save those who love *Hate*.

IV.

Be that unexpected Xian, never hostage
To *Religion*, but hostile to bavardage.

Truth is torment. *Truth* is torment.
Truth is torture never dormant.

Set hearts afire on every side,
Scourge us of *Lust*, purge us of *Pride*.

Hew from *Scripture* bright pearls of *Verse*:
New stars to light th'Ethiope universe.

V.

From time to time, lead poets back to *Poetry*:
Let each scribe torch the Bastille in the Library.

(Damnable poets speak volumes and say nothing.
Their "revelations" disperse in gaseous vomiting.

The disciple of negligent hand, careless
Of a pure style, serves malicious palaces.)

Thy true poets press ink from crushed wasps' nests.
(Books father books: *Knowledge* is promiscuous.)

The Trumpet of *Poetry* sounds ever hideous.
Thus, if honest, preaching sounds insidious.

VI.

I have coffee and cocaine, my solitary pension:
Suppose it's how I oppose decomposition.

I eat pastries, drink *pastis*, and parley with all—
Heretical histories, Salmagundi intellectual.

My café face looms bold from the crowd
When brittle light—grimy rime—is the little that's allowed,

And my useless mouth amuses bitches and sluts,
The stalkers of vineyards and the tavern poets.

My scorpion of black ink stings the sugar page:
My verse is vinegar—or wine of bitter vintage.

But *Art* is cruel—
And *Eternity* is uninhabitable.

—*Septimus Clarke, Halifax, Nova Scotia, 1854*

[Montréal (Québec) 28–30 *décembre* mmx]

Meditation on the Babylonian Harlot (Rome)

Rome—Babylon—is Satan's Whore.
Won't God tear down her ass,
her façade,
so Xians can split shit from sugar?

This cake-mix succubus, pastel icing
of clothes, with her *papier-mâché* face—
is a fat wasp, a loathsome vampire,
as cadaverous as a mushroom.

Believers spy a female butcher
who makes God's *Lamb* kneel
and slashes the throat so blood gushes up—
fountains up—blustery.

That succulent, maculate bitch,
her dirty buttocks straddling gore,
would only burgeon in suttee,
emerge flame-polished,

as golden as the golden calves
that trinket and gild the *Papacy,*
and guffawing in her insolence.
(*Sin* is the triumph of laughter.)

This sluttish theologian changes her meanings,
sheet after sordid sheet:
All Protestants puke and shiver
to observe "Miss Fine Style."

Her Apocrypha spits sparks and flames—
the black *et cetera* of burning.
Her sect (her sex)
yields noxious insects.

—*Septimus Clarke*, Halifax, Nova Scotia, 1854

[Cairo (Egypt) **15** & **18** *décembre* **mmx**]

Aesop of Three Mile Plains

April is *Anguish*—if sun blooms not.
May must flourish apple blossoms,
if September will brandish apples.

What gut don't want a good harvest?

This March, earth is colourless jade.
Gardens flaunt dark brambles.
Hardly a red bird or blue bird shows.

April moonlight shimmers like a balm;
next, crocuses blaze against the final snow;
and spring water tastes like mead.

Still, a blizzard whitens again the air.
Against this blighting tax,
does the sun loom gold enough?
Does its *Radiance* overflow?

I want—soon—gold sunflowers on jade stalks.

Must I fetch wine from Niagara?

(Wine-drunk, the poet cannot write.)

I want the crab apples and spruce of Three Mile Plains,
the blackberries and pines of Three Mile Plains,
the white lightning and molasses of Three Mile Plains,
the fiddles and banjos of Three Mile Plains—

a sprinkling of poets, the braying of pens!

—*Septimus Clarke*

[**Windsor (Nova Scotia) 22 *mars* mmxiv**]

L'Ésope de Three Mile Plains*

Avril est Angoisse— si le soleil ne point.
Mai doit épanouir les fleurs du pommier
pour que septembre en vienne à brandir des pommes.

Quel ventre affamé ne veut pas récolter?

Là, en mars, le sol est d'un jade incolore.
Les jardins ne font voir que leurs ronces sombres.
À peine un oiseau rouge ou bleu qui se montre.

Clair de lune en avril chatoie comme un baume;
les crocus flamboient sur la neige finale;
et l'eau du printemps a saveur d'hydromel.

Malgré tout, un blizzard blanchit l'air encore.
Pour contrer cette imposition ténébreuse,
l'or du soleil pèsera-t-il assez lourd?
Et son rayonnement va-t-il déborder?

Je veux—bientôt—
des tournesols dorés sur des tiges de jade.

Faut-il quérir le vin du Niagara?

(Enviné, le poète ne peut écrire.)

Je veux les pommettes et les épinettes de Three Mile Plains,
les mûres et les pins de Three Mile Plains,
l'eau-de-feu et la mélasse de Three Mile Plains,
les violons et les banjos de Three Mile Plains—

quelques rares poètes, un braiment de plumes!

—Septimus Clarke

[Windsor (Novelle-Écosse) 22 *mars* mmxiv]

---

* Traduction : Robert Paquin, Ph. D.

The Poetics

By Louisa Bailey[*]

Moonlight's a buzzsaw
(mute), sharpening serrations;
thus, pines needle night.

Meanwhile, dusty prayers
wither on coffin-dumb mouths.
Fulfillment? Hopeless.

Meaningless be sighs—
like the last scrap—gasp—of dusk,
the sun drowned, salty—

its careless dipping—
sunk—like a last drip of rum
in a sailor's jug.

I shrug off a cloak;
tug off a petticoat; cross
into nooked shadows

that crosshatch my books,
their now-vitiligo spines.
But ink's deathless gleam

can't hold a candle
to the moon (that honeyed sheen—
ubiquitous now).

---

[*] The sanctified poetess of the Africadian Baptist Association.

I'm an architect
of ink; implant foundations
amid a white sheet's light;

concoct silhouettes
of *Thought* (archly beautiful),
to secure a fast

Reputation, eh?
Each stanza's a paced-off space—
squared by *Time* and *Death*—

a psychedelic
moiré—like shadows splotching,
botching, stiff-spined books

in their ranked banks (or
banked ranks), lined up on my shelves.
Death is always

an eccentric dump.
However, wherever it
alights (or may dawn),

the corpus (corpse) is
as constructive as portraits.
I will away soon— .

I will away soon—
pensively apprehensive—
but a dose of gold—

pages illumined—
to ford unfocussed blackness—
just behind your eyes.

[**Granville Centre (Nova Scotia) 24 *août* mmxxi**]

25

Settled?

We're the independent remnant
of America's once-and-nevermore slaves.

Got no surplus pastures—
or pastors.

In "Nova Scarcity,"
snow falls faultless,
but lands all dingy;
its dirtied *Purity*
be a hostile stain.

Too many of us slog inarticulate to/fro taverns;
wind up winded and maculated under trollops;
prove newfangled fools for old-pro whores

off "Got-a-gun" (Gottingen) Street,
but trawlin, trollin, strollin,
right down to the wharves and docks and piers.

(Enormous church bells
are less convincin
than expressive beauties—
"fine-ass" belles—

who bring big-tit *Ecstasy*—
plus fishy kisses—
to a climate, clammy,
due to swilled and vomit-distilled rum.)

Those grievous Powers—
Brit or Bostonian

(George III *vs.* George Washington)—

banded, landed, and stranded
us here—

after th'ocean-tousling business—
Slaving, War, Evacuation—

to be conversant in soil all stones
and, thus, *Starvation*

(either potatoes or *Privation*).

One must say that this entire colony
persists in a coma of *Dishonour*!

Nova Scotian rum, Nova Scotian molasses,
Nova Scotian seaweed, Nova Scotian lasses,

all bog us down;
leave us groggy;
we end up as dregs:

Vehement drunks and *Sensuality*'s sycophants.

Hypocrisy is *Deception*.
Acts of *Atrocity* are precocious.

(Rudimentary bugs scurry
in complex swarms,
scour every scintilla of dirt
for any edible germ.)

Our dusky muse (Louisa Bailey)
jets letters that splinter
the flimsy panes of newspaper columns.

Mainly spurious Believers, eh,
we be?

We display the pomp of donkeys—
the groaning *Majesty* of oxen:

Yet we lack both asses
and oxen!

We've survived merciless cannon—
the wild waves of altered maps—
and unscrupulous disciples

of Kirk and King.

But still we shuffle along, shiftless, here—
as lice-infested Romantics,
havin to chisel a meagre meal,
eke out a marginal breath,
scrape at dirt like chickens,
tug at small-beer,
bleed through blackberry bramble,
squelch through cranberry bog,

pursuing our down-at-the-heels,
mouth-downturned,
God-turned-down
Messiah—

despite the indelible chirping of our choirs!

And we discover this latent Hell,
this blatant Hell!

—*Septimus Clarke*

[**Vicenza (Italy) 23** *septembre* **mmxii**]

The Poetics (II)

By Louisa Bailey

I'll jet inkwells into chaff faces—
bossy—Caucasoid;
dissolve their characteristic tinsel:
Bible sheets as thin as cirrus clouds.

Let mindless, brainless top hats
go heedless unto guillotines,
emerge headless.
Still, I'm as infallible as sunlight!

I see insects digging into, excavating,
digesting cadavers.
Thus, a picture-book *Xianity*
ends in pettifogging doggerel!

Is there effective *Damnation* in *Poetry*?
I pray to be ruthlessly exquisite,
wield a big-mouth pen,
so cathedrals parade crumpled demons' wings.

I don't grieve for pig sties!
What martyrs wallow therein?
What saints dwell in mud?
Better to live on margins of canons—

Fraternal to every rebuttal;
incorrigibly non-conformist.

[Point Pelee (Ontario) 12/11/21]

Louisa Bailey's Critique of the
Lieutenant-Governor of Nova Scotia

Regard the Lieutenant-Governor's frivolous plumes!
He's a picturesque, carnival emperor—
whey face tethered to a scarlet tunic.

The garrulous womanizer, eager to join
the *Aristocracy* of portraits
squaring the legislature's walls,

should merely cut taxes
and parcel out lands—
all he has to do.

But he governs for nodding, satisfied slaveholders—
the gentry of the university
(Haliburton and his ilk),

each one an appalling crocodile—
bawling tears—
grinning at black folk—

all gargling, ungrateful gargoyles—
intellectuals, cynical—
irredentist boosters of *Slavery*—

a ballet of facial expressions
(not one expressive of a blessed emotion).
The Viscount Falkland is an emperor

of receptions and toasts—
the eruption of acid reflux, malleable, but stylized—
rosewater flattering floating turds—

all to solicit pompous *Adulation*
from *usocchi* (pirates)—a dictatorship
of hypocrites and *conneries**—

lies never short of tongues of ink—
the cesspool *Grandiloquence* of a bidet—
the dirty ethics of his poetics.

Falkland's *Psychology* is predisposed to wine—
the oinking, snorting, farting, of a bordello.
Lust is the setting and Sade is the hero!

That astonishing libertine—
his *Debauchery* never botched—
is unadulterated *menefreghismo*,**

ideal for a pestilential government,
plus an alliance with deranged syphilitics,
who beatify the vicious and sanctify vices.

How *indegno!***
The jerk is as intangible as Champagne bubbles.
His gut is his cock, his balls!

I view *la cimice* (the bedbug)
with unshakeable *Contempt*,
though he exemplify the arrogance of stone.

About that worthless *stronzo*****—
that exemplary human waste—
light is scratchy, rats are squeaky.

He is *Lust* in its apogee!
Not just lousy but unhygienic!
Nonchalant in *Vice*!

---

* French: Bullshit.
** Italian: I-don't-give-a-fuck-ism.
*** Italian: Shameful.
**** Italian: Turd.

Lackeys and yes-men
and sycophants and psychopaths:
Such bandits orchestrate a candid *Tyranny*.

[**Point Pelee (Ontario) 13** *novembre* **mmxxi**]

Articles of Faith and Praxis

I—Articles of Faith

1. One God Supreme only—a Spiritual Intellect
uncircumscribable, even by the Cosmos
(which He hath authored),
instrumentalizes every occurrence of *Love*,
Truth, *Virtue*, *Wisdom*, *Justice*, and *Beauty*.
Period.

2. The Godhead is triune, a Triumvirate:
Three Beings: "Father," "Son," "Spirit,"
all equal in mutual *Authority*.

3. The Divine Scriptures are Hebrew and Greek
(also in Africadian translation).

4. God keeps *Time*, exceeds *Time*,
and knows every origin, every cause,
every course, every act, every event,
and every conclusion,
before slotting *Time* as *History*
or reserving *Time* as *Prophecy*.*

5. God's Government is *Creation*,
i.e., *Making*, i.e. *Poetry*.

6. God deemed Humanity eternal—
if obedient, if righteous,
if sinless, if flawless.

---

* Here is one: America will sweep across the skies of Europe, burying her wealth
in flames!

7.   But the First Man and First Woman
thought *Self-Consciousness*
superior to *Innocence,*
and so brought *Deceit, Greed, Wrath, Lust,*
unto the world,
and so also initiated *Entropy, Decay,*
Disease, and *Death.*

8.   We are thus born "dead" or dying—in effect,
and can only expect to remedy *Mortality*
in *Eternity*—
if so blessed by God.

9.   God hath already secured an innumerable portion
of doomed Humanity as His salvaged saints,
out of every culture, continent, and tongue,
and this polity—
the Kingdom of God—
is all colours and conditions of *Humanity,*
but appointed peculiarly
to preach the Gospel equitably
to all rational beings,
to establish the Empire of *Righteousness*
in hearts, minds, behaviour, attitudes,
and in dreams and in deeds.

10. Being God's once-mortal offspring,
X was commissioned to perish,
but also to overcome *Death,*
so that sinners could convert to His Example,
beg forgiveness for previous sins,
commit to not sinning further,
and be ransomed and redeemed unto *Righteousness*
and Eternal Life
immediately upon cessation of *Mortality.*

11. Only the Spirit of God administers
the benefit of *Atonement.*

12. The Spirit of God proposes to supply
the merits of *Grace*,
once the beneficiary confesses faults,
realizes the necessity of X's intercession,
accepts the Glory of *Salvation*,
and prepares to live evermore
in *Righteousness, Wisdom, Sanctification*,
and to urge *Redemption* upon all.

13. The truly religious life alters
every deed and desire
of the truly converted.
Instead of living in the shivering shadows
of Hellfire,
upward turn our eyes to view divine Light—
sunlight magnified beyond measure.

14. True Believers exercise ideal *Communion*
in *Spirit*—
and *Communism* in practice,
sharing *Labour*, sharing talents,
partaking of each other's offerings,
the common *Plenty*,
so that *Prosperity* and *Abundance*
circulate in tandem with *Charity* and *Mercy*.

15. (Thus is God's Government evident on earth.)

16. The Sabbath must be kept holy.
Believers must worship *ensemble*.

17. God grants mortals Free Will to govern
our societies,
but a Xian order of Government
serves the poor, never the rich;
and upholds Civil Liberties,
even for infidels and dissenters.

18. A mass Resurrection of the Just
and Unjust will be tried before God,
Who will cast the miserable
unto everlasting *Misery*
and usher the Salvaged unto deathless *Joy*.

[Dorval (Québec) *Le Jour d'Aurélia* mmxviii
& Paris (Ontario) 30 *juillet* mmxviii]

Articles of Faith and Praxis

II—Articles of Praxis

1. Our Church must be distinctly visible,
flagrantly alive, brazenly vivid,
and proudly loud,
for it clusters and convenes
actually existing saints,
lustrous in Pentecostal fire,
communicating discipleship
and devotion to God,
to flaunt His irrepressible *Glory*,
inspire in the Believer the most edifying *Fervour*
in the correctness of the New
—and post-mortem—
Eternal Life,
plus frustrate *Evil*.

2. Baptism and the Messiah's Feast
are commandments of X Himself,
and are to be observed
unto the Second Coming,
and the former ordains the latter praxis.
One cannot partake of what is
(currently)
"The Last Supper,"
unless one has been immersed—
submerged—
in the waters both purifying professed *Iniquity*
and sanctifying the onrush of the New Life,
i.e., the burial of the sinner
amid blessed, holy fluid,
and his or her resurrection unto a temporary
and then an eternal Life of *Righteousness*,
in the witness of that perfect Trifecta—
Father, Son, and Spirit.

3.   Candidates for Africadian Baptist rites
of *Admission* to the Congregation of the Salvaged
via Confession of Sins
and receipt of Baptism unto the New Life
of *Righteousness,*
are expected to fast and pray for three days prior
to the Interview preceding Baptism,
and to express/relate
the Dream or Vision communicated unto each
as he or she approaches
committed *Communion* with X and God
via the Spirit.

4.   Only the veritable Believer may accede rightly
to the pinnacle of submission
which is full-body Baptism
plus partaking of the Sumptuous Feast of Crucifixion
("The Last Supper").
We must bar all pretenders to *Sanctity,*
and exercise fearsome *Jealousy*
in *Love* of our Lord
in preserving Sacraments
and preventing False Communion
(which is to league with devilry).

5.   Thus empowered in governing itself,
our Church may appoint those officers
that X hath approved
(Bishops, Elders, Deacons);
and may depose, discipline, and/or expel
all those whose acts reveal
disavowal of *Redemption,*
eschewal of *Salvation.*

6.   Our Constitution forbids individual judgment—
(*Autocracy*)—of Bishop or Elder
in regard to any *Controversy*
of either person(s) or of *Faith.*

However, superior training in *Theology*
may yield superior instruction
and/or judiciousness
(or so we pray).
Thus, so long as decisions-in-*Congregation*
prove beneficial to all Baptists,
so may the Bishop or Elder
be deemed responsible
to administer the ordinance of *Grace*,
exhort the Gospel,
lead Believers,
warn backsliders,
and rebuke those in peril of Hell.

7.   The Deacon must deliver *Charity*
as *Prosperity*;
become rich in *Joy* in feeding the hungry,
housing the vagabond,
clothing the ragged,
nursing the sick,
and teaching the unlettered.

8.   Every Believer hath the *Duty*
to profess the *Faith* (with exuberant *Panache*);
to enjoy the Freedom and Fruits of *Salvation*;
to do right, to uphold *Law*,
and to improve circumstances,
so that the whole community flourishes;
and to banish *Injustice*!

9.   Each minister must correct "Contradictions
among the people";*
be devoted to their spiritual (real) selves;
promote the channelling of natural *Usufruct*—
bread, wine, milk, honey, fish, gold, myrrh, etc.—

---

* Cf. Mao.

to satisfy the Communion,
so that the Body of X is fed, watered,
clothed, housed, nursed, taught, healed,
and moneyed and pensioned,
and all Believers dwell easily
in *Holiness* and *Righteousness*.

    10. Yet, none of the above Articles
is to be backed violently,
or enforced by the batons and bullets
of bullying, secular *Power*.
Belief is a freewill Offering—
by *Faith*—
accepting the strictures of Gospel.
Members deficient in *Faith*,
in good *Conduct*,
or any breach of fundamental *Duty*,
will realize the subtraction of *Fellowship*,
i.e., *Abandonment* to Satan's claws.

    11. *Shekinah* is the visible *Glory* of God
hovering bout the *Mercy*-seat!

[Batavia (New York) 31 *juillet* mmxviii
& Niagara-on-the-Lake (Ontario) 1/8/18]

[A Preface to the Africadian Baptist Association Covenant]

W ho is as theological as the Devil?

Legalistic, only Lucifer insists
categorically
on a dehumanizing *Purity*—
that *Rectitude*—
invective—
the white churches preach.

In their grotty cloisters,
their damp crypts
(smelling brownly like the doggy-poo smell
of decapitated mice),
find dysfunctional *Cheer.*

There's a lot of brass, china, crystal,
even gold-foil Madonnas,
but, to their congregants,
each virgin is just fresh meat—
an unsmiling—
because unpracticed—
jade.

But who wants a wife who's a talkative, rebarbative bitch?
I want one who's blessedly less a bluestocking
and more a bar-maid,
who's glad to exchange tea for whiskey!

I don't want some pale, wrinkly-assed church mouse,
with wine-coloured lips and snout.
She'd be praying as we communed,
and it'd be one damned thing after another!

The white man's pride of *Sexuality*—
his *Woman*—
is also low-grade, marginalized,
and prefers to be forcibly demeaned,
to be a Negro's personal plaything!

Tis a misfortunate situation:
That ivory women desire charcoal men.
But neither can have the other
unless one elects to be hurt.

The pasty-face clergy swear by *Celibacy*,
but don't swear off *Adultery*, *Buggery*, *Contumely*, and *Debauchery*
(etc.),
though unwilling to say so stridently.

But I don't see why lovers should
compact a cabal of saints.
Leave such posturing
to the maggot-ridden, maggot-sodomized *Nobility*.

The Caucasoid Xians recycle
always refreshed garbage.
Each church is a gleaming dump-site.

Milton's Satan is an aristocratic rebel
of baroque *Majesty*;
Dante's Satan is an effete playboy.
Both are obviously ofay men.

Our *noir* Bible's different
because it's true.

I'll wield X's sickle against priests' tongues!
I'll sink into my love just like sword-points sink into skin!

—*Septimus Clarke*

[Essen (Germany) 2 *mai* mmxi]

The Africadian Baptist Association Covenant

1. We are devotees always of the Party of God,
and witness thus before angels and mortals,
acknowledging God as our Creator, Saviour,
Judge, and King,
and as Omnipotent and Omniscient.

2. We declare X to be our Lord and Prophet
and Priest,
and we are His partisans too,
connected by the Spirit of *Grace*.

3. Our lives now commit to glorifying God
in the usage of our bodies,
the spiritual and practical application
of our talents and capacities,
the diminution of *Sin*,
and affirming *Righteousness* at home
and *Charity* outside.

4. We also covenant, being Xians,
i.e., children of God,
related by the state of *Grace*,
to undertake to rebuke,
reprove, admonish, remonstrate with,
and correct one another,
to eradicate misconduct
and affirm *Rectitude*.
If any one appears to backslide,
the just action is not to gossip,
tattle-tale, or backbite,
but to labour to restore—
in *Communion*—
a moral orientation.

5.   Our Church also covenants
to avoid these maladies:
Violent evils; iniquitous chitchat;
cussing and dirty talk;
vain disputes about *Theology*;
disregarded promises;
unkept appointments;
inessential labour on the Sabbath;
idling in taverns and/or brothels;
ignoring the *Communion* of *Salvation*;
and refusing to seek *Forgiveness* for errors.

6.   But our Covenant insists
that the glories and mysteries
of *Redemption*
belong solely to the Redeemed.
Via X.
To Whom be *Glory* forever and ever.

[**Windsor (Ontario)** 5 *août* **mmxviii**]

Discourse on The Devil

To the Believer, Satan's a joke
as an enemy,
and all his *Theology* sounds hollow
as a fool's howl.

He has torn apart lions—
rendered em carcasses—
golden, bloody, dismal rust,
but can't make em roar again.

He's weak—unrooted, rootless
as a portable, pagan god,
easily uprooted like a wooden idol.
He's a pushover, topplin like lead.

So, he bad mouths saints?
So, he hisses at martyrs?
So, he cusses, spits at, prophets?
A mutt's gutter deathbed will be his.

Come some aeon, Satan will scuffle
bodily, ineffectual, *versus* angels,
who'll doom the burly grub,
let him wriggle in his native flames!

(A rough mirror
Beaming *Error*:
His tombstoned face?
Gleaming *Disgrace!*)

His scheme and plot is always
to invade mortal flesh, to chomp
and gnaw all down to carnal meat,
to bite down to the bone.

Always, he's as habitual as breath,
yet impersonal as a urinal,
as *Sin* slinks in, wrinkles a brain,
diseases tissue, lecherous as cancer.

Always, he musters beetles,
locust flocks,
an extraordinary cluster,
Creepy-crawlies expert at destroying!

Woe to all who award *Succour*!
Quick is that personage
a derelict being,
cast out amid thorny *Desolation*.

Beezelbub bruits the hubbub
of pin-striped sloganeers
(slave auctioneers of yore),
monologuing *Pettifoggery*.

Obstreperous, the impish pimp,
impervious to groans of *Pain*,
shrieks of mourning,
guffaws—raunchy as a blackface minstrel.

Despicably—but pseudo-biblically,
Satan expounds heresies
to the stubble and prickles of headstones,
to solitary, astonishing ruins.

His auditors—the hellish damned—
feel already God's implemented *Punishment*
of that boyish rogue,
to bake and boil and broil in blaze.

The Devil squawks like a cock,
encroaches like a cockroach,
but will crackle down to
anonymous, ignominious ash—

a tumult of smoke—
to be exacerbated by lava—
the sulphurous design
of his senseless premises.

—*F.R. Langford**

[Roma (Italia) 9/11/19]

---

* Avid disciple and apostle of Father Preston.

Discourse on Original Sin

Original *Sin*? Rosehip-infused gin!
Or out-hollering queans' mouths
in churches rent by hallelujah battles
set to score the heaviest bulk of humid silver—
the gross sediment of the well-milked collection plate.

Better the spunk-freighted, unhallowed hips of a bawd—
a stray melody snaking from a bar—
than a saint's gaunt tongue
fat with screams;
or the rickety lungs of a parson,
crying "Arson!"
when it's Hellfire swallowing his soul!

Avoid hearsay *Wit*—
the god of the taverns—

plus springing kisses
unhinging lips!

The Caucasian church? There's the arsenic,
the rot, the fecal *Invective*.

(Although *Lust* unlocks even baby-powder'd pores,
and ladies the tint of snow and moonlight
bust into motherfucker smirks.)

Fragments of foam—
a collage of clouds—
pastel light pasting water—
conjure smoky haze.

The Gospel is undisturbed *Luminosity*—
virtuoso chiaroscuro.
(Nothing even sweetly dingy.)
Robust, unflustered.

—*F.R. Langford*

[Granville Centre (Nova Scotia) 23 *août* mmxxi]

About the ABA Pastors....

The divines crop up
where least expected,
but most needed—
in climes arid, gloomy, dreadful;

they descend from horses;
disembark from iron horses;

to drive out incorrigible *Folly*
before it hardens to irredentist *Perdition*.

They face down drunkards—
intemperate—
as grumpy as dethroned gods,
no matter the insolent bavardage
of the frivolously slanderous,
the inexorably foul-mouthed,
whose gospel is "effin this and effin that"!

The Africadian Baptist pastors do not trivialize
extremities of *Dereliction*
(I speak of sybarites and their building up of *Disgust*);
but nor pray they for each sinner
to be bitten and killed dead by rats.

But nor do they teeter-totter,
shilly-shally,
or go off-kilter
or off-message.

—*Louisa Bailey*

[New Orleans (Louisiana) **27 *mars* mmxxii**]

Notes Re: F.R. Langford

No slave to *Technique*, he screams out prayers,
spanks the air with growls.
He screeches first and/or later scowls.
He battles down Satan
like any Sat'day-nite gladiator—
in a busted-bottle bar brawl.
All truculent knuckles—
and succulent blood accumulating on towels
(scorching em brown—
the tint of sumpin burnt by smouldering)....

I have a slim hand, sly with letters.
I pen an itty bitty notebook
of (maybe) penny ante verse—
every word a nocturne
out a smoky blot of ink;
every poem a signal assertion,
and no claptrap contraption.

But Langford? A heavyweight thunderer!
His Gospel is lethal *Generosity*—
tactics of *Surgery*—
to cut out the wound—
the *Sin* entire—
while his venomous words leech
at the weeping self-sorrow,
so *Poison* medicates *Bilge*,
and perplexities of excuses turn futile.

Indecisive measures breed *Anarchy*.

But Langford is the oversized masculine—
a grisly harmonica,
notes hacking at air.
Monstrously gritty!
His black frock coat looks like an umbrella
turned to molten licorice.
He be solid sweat.
Blunt *Brutality* is all he ever broach....

—*Louisa Bailey*

[Point Pelee (Ontario) 7 / 11/ 21]

The Whylah Times *Editorial on*
The Candywine˙ *Bandit*˟˟˟˟

A series of petty but impudent larcenies
have lately been perpetrated in Whylah.
The pilferer—"The Candywine Bandit"—
entertains a judicious predilection for
(we suppose) delicious edibles and fine
wines.

Thus, one store has been despoiled of
fior-de-latte cheese and seven pounds
of *fois gras*; another has been plundered
of a jar of pickles, a drum of figs,
and a plump, juicy duck.

Next, a wedding fiesta was derailed
when the wedding cake
mysteriously evaporated
out the premises of the bride's
already disgruntled father.

In a "Coloured Baptist" household,
pastoral calm became apostolic fury
when a churchgoer,
after warbling spirituals
and imbibing a sermon,
returned home to find
his roast turkey having sprout wings
and flown,
ruffling his usually benign *Temper*,
thus confounding the balm
of the *Religion* he'd just digested.

---

* Cf. John Hearne.
** Cf. Robart-Johnson, *Africa's Children: A History of Blacks in Yarmouth, Nova Scotia.*

These instances of hunger pangs
and belly-aching,
disturbing the felon and victims alike,
must soon come to a finish
because the criminal of kitchen
and cupboard
is known to be that rascal extraordinaire,
that most indelible "cullud pusson,"

retired farmer (George),
defrocked preacher (Elliott),
and dyslexic clerk (Clarke),
otherwise known as "Four-Eyed Dick."

The reward on offer
for the apprehension of "GEC"
is the goodly sum of 30 dollars.
He cannot presume his Whylah Falls
abode a redoubt,
for the *Law*'s soon to cuff his hands.

To avoid any needless harm
to his domicile or to his frame
(or his four-eyed face)
during the process of apprehension,
we advise the scoundrel
to "cakewalk" voluntarily into prison.

He should not insist on *Innocence*.
The proof of felonious "shoplifting"
is as one-sided as an empty pie plate!

Indeed, in addition to the forgoing menu
of "levitated" foodstuffs
soon abbreviated in his gut,
it is now alleged that Four-Eyed Dick
trespassed upon a doctor's office
to make off clandestinely with opium

and laudanum, proving his proclivity
for the medical arts,
and a hankering for pharmaceutical
Bliss.

Also, Four-Eyed Dick is wanted
for practicing *"Law"*
by entering an attorney's office
and pocketing a watch—
all to make him a better judge
of *Time.*

In balance with due condemnation
of GEC's hand-to-mouth stealing,
let it be known that the miscreant
has left behind at one site of loss
a silver-mounted meerschaum pipe
(bearing the pseudonym,
"Austin Chesterfield Clarke");
and at another a woollen jacket
so colonized by imperious insects,
it would make an instant laboratory
for a savvy entomologist!

We trust that Four-Eyed Dick
will not take umbrage at our plea
to imprison himself
because he is a menace
to household *Economy*
as a ravaging pest—
no better than a rat or mouse,
and worse than they,
given his intimacy with every pantry
in town
and their length, breadth,
and contents thereof.

Too, it is his custom to select the best
specimens,
and leave the starving the worst aspects
of *Culinary Art*.

He is murder on wine—
leaving no bottle standing—
and an assassin of pies,
even doing away with crumbs as witness
to his malicious *Consumption*!

(To wax classical,
it is not that he loves cakes less,
but that he loves pies and *vino* more.)

If he hits upon a destitute larder,
he scrawls a note—
a plain "X"—
scratched into the nearest, pliant surface,
to inform the scantily-provisioned "host"
that the sable finger has judged,
writ, and moved on.

So, Four-Eyed Dick, or "GEC"
abandon the cloak-and-lockpick *Gloom*
of *Robbery*,
vanish from the public gaze for a spell,
until thy notorious exploits
become obscured by subsequent events.

Besides, should you resolve on *Surrender*,
might you be entitled doubtless
to the $30
offered for your apprehension?

May you, a criminal of darkest hue,
become a penitent,
eager to recover the lily *Character*

of every soul at birth,
and nurse a *Reputation* fed by hard work,
not purloined pastries
and stolen spirits!

We hope that the feeling of *Regret*
occasioned by the loss of the Emperor
Frederik William III of Prussia
and the Empress Xiaoquancheng of China,
which has pervaded this parish
all winter and spring,
will be assuaged by the capture
of "The Candywine Bandit,"
so that no longer will our tables
be subject to a state of chronic alarm!

Or vitiation of *Nutrition*!

[**Tropea (Italia) 20** *juin* **mmxxii**]

F.R. Langford Prepares his Sermon

(As if with brushes, rain strokes mud softly;
ink streaks from my speaking pen:
It circles, alights;
the nib troubles the white field:
Another killing or seeding?

Issues yet the sermon,
whose issue is,
Beauty destroys the unwary.)

Lovers bumbling in sheets muss
tumbled-off shrouds!

All the living all compose
an unprecedented cemetery—
a brand-new, unplanted (unpeopled) graveyard!

Notice?
Champagne determines to be frivolous
but ends in the frothy purling of piss!

(Light leafs through trees,
and gin chills me violently.
The biting sparkles of ink
reverse the colours of lightning-tainted night
as they dart, darkling,
into Bible-illuminating letters.)

I need to warn all ye who loaf
and lounge in *Lovesickness* (and *Lust*),
thy *Pleasure* waxing and waxing
and climaxing in greater *Pleasure*,
that in thy taxing labours,

y'all still be lousy insects—
like flies begetting maggots.
All *Sex* is lethal!
We be but skin-encased bones—
as random as a cat's litter—
as arbitrary as discarded flowers....

(Yes, that be an ice-cold *Monologue*!
Diatribe!)

Our caste is cast-forth blooms
that undergo various wilting—
perishable blossoms,
unpoetical botanicals,
or even disintegrate into smudge-fringed,
ash-clotted urns.

Nor is there any easygoing, "conversational,"
toast-and-tea,
theological "fixes," eh?

(Now, I am drained of ink-and-think.
I'll lumber among the umber pear trees
to scuttle among the slumbering limbs,
seeking the peerless fruit
via hostile squeezes—
as discriminating as a diplomat.)

[Sheguiandah First Nation,
Lake Manitou, Manitoulin Island (Ontario)
22 *août* mmxx]

Warning to the Grass Roots!

Nothing is as unforgivable as *Damnation*!
Best swing your clock hand toward *Salvation*!

Lookit! The gavel is droppin on ya every second:
Every foul deed's counted, every foul thought's reckoned!

Each tick-tock echoes with ramifications:
Your heart's booming gross amplifications

Of grimy *Crime* and slimy, climactic Sins.
(*Wisdom* is sulphurous to fumigate *Innocence*.)

We honest Xians are an elated phalanx:
Fish who loathe this desert world and seek Baptist sinks.

A surge of Joy is our *Faith*—
Insurgent against purging *Death*.

Every Xian demise is suicidal *Art*—
To dodge the peril of a pissed-off heart—

So we can hurry on to Heaven and meet
Our Lawd, whose realm be perfumes extra sweet.

Unwanted, but as wanton as rats
Be our opponents, breeding their swinish brats.

They believe they are unkillable,
But each will expire, speech and syllable.

—*F.R. Langford*

[Wiarton (Ontario) 23 *août* mmxx]

Randall Day Invents the Blues

The mahogany tint of sensual leather,
I navigate a pine-green, spruce-green jungle,
but the branches, needles, the fur of fir
and conifers
beat back at me,
almost perforate and/or lacerate
my pretty visage—
my lady-panty-remover visage—
to smite me a smallpox-foxed face—
pocked and pricked or scraped and scratched;
I gotta worry that these tree limbs could thrash
and/or gash my visage;
coerce cuss words to glug and gouge my throat, eh?!!

Such *Pathetic Fallacy* would make my phallus pathetic—
fallacious,

and then I'd be sick-to-death of *Life*—
and sick of *Nature* and how it frustrates *Desire*—
and sick of how *Society* militates against *Joy*—
and sick of the huge hammer (*Mortality*)
slamming down my cranium....

I'd fall—incredibly—sick of maidens and matrons,
virgins and sluts, mamas and mistresses,
brides and bawds, wives and whores;
I'd be sick of that split-second of *Bliss*
and that afterlife of "Sorry!"
I'd be sick of Venus, venery, and venereal woes.

I'd be sick of gold and sick of accountants!
I'd be sick of rolled quarters and bottles glutted with cents.

I'd be sick of good English sunk down into the gutter
as words drop out bad-breath, bleeding-gum mouths!

I'd be sick of dickering docs and rotgut medicines!

I'd be sick of bourgeois peasants
(puffed up and unpleasant).

I'd be sick of washing laundry and sick of tending fire.

I'd be sick of X-quoting, Devil-devoted preachers!

And I can't stand flowers, anyway,
for they preen as if unbothered
by being jailed in soil.

And *Society* is *Crime*;
folks is *Crime*;
guv'mint is *Crime*—
is cartel, is mafia, is syndicate,
is *Murder Incorporated*,
is bullet manufacturers,
ballot counterfeiters,
is pin-striped pimps,
is hos in power-suits and pumps,
is deficits, defecate, deficits,
is assassination by paper
(*Death* by a thousand paper cuts
at the end of the paper trail),
is white-collar, red-handed killers,
is *La trahison des clercs*,*
is the (renewed) treason of the intellectuals,**
is gamblers accessing the Treasury as their bankroll,
is a conspiracy of price-fixers
and a coven of liquidators.

---

* Cf. J. Benda.
** Cf. P.E.T.

Guv'mint is *Crime*—
is fat-butt trolls defecating deficits,
is toothless cocksuckers
(useless as eunuchs, but good at hoovering up
*renminbi**),
is damned rats, vipers, hyenas, piranha,
is *Inanition* (or *Ennui*),
is blossoms of Caucasian-flesh-tone skulls:

Is so!

[Roma (Italia) 29 *juin* mmxviii
& Ottawa (Ontario) 31 *mai*
& 15 *juin* mcmxciv]

---

* Chinese: The people's money. [人民币 or ¥.]

A Xian's Complaint*

I drool at church ladies finery:
Damn! How they pray and sway and swoon!
I don't blab no chic *Chicanery*,
I seize my Heaven night and noon:
When Jezebel down-swivels lingerie
And we revel in *Revelation*.

Yep, Jezebel dances so teasingly,
Make me yearn for when I was young.
She romances me so pleasingly,
Geez, wager her kiss is just pure tongue.
God! That gal with the brass hair clasp
Be slippery *Truth* I must needs grasp.

Done been baptized—soaked to marrow,
But, I's crooked, crippled, and bent;
Rebo'n right upright as an arrow,
I's now busted, broke-dick, and spent:
Women and wine mint no worse sorrows:
Black blues worth not even one red cent.

—*Randall (Randy) Day*

[Banff (Alberta) ? *juillet* mcmlxxxiii
& Nantes (France) ? *février* mmix]

---

* *Pace* The Right Honourable Gilbert R. Daye, PC, D.Div., LLD., etc.

Love Ditty

Gonna lay down my coal shovel,
And skedaddle to your hovel,
To growl and grunt and grovel—
Like a Romeo in a novel!
Yessum, like a lover in a novel!

Gonna make your backbone shake
Your brass bed squeak and break.
That's the sort of love I like to make—
So you squeal feelin hips quake.
Ya squeal feelin your pelvis quake!

Your bedsprings crackle, crack, creak:
Your loins—my groins—too sweaty, squeak,
Language mangles so ya can't speak.
I'm lovin ya in French and Greek.
My tongue all French, your "backtalk" Greek!

I'm no bumbler—inopportune!
Gonna put ya, gal, o'er the moon.
Chuck down your Bible as you swoon—
Sweat gallopin down like a monsoon!
Sweat scallopin down in a monsoon!

—*Randall (Randy) Day*

[Roma (Italia) **30** *juin* **mmxviii**
& Ottawa (Ontario) **9** *janvier* **mcmxc**]

Reflections of a Natural Man

By Randall (Randy) Day

I.

So I follow the round song of the seasons—
of the seven seas and the sun:
I mean X no disrespect,
nor would I scrap the Scriptures.

A Gospel wind doth summon me:
I admit the Lord is tuggin me,
but Satan's holdin me back.

The preacher at Cornwallis Street—
Reverend Father Preston—
thrills my ears with spirited sass....
And I like shoutin spirituals—
they're medicinal
like red wine windin down the throat.

II.

Regard these bottles cracked open
like fortune cookies—
my *Cornucopia* of poison—
I heft and sound
a pound of rum—
my steady medicine:
dark rum—
beverage and *Intoxicant*.

The enamel cup on the pine table,
topped with either alcoholic coffee
or pure spirits, a rotten gold,
explains my rum-flummoxed stomach.

I don't booze; I drink—
nectar.

I also swallow coffee and cheese
and various shades of wine.

(The poem of Three Mile Plains be
molasses scribbled on bread.)

III.

Don't blame me for my attitude!

In Nova Scotia,
Music is drinking,
Art is drinking,
Sport is drinking,
Science is drinking,
Engineering is drinking,
Medicine is drinking,
Law is drinking,
Theology is drinking,
Sociology is drinking,
Economics is drinking,
Agriculture is drinking,
Fishing is drinking,
Nursing is drinking,
Teaching is drinking,
and *Forestry* is drinking.

Every faculty is devoted to drinking,
and so's the government!

IV.

Do excuse my messy pleasures,
please and thank you:
I do.

Because nothing is as definite as shit—
or as deafening as *Death*,
I eat fine liquor or go hysterical,
run with night-time rats
or daylight rats,
catch a bitch by the tail,
a pussy by mouth,
cuss like a dog
and tussle like a bull.

A zigzagging, lollygagging drunk,
I sniff out a red-wine scent
to trail a brazen, brassy hussy
and nail her brown behind.

Or I leave my falling-apart room,
as stars gleam like bread crumbs,
to venture into razor-sharp cold,
trade tobacco for groceries, greens, gin,
"smokes" for smoked meat,
and then walk into a house
where china doubles for ashtrays,
and spoil good-tastin liquor
with bad taste in ladies
as erratic as perfume.

V.

"*Love* at first sight" just means
mating on the second date—
even if the gal be as humdrum as a bruise
and as listless as drying mud.

"The King of *Love*"?
Tyrannosaurus Rex.

VI.

Home is where breakfast, bed,
and broad are had.

Mine's infamous for wine twaddle
and whiskey drool.

I love barbarous *Luxury* too much.

I'd take a bank for every cent
they ever took,
payin em back in spades
(pun intended).

I'm a sugar-plum rat
and give off a pepper perfume.

I try to keep on the sun's good side
and stay off the rain's nerves.

VII.

Let some fool step through my doorway
and start up a ruckus:
I'll muss up his wretched face
befo ever I ratchet up and retch out tears.

My ten knuckles will buckle his mouth
so it's as red as a mandrill's rump.
There'll be blood-soaked, bone breakage.
My manly rights—
and lefts—
will set him feeling as righteously wronged

as a left-behind wife.
I'll show him he's as meaningful to me
as a po is for my piss.

Say some shit-hole come spoutin
ostentatious *Crap,*
or some pantin puppet
with flushed look and cracked brain,
wanna frazzle,
rassle,
with me,
well, I'll attack em like dogs,
give em coco butts
hard enough,
bloody matter storms down
and each dolt faints
as pretty as a shipwreck.

VIII.

After the pallid, well-fed rats finish
dining on party cake,
that's when "cullud" folk can swill swamp slush,
gobble sugar and fat spewed into a pot,
and drink a few, dewy drops of poison,
until everybody gets trapped
in a crypt of *Vomit.*

But my exaggerated heart won't let me droop
like a sick, old man—
nervous, ravenous....

I accept *Lust, Anger,*
and dive straight into "muck,"

dip my spear—
my panther rod—
in some gawky, giggling, fidgeting gal,
even some shy, drab nun,
and make our feuding bed a festival,
so the night leaves us mute, weak,
all fagged out, afterward.

I'd rather breathe out-of-character
than be a character outta breath.

IX.

My wife?

See my tan eyes?
They ain't seen her black duff yet:

All I ever see are her tears,
moanin for yours truly,
a catskin banjo man,
who don't do no pussyfoot playin.

I like my songs as pensive as bartending,
with style as expensive as cathedral tithing.

X.

There's nothin perfect under the moon:

Every face gets rained on;
many books get pissed on;
and sometimes faces catch piss
as books do rain.

Stars be the only *objets* not turbulent.

XI.

Say the world is autumn and winter,
Decay and *Death*.

I say,

April—*Nisan*—is coming,
with surprise on surprise,
with velvet dusk,
ornate dark blue,
and then a moon-broken night,

and a widowed Cleopatra
craving a gentleman

plus his wedding-cake blade....

And summer prepares fruit
outta undoubting green.

There's time for church when I'm dead.

1854

[Nantes (France) 26–28 *janvier*
& 6–7 *février* mmix]

Rumours of Rum / Hum of Humours

By Randy Day

I.

Quaffin gold rum come indigo *minuit*
is *Beauty* solidly fluid,
and no albino liqueur,
but medicine more like mama's milk—
silk to a sucker's throat—
palm wine, even, a tad salty....

II.

Rum of the Atlantic—dark like oil;
rum of *Resurrection* and *Insurrection*;
rum of railway runnin under night soil;
rum of unorthodox, bloodhound *Indirection*;
rum of rain floodin yieldin sodden *Nastiness*;
rum of majuscule *Innocence* in distress;
rum of incurable *Love*—disease bards catch;
rum of duellin virgins fuellin epics of pitch;
rum of oysters gulped in Curepe, Trinidad;
rum of sordid massas and each dirty white bitch;
rum of Caligula and the Marquis de Sade;
rum of rheumatism and arthritis;
rum of *Destruction* and massacre;
rum of bush-baths and Black Magic panaceas;
rum of noose and cutlass and arsenic murder.

III.

And when I have no more rum—
zero is *Love,*
zero is *Sex,*
zero is *Joy,*
zero is wine,
zero is ink;
gone is *Poetry*
gone is *Clarity,*
gone is *Justice,*
gone is *Wonder,*
gone is tin, brass, bronze, gold, black;
nothing is sense,
nothing is *Time,*
nothing is *Life,*
nothing is cream,
nothing is *Speech*;
zilch is *Salvation,*
zilch is tambourine,
zilch is *Electioneering,*
zilch is piano,
zilch is *Baptism*;
nada is *Light,*
nada is *Peace,*
nada is *Church,*
nada is *Song,*
nada is milk;
zip is *Melisma,*
zip is *Economics*;
zip is So-and-so;
zip is *Prophecy,*
zip is *Music*;
nugatory is Purgatory,
nugatory is the hymnal,
nugatory is thingamajig,
nugatory is thingabob,
nugatory is this-and-that;

nil is stainless steel,
nil is satin,
nil is *Moolah*,
nil is *Memory*,
and nil is *Anaphora*—

whenever I have no more rum.

[Curepe (Trinidad) 15 *décembre* mm
& Washington (District of Columbia) 31 *décembre* mm
& Tropea (Italia) 5–6 *juin* mmxviii]

Wisdom of Randall Day

Come *avril*, once the caterpillars creep,
women won't slog through snow drift
or stumble into potholes,
but'll prance, their butts dancing,
their coats undone,
while breezes fondle em, feel em up, blithely....

★

Stopping outside showcase windows,
spying mannequins, undressed for May,
but sporting gaudy blouses,
the shopping ladies imitate butterflies:
A coat drops off, a chemise shimmers;
cleavage steeps where the cocoon splits.

★

Down by the salty harbour (Haligonian),
female eyes sop up salty sailors—
like toast slices dunked in tea.
March they then to April markets,
to purchase every brazen, fragrant lily,
to blaze and perfume their dock-side, for-sale baskets.

★

---

* Cf. *Cold Mountain: 100 Poems by the T'ang Poet Han-Shan* (trans. Burton Watson).

Hey, Preston! Chat up *Eternity* all you like!
I's content to stand here, ask no questions,
but bask in the sun-burnt pleasure
a sailor feels, ashore, at ease, ogling gals,
those rainbow butterflies fluttering free
from split-open cocoons of church—or childhood!

[Roma (Italia) 29 *juin* mmxviii
& Ottawa (Ontario) 7 *février* mcmxciv]

Moral Reflection

Could I have been the darling of the Church—
Glossy Heaven my irresistible
Direction? Omnipotent in office,
If impotent in bed, but truly *saved?*
        No: Too often, I filled my coffee cup
With Scotch, made oily sounds—*Sex* fluting *Sex,*
And never interrupted *Corruption.*
(I like fat ladies's preposterous *Softness!*)
        Ideas aside, my ideals proved
Surreal. I preferred dim cafés
To cathedrals. I was religiously
Egregious, outrageous, gregarious!
        To improve, I keep one command: Heal thy
Heart of *Love* that's false, *Love* that's unhealthy.

—*Randy Day*

[n.p., n.d.]

Randall Day Preaches Bout Solomon (Apocryphal)

1.   Now, Solomon's kingship was total *Peace*.
His enlarged *Fame* engrossed the globe.

2.   But Solomon enjoyed sobbing harps too much,
plus bare-naked nymphos way too much.

3.   He forgot his own *Wisdom*:
Neither spurn a relative nor favour any woman
not thy wife.

4.   Yet, in ale-amplified stupors, he stumbled
into jumbled up beds, mumbling.

5.   (What giggling gals didn't wriggle their tits,
to feel his eel wiggling betwixt their jiggling mounds?

6.   Lookit: The womb is the pinnacle of *Want*.)

7.   After all, Solomon was a king!
And loved he much-much-much
the creeping, tippy-toeing babes!

8.   *Honour* thus corroded;
family life got corrupted.

9.   Each two-bit ginny has her bikini bottom
shunted aside, slippery sausage shoved in her c***,
while the crowned galoot squashes her down
into a scummy mattress.

10.   Until he unscrambles from under her topping,
and lies convulsive aboard the bitch....

11. Yet, jets of his cream even flooded
boozed-up, heathen *queyntes*;
each quim quivered with the fatalistic germs.

12. Soon, *Genealogy*'s bout as cohesive as Morse Code.

[Vicenza (Italia) {?} 7–8 *mai* mmxvii {?}]

The Poetics (III)

By Louisa Bailey

Oui, my penmanship be sly,
my style pure *Cunning*;
and thus, I carve out *shy*—*
classic verses—unshy—
letters earnest in sagacious punning.

I trust in moral backbone
to keep my *Poesy* keen:
Thus, no line needs further hone
(it's clean as a well-picked bone)—
and words say what they mean.

A reedy flute shoots out notes
in mutual *Tumult*. Likewise,
upon my ink *Contention* floats—
ideas war as my pen spouts—
Truth shining neath inky guise.

Ain't my ink both bucket and axe?
As bottomless as the brain
and as sharp as blades biting backs!
Blunt and brutal are my whacks—
my contrapuntal blows of cracklin *Pain*!

[Point Pelee (Ontario) 14 *novembre* mmxxi]

---

* Chinese: Poetry.

Langford's Missionary Report

Black horse hooves shatter a ledge of snow—
batter a wedge of congealed light—
to ferry me to unhealed *Injury*—
so I befriend, defend, X—with a fury!

But best to be abrasive,
not evasive:
I'll not be shunted aside,
cantering, sauntering,
but rather must have horse hooves hammer
snow, stone beneath,
or slink through slush,
the hot-steed breath upturned—
a gaseous vesper or prayer....

I'll pour black thorough blizzard—
ford black through blizzard—
like India ink slinking across paper:
The clinging residue is words.

Or let me go hunchback on this horse—
hunchbacking black through blizzard—
never to know lull—
to loll like a dullard—
a sullen *Nullity.*

I cannot be unterrifying
for I go to go on:

I fracture every hush-hush façade,
never let sleep padlock eyelids.
I imitate the violent steam
hurtling the locomotive down tracks—
as irrepressible as surf stoving rocks.

I am scary! I admit it!
I act on unpronounceable, theological principles,
to oppose preachers better at philandering
than acting like Ph.D.'s!

So, let me brush aside snow-chalked leaves,
push aside the parish discourses
of *Sin*-bred perishing
this undreamt-of winter.

My horse's eyes are headlights challenging night;
his hooves—splashing spades—
dislodge emboldened gravel;
and I am the blessed *Blackness*
to harry this snowy Caucasian state!

[YUL—Dorval (Québec) 1 *septembre* mmxx]

I. Testimony of Septimus Clarke

I.

No gross of books
assembles a library,
let alone a church.

All books and papers are useless
beside / except
The Holy Bible—
that blast of cold air,
that blizzard of light.

Verily, I talk for folk
whose *Faith* effects no temple,
but respects fiddles that siren like flutes
or drone as resolutely as drums.
My peoples trust *Worship* means,
"Ya jus start singin n singin,
then the sun jump up
blazin black midnight as gold as noon."

Yes, they stomach eatin only raw corn,
so long as they believe their soul's
got just the right sparkle
to attract Heaven's ogling.

Their / our spirituals—
innumerable poems that deny reading—
certify
no howl or moan needeth *Translation*.

Sides, how else can we know now
X's human ecstasies
or agonies,
if not by a shout, a cry, a clap of hands,
a swoon, a foot stomp?

The people hath *feeling*, hath music.
They be *un popolo di poeti.**

My post is marginal:
A *clerc*, a cleric, a clarke,
Clerk of the Association,
I scribe merely spontaneous *Elegy*,
the fluxing inspiration of a stump holyman
(Preston),
a minister high up on horseback,
or stuck knee-deep in mud,
preaching, *plein-air, al fresco, ex cathedra,***
hollerin, snatchin *Spirit*
fresh off the wind,
"rasslin" with the Devil (him bad self),
to prance, shinin, in princely *Light*.

No commonplace orator,
Preston answereth
Black Death,
yellow fever,
gangrene,
white lynchers,
and blues—

with red-letter miracles.

Yes, everybody thinketh by words.
Tis also true that *Discourse* smoulders
to charred bones of letters
entombed in the crypt of each page.

Tis also true that every text
hosts subversive catacombs,
whose excavation can sink
the seeker
way past bedrock *Truth*
straight down to deepest *Hell*.

---

* Italian: A race (nation, people) of poets.
** French: In the open; Italian: On the grass; Latin: Outside the church.

(My point's literal:
Consider the marble Roman emperor
unearthed latterly from a dug-up sewer.)

And yet,
ink can be flush with talk;
scribbled *apercus*
can unfold lightning;
moulded verses—poetry
—pottery-fragile,
but never outmoded—
can pour out (*verser**) *Law*.

II.

Outside, snow consumes earth in white gulps;
the raining snow damps white the streets,
rinses night from trees, washes out the stars.

I put my chapped lips on my chipped cup,
chug a taste of tea.

My candle thaws the night.
(Slowly, it'll melt to daylight.)

I recognize my estate's only gypsum,
an acre of gravel,
topsoil that's muck,
only a dead piglet on the table,
the surf of thistle where there's field....

I dwell in a *noir* Halifax—
a watery, sad citadel,
whose streets cascade to ships
and zigzag, drunk, twixt pub and brothel.

---

* French: To pour (out); to versify.

(Halifax is a miniature Edinburgh—
but with greater garbage,
more typhoid-prone prostitutes,
more avid alcoholics!)

My era sets out
a sunset empire, cannon, and rum,
thuggish economists
(comic cons, mistaken mystics),
and ecclesiastical harlots:
For a fat purse,
both are keen to cut throats
or spread legs.

Apocalyptic, bloody,
is this age,
infertile is
my acreage.

But I must articulate my people anyhow,
for *Poetry* devours *Cant*
until only *Scripture / Revelation* remains.
We do what we can't.

It was not enough to slip
that stock-exchange republic
that turns babes to corpses,
that legislates *Manhunt* and *Rape*.

I must answer the white-collar hypocrites,
who acclaim *Slavery* as righteous *Law*,
who use Latin cant
to buttress British-American *can't*,
whose babbling excuses
are so subtly corrupt
and so brazenly postulated
as to baffle detection.
Yet, they are not just diabolical,
but diabolically theological.

That's my learned duty—
to take elastic jottings
and stretch them so far they snap,
exposing invidious *Idiocy*.

Profit is their only interest.
Mammon is their only prophet.
Their *Ideology* idolizes
idylls for themselves,
sullied lives for all others—
the black, the poor,
the brown, the unlettered.
Their premium belief is *Greed*.
Their premier bugbear is *Public Spending*.

III.

I confront here Bishop Inglis Stairs,
who distils sweet ink into bitter words,
whose black silk script—
flashy as Babylonian scarlet—
stabs as insidiously as a stiletto.

Some wager him "sincere":
Yes, he's as sincere as an unclean stable.

Stairs argues, "either the blacks hath no souls,
or their souls are finely fiendish.

"Each black child delivers a mortal blow,
entering this world to grab—to thief—its share
of what it merits so little of—
our love."

I can only be pleased that all his pages
(like mine)
come from wood
and go from wood
to fire:
his inspirations retire as smoke,
prove globs of ink can't job a faith.

His *Intelligence*, hellish,
takes poems and sets them afire.

(O! The Caucasoid-Maritimer theologies,
variously erroneous,
get snarled through ruddy fangs!)

IV.

Outside now,
snow
yields to smoke.

The moon bleaches
a whirl of white, sepulchral churches—
Anglican, (Caucasian) Baptist,
Catholic.

(Anglicans, Lutherans, and Methodists practice
the most catholic sins!)

The pasty pastors are Sisyphus at Golgotha:
They heave and heave to roll the stone away
from X's should-be-useful tomb,
only to watch it roll back again
as their congregations fall
into a drowsy mood
and then blissfully into sleep.

V.

For the Africadian Baptist Association,
Xn,
my words must drum tom-toms
to thump out the extinction
of *Colour Distinction*,
what stains lily-white religion as crimson as a vampire's jaws.

What do I believe?
No one is *finally* sovereign.
Life is elitist, *Death* democratic:
One man, one vote, one church, one God, one grave.

Grass outlives us;
rats best us for breeding.

I grow to sun and prayer.

Damp fog clears,
debuts the diamond-studded sea.

Outside, the harbour shows broken panes of fire.
Campbell Road's / Africville's
wooden houses slope down to the water;
sidewalks tilt past terraced gardens to the sea;
now robins peep their *Treasury of Verse*,
and my words coalesce
as a temporary Bible—
al-Qaeda
(The Foundation)—
to shore up our black folk's still-unsure church.

I spy out births to come—
prophetic profit.*

[Corpus Christi (Texas) 19–20 *avril* / *Nisan* mmviii
& Nantes (France) 26–28 *janvier* mmix]

---

* Each object's an encyclopaedia; each person houses an archive....

II. Testimony of Septimus Clarke

Even easy-come-easy-go, juicy floozies,
out-and-out in-takers of dudes-and-booze—
their sexes mere poison pits—
have the power
(after the lavish, moneyed moment),
to hang any "well-hung" boy,
by a pretense of *Rape*,
then look at his dangling blackness
with jaundiced eyes,
as he's cut down from a rope,
and junior white fiends jest,
and play taps on penny whistles
and kazoos,
while the charred or mutilated being—
carbon skin, sooty wrapping,
a figment of pigment—
represents an abandoned blackness,
when once he was viewed
as a blackness of abandon,
of *Abandonment.*

[Ottawa (Ontario) 25 *janvier* mmix]

A Russian General Re: the British (and Allies) at Sebastopol (1854)

The Brits, Turks, French, Piedmontese, and Sardinians?
A lot of stinking, drooling cunts!

Their massed forces wriggling about Sebastopol—
besieging, beseeching, like maggots aboard a carcass—
are schoolboys, pupils, spineless as eyes,
who we will cannonade unto *Capitulation!*
They'll be cannon-decapitated, rendered sludge—
some catastrophic, indescribable, but flushable bilge,
a sewer mess!

(A pretty postcard for lamplit Florence Nightingale
and/or Mary Seacole—"Saint of the Field Hospital"—
to perfume and post to London!)

What Shakespeare will eulogize these lads if not Sade?
To salute their incineration *via* burst-open naval shells?

We shall see the Brit lads and Ottoman cads
frayed up like worn-out, cardboard puzzle pieces—
or scorched and seared
like playing cards pitched onto a barbecue!

All will be irrepressibly depressed.

Tis strange how stranded cadavers become gossamer—
become stew squelched by boots
and feasted upon by flies—
as each Frenchy frog and Italian minion sinks,
breaching mud-beds,
then flushing black as soya sauce—
the oceanic expanse of their blood gone black—
a flood so deep that larvae flounder!

(Empire is emphatically a pyre,
and every *Victory* pyrrhic.)

[FRA—Kelsterbach, Frankfurt am Main (Germany)
Independence Day mmxxii]

Alfred, Lord Tennyson Drafts
"The Charge of the Light Brigade"

That valley of *Death* was a char-smudged, burnt-earth zone
reeking of scorched, electric-ozone stench,
the streaked smoke of lightning-launching arms—
Russian vodka oiling thundering, boiling cannon.

Hard to tally robust *Altruism* of do-and-die *Courage*
from a London study, where the only "body"
broken is bread—
a crumpet, a croissant—

and all the bleeding is ruddy wine
shipped past lips and gorged in the gullet.
How do I draft tsunami of hooves and flame of swords
commanded to hand-to-hand stymie,

i.e., exterminate, Crimea's Russians?
How to award a prize to a self-abolishing charge—
insupportable (French pronunciation)—
versus contemptuous, cursing cannon—

while our British bawled shrieks, yells,
three-hundred-plus horses splintered—
or splashed open—by the marrying barrage,
while the smirking *Foe* hunched contentedly

behind their cannon, crunching stalwarts
and stallions down to mulch and *merde*?
Rococo were the ranked corpses—
an exceptional alabaster splayed

amid the general khaki smog and turgid smirch.
Romanesque were the stilled, stiffened limbs—
sprawled bits of broken statuary
intertwisted with smashed equestrians:

Spy a beauty that betters *Beauty*!
Intense *Mirth*, that juvenile *Emotion*, thrilled
the hill-top Russians cropping the downhill Brits:
Their cannon swivelled half globally

to pell-mell pick-to-pieces heroes
unperturbedly upright in superb saddles—
these Albrecht-Dürer-Apollos in newsprint black-and-white—
who were Red Serge, Blue Serge, surging

and white marble battered back
by the indefinite hail
of hit-or-miss *Fact*,
their titanic hearts encouraged by satanic *Hope*,

until half got swirled milk-white
into the tar-black, char-black *Catastrophe*,
thus surfacing as the deathless cream
of a guiltily grimacing Gilded Age.

I shan't write out of accumulated *Vanity*—
our Victorian *Grandeur*, all *haute-bourgeoisie*—
that sees us tramp and clamp the seas
to plant our truculent—succulent—youth—

lilies rendered poppies—
to decorate vulgar trenches
after heeding the bleating sirens of drums;
to be such impressive suicides—

our trenchant, imperial signature—
the impress of our Empress.
I do not seek to oust anti-monopolists
(Marx doth have a point about our Blake-damned mills);

or outdo the parochial buglar of the Elysian Field;
or codify preening for *condottieri*;
or quoth *Eloquence* camouflaging *Nonsense*.
I will say nothing derogatory

about their characters—
gods in human shape—
but only register how the Light Brigade
unscrolled *Scripture* over fire.

2 *décembre* 1854

[Guelph (Ontario) 25 *juillet* mmxxii]

III. Testimony of Septimus Clarke

I.

Fine snow filters from a ground-down sky.
*Le refroidissement eolien**
freezes Halifax,
breezy burgh.

Plunked before me like an iron,
a cup puffs steam:
It's coffee in black and white.

And a luxury.

Other black folks suffer pretty good starvation—
a "stiff-upper-lip" kind of diet.

Their axes, hoes, and oxen trundle
into hardwood lands,
feed fragile forests to fire,
carve out honest, upright places,
plough, plant, and pray
for gilded wheat like brass,
and fields gone gold with corn....

At Preston, ex-slaves heft huge trees
from fat forests,
strike them into log cabins
and lumber and firewood.

But God is slow
to hurry on *Remit*.

---

* Québécois: Wind chill.

Would-be ranchers, beekeepers,
dairy maids, apple orchardists,
must settle for raisin a few hogs,
stockin a few chickens,
bending oakwood into rum barrels,

or go slavin for pale peckerwoods,
without benefit of coin,
in this Newfangled Scotland
of sauerkraut, beans and wieners,
and rapure pie.

Thus, our planting implements rust;
eggs are as good as silver and gold.

Nourishment out of Nova Scotia *Wilderness*
is fog, brine, mushrooms,
but even rollicking, feel-no-pain Baptists gotta eat.

Hear the squeak of shoes in blue-blanched snow.
Snow panders to all shapes:
Like *Democracy*.

Widows congregate,
monuments in a graveyard.
Our black bouquet of ministers
blossoms like umbrellas—
robes as black and thin as crepe
among this sparkling Eden of snow.

Ice, a lead glaze, blazes everything,
weighting down dreams.

II.

Africadian Baptists may break
from our wood cabins,

wade through stars,
desiring Heaven,
sweating to build it,
despite glowering snow,
roads snarling with bears,
but all our muscle
is useless against zero pay,
gallows prices,
blood-from-stone *Credit*....

History undid us—
as Europe did extra well,
pushing peasants
up to presidents,
thanks to red corpses
ploughed under black soil.

The state the Brits gave themselves
was not Greco-Roman marble,
but Kindergarten *papier-mâché*,
a model republic hollow with *Hypocrisy*—
"one man [white plutocrat], one vote,"
with white women as serfs
(when not privileged as "ladies"),
black women as concubines,
and black men as porters.

From the wasteland of monarch-saddled Europe,
paupers, peasants, and protestants shipped out
to the Americas,
their tears ferrying the smoke tang
from burned-out empires,
the pall of pogroms,
girls catching fire as "witches,"
whole towns besieged and torched
for singing the "wrong" hymns,
and yet, the byword of *Prosperity*
on these shores was,

in effect, the by-law,
"Love Thy Neighbour
and Lynch Thy Nigger."

After the Cajun Dispersal (1755),
Yankees invaded Acadie,
brought in pastors and Planters,
while the Royal Navy imported prostitutes
(a few poets too)
to this fishy outpost of "Last Post" pipers,
and everyone wanted slaves.

Even now, Africa creeps whitely
to Nova Scotia's black rocks—
the whitecaps—snow-headed Negroes—
came ashore, fainting....

Africa became Africa
in relation to Rome,
then Lisbon,
then London,
and now the "Negro" got no home.

Piracy plus *Plunder* produces plump profits.

Pitiless Europe—
methodically diabolical—
pitches a *Political Economy*
where blacks are pitifully *Lumpen,*
crow-faced clowns,
sad-mouthed Sambos....

No wonder we all seem
as tired as faces
in old paintings.

Now, Nova Scotia is a *salon*
of snow and shotguns.

III.

Even our Negro successes
fall tragic honestly.

Impresario Farmer
scraped together dollars for a lumberyard,
put up a wharf,
then, quickly, a whorehouse,
and with cash heaping up,
put up a play house,
and then, in his dotage,
was primed to bankroll a cathedral.

His skin was the colour of mucus;
His drunkard's face was as ruddy
(bloody)
as a boxer's following a bout.
He was a zebra-tinted schizophrenic,
half-European and half-African,
and all Zombie.

Inoperably obscene in *Hypocrisy*,
this ex-Baptist was a hunky-dory capitalist.

He knew a wharf is only wood
slapped down and nailed roughly together,
unless it lands stogie-fancying, ulyssean sailors,
lonesome for ale and a lady.

Farmer even smuggled in tax-free booze
by filling hollow cannonballs with whiskey.

He prospered, but not as one of us,
I mean, not as a Xian.

His Maritime, good-time cathouse,
slinging hot-house wines

for ex-jailhouse wantons,
inspired energetic chatting in taverns,
persnickety talk in pubs,
elaborate gentlemen's jokes in the legislature,
so silver clanked into Farmer's pockets,
enough to let him erect White Star Theatre,
and "pass" as a gilded, European monkey,
yapping innocuous, middle-class words.
Then, thanks to eavesdropping,
on his scarlet premises,
on the low-life pillow talk
of high-class politicos,
tasting a rum and a tart,
Farmer tried to pocket a political party.

Molto* awkward, mucho backward,
he ventured to blackmail
a private financier to the premier.

Farmer presumed he could connive and campaign,
wheedle, wheel and deal,
bribe and booze and bootleg himself
into a (back) seat at the Cabinet table.

Instead, his maple tree soon drooled
a brown, brutally broken thing;
it dangled from a branch by a piece of string,
dangled broodingly,
moodily,
this tendril of gilt spittle.

And the Government seized his *Treasure*
for supposedly unpaid taxes....

---

* Italian: Very.

IV.

Any bloodshed is too much for comfort.
But *mordet** shapes our down-and-out Cosmos,
even if Halifax swirls a whirl of white churches.

Consider the inherent brutality of wars,
so many bloodletting ideologies,
and the huge imperial bloodbaths,
as in Lucknow, India.

(Plans for new crypts
are drawn up with battle orders.)

Eye the red-waved British globe,
so many battlefields of yellowing grass,
or the silence of snow
and the pain of jagged splinters of ice,
blades glutting themselves in blood
while ashes blow in from a new, earthly Hell,
and a fresh cannon blast
seems to heave this orb from its orbit,
and each mindless army asserts desperately
the suddenly needed faith in *Death*'s powers—
to kill many and kill quickly,
until one hears the scrape of rat teeth
on human bone.

A shell could bam down a church,
accidentally spill oil
that meets an unluckily lit fire,
so worshippers become living torches,
and unpolished screams erupt.

Soldiers get squashed, crushed, like roaches,
ground down in gritty muck.

---

* Danish: Murder.

(A soldier accepts rank injury, damage;
Music bites his ears.
How is such a man a councillor?)

Open graves resemble
so many laughing mouths.

Sermons, anthems, poems of holocaust!
Crimes of tombs!

See the carnage of horses
instantly made leather,
their riders made pudding.
Castles smoking.

April maples may jizz juice—
as war-ripped corpses—
the Crimea's harvest—
ooze fly "rugrats."

Flowers from gardens, weeds,
cover up cadavers—
as colourful as a dung heap.

Blood spatter's often likened to rain
because it falls so steadily red,
so steadfastly oily, wet, and red,
with any tumult of bullets:
a shower of *Gore*—
as logical as Dante's tortures.
(See the Siege of Sebastopol:
Omnipotent *Hell*.)

Empires erect cannon
in gardens.

Rash, hurtling fires
thud—like tears—to the ground,
or incinerate home, school, church and shop,
that ashes do a very poor job
of remembering.

In America, even now,
across the south, Dixie,
congregate white hoods,
loud hooves,
to accompany the vehement stench
of flaming flesh, smoke,
swinging black corpses,
until the end of the Republic.

Violence *partout* is as unsettled
and as unsettling
as ash spilled from an urn.

The Age stages
the usual pitfalls, downfalls, windfalls.

Criticize me, if you wish,
for delving into politics, yet

"*Truth* opens the graves
Hate wants to cover,
And unearths all the gold
Greed cannot discover." (Tennyson)

The point is, to pry hands
from private piggy banks
and then to pry them
from guns.

V.

This eve the sea will seem copper and gold.
I expect a sea of silver and gold.

The harbour scuttles gold
under the corn-yellow sun;
but the Atlantic fields
a long, leaf-green sea.

Firs, frozen, gleam in the pond—
a mirror of glaze.
Yet, outside my window,
a grass blade pokes through ice.

Across the frosty wilderness at Rockingham,
a locomotive exhales smoke and ash.

I take naturally sweet tea,
honeybush plant (*cyclopia spp.*),
brewed by the San people of the Cape.

Lookit! I'm short on tea currently,
but I'm not big on rum.

(Taking scrambled eggs and tea
calls to mind Europe's "Scramble for Africa"
and Britain's tea-rum-and-opium Empire.)

I snuff my lamp milking kerosene.

VI.

The casual anarchy of perpetual motion
makes stillness seem like going backward,
and so, for this *Progressive* era,
church construction must seem regressive.

Yet, I laud us Africadian Baptists,
our new hammered-together churches,
our saints imagined out of ex-slave
and common labourers,
and our hymns—
about as Canadian as a canary....

As Br'er Ambrose
baptized St. Augustine (African),
so Preston,
blessed by the West London Baptist Association,
homed from England,
while leaves gave up the ghost,
dropped dead,
to rail against "man-manufactured gods"—
booze, brothels, and bullets—
and even convert "King George's Negroes"—
West Indians—
to the indigenous, Africadian Baptist cause:
Church, School, Temperance,
plus a pinch—or pound—of *Spirituality*,
to oppose "a civilization of tinsel
and barbed-wire."

Preston zeroes in on a crisis,
like a focus on a microscope.

He's intellectually homely homiletics,
is Preston.

"Politics is an illusion:
what matters is doing—
using scripture for light,
other books for fire:

"School is a scribbler and a pencil—
nothing is as pregnant as a blank page,
but there's, for us,

rare singing in classrooms.
Rather, the metaphysical brewery smell
of the Haligonian wharves,
flavours the prayers
of too many Coloured husbands
and fathers,
becoming bad Xians, bad examples,
and, though too many of em are poets,
they can't write
because they'd rather drink.

"(In public they are pious,
in private poets,
but everywhere propagandists
for every *Vice*.)

"Some of you are like pretty flowers
and dainty, ivory blossoms,
that, when they open,
are black inside from frost.

"Remember your Bible:
To preen, first prune.
Cast off sins,
coast up to the Son.

"Forget about the world,
its boasts and its treasuries:
Proud statues are soon plastered
with gulls' tributes and pigeons' applause."

Some of our preachers can't read,
but bang big black Bibles
with blood-red words,
scarlet letters spelling out
who's been mixed
with Micmacs—
and "Mc's" and "Macs"—
and who's been nixed.

Preston repairs all *Lack.*

He's favoured churches
where splintered keyboards' ragged rhythms
tear songs to pieces.

VII.

Clouds exhume a down-to-earth lantern:
The moon.

Under it, the iced beach shimmers
like billions of grounded stars.

Ice tucks in the streets.

A locomotive, burning, black,
screams out of nowhere.

All the world beds down in this fur—
snow.

I go out, stroll the strand,
thin sand fringing the rock-bordered beach.
Between boulders, the harbour heaves
and humps;
waves speed back and forth, bump,
form lumps.
Moonlight fires on the indigo water.

I await Spring:
Trees blaze from black to green,
or a scissor fog lops treetops,
or rain shines,
wind soaks,
the molasses surf creams on rocks,
and we jig tinkers and fat mackerel.

VIII.

Indoors again,
I take a touch of Scotch;
the harbour flares moon-white.

Another sliver-thin, ebony night train
howls through Campbell Road
("Africville," some call us),
rattling the tiny bones of snow
over Negro Point.

Yes, now snow's blowin
cross the road:
startin up a blizzard out there.

December 1854

[Ottawa (Ontario) 24–25 *janvier* mmix
& Nantes (France) 26–28 *janvier*
& 2 *février* mmix]

Minutes of the Proceedings of the Africadian Baptist Association of Nova Scotia, Held at Granville Mountain, September, 1855 A.D.

★ ★ ★ ★

Resolutions (1855)

B e it resolved that our Missionaries—
who so water and refresh our churches,
scattered about so large a portion
of our African Nova Scotian *Race*,
and looking wholly to our scanty resources,
call upon us unceasingly
to set down seeds and roots of *Faith*,
thus increasing the Redeemer's Garden.
Resolve further:
That *Gratitude* be extended the Rev. R. Preston
and Brother Septimus Clarke
for the excellent *Diligence*
with which they have fulfilled our *Trust*,
and for the *Poetry* of the Report
recounting the bounteous *Benevolence*
of our Lord in shepherding our Association,
our organization,
so necessary for drawing down the *Philanthropy*
encouraging our exertions,
so the "New Scottish" Africadian Baptists
achieve sustained *Action*
and permanent *Success*.
Resolve furthermore:
That the sincere appreciation of the Association
bless the Baptist Church and Congregation
and Associate Community of Granville Mountain,
for their spirited *Hospitality* and *Kindness*
bestowed upon us ministers and messengers
of the *Faith*.

Resolve furthermore more:
That Bro. Septimus Clarke oversee
the Minutes printing
down to the second of *Scruples*
and the instant of *Scrutiny*.

Adjourned to meet
in the Meeting House
of the Africadian Baptist Church
at Bear River,
on the first Sunday in September,
1856.

Until our *Reunification*,
Let us avoid *Rage* that eggs on Elegy,
Lust that urges Eulogy.
Amen.

—*Septimus Clarke, Clerk of the ABA*

[Sheguiandah First Nation,
Lake Manitou, Manitoulin Island (Ontario)
17 *août* mmxx]

Haliburton Negrophobic Fulmination (1857)

Exceptional labourers are the Nova Scottish Calibans—
better than free darky fops
who ape their Caucasian superiors.

Yet, they are worthless soldiers,
just jujubes for cannon to chew on.
Indeed, enemy snipers would have a field day
cutting down every distinct Negroid—
if indistinguishable—
pug mug.

All black eyes, black hair, black soot—
bootblacks and chimney sweeps—
swarthy as coal—
the colour of dug ditches
and asphalt roads.

Better that they get fielded as advance guard
to intake every askance musket ball
or cannon blast.

Despite the alleged *Valour* of Bill Hall
at Lucknow,
these Hades shades don't seem to merit
any medal, any trophy,

save to staff any minstrel show

or boxing exhibition....

[Halifax (Nova Scotia) 31 *mars* mmxxii]

Preston Re: Haliburton

I.

The man ain't bovine, but swinish—
a blue-eyed brown-noser—
a scum bag
who likes to drag shit about.
Not a bard of the brogue,
but only sly as an ogre.

(More like a corpse throbbing—
but only with bugs.)

Regard his gin-squeezed-to-slits eyes:
The disproportionately boozy waste of a face;
the constant thrust of tooth through meat.

II.

It's too bad that bullshitters like Haliburton
enjoy "parliamentary immunity,"
or I'd hit and knock im down.

(The fouled heart
informs a befouled brain,
and his ejaculate befouls.

His inklings befoul—
both as flashy
and as pedestrian
as tinfoil.)

Unemancipated, indecently hierarchically
"Golliwogs" are too rank
to rank.

So Haliburton's venomous verses be writ
on wasp-nest paper.

(True greatness brooks no quarrel
because the expressed thought is true).

His heart is a *cul-de-sac.*

He wants to thump and smite abolitionists,
suffragettes, communists,
but all his markings are fractious soot.

The trove of ink is an evil rinse:
The page goes black,
spiked with exclamations!

His gritty harangues notwithstanding,
Socialismo is the gifted guillotine—
and his head should topple—
head-first,
off his shoulders!

(One hears the keen and bark
of hammers upon nails;
one hears untranslatable,
cabalistic, saltwater yinkyank.
Unlovely exhalations!)

[YUL—Dorval (Québec)
Quatorze de juillet mmxx]

On William Hall, V.C.

That African cavalier did *Imperial* duty,
chiding—
by snarling cannon, zealous flames,
aroused fumes,
and pitch and vibrant arc
whealing (flogging)
the Muslim fort;
and by thumping breathless at the keep
until worthy chinks got birthed
and four walls became,
no longer a stymying *Quandary*,
but worthless.

Unlike the fallen, Haligonian valiant of Sebastopol
(Messrs. Welsford & Parker),
it was our William Hall of Hantsport,
whose booming fumes and sparking arcs
committed multifaceted *Injury*,
breaching a stony girding,
so that solids dissolved to rubble,
and a domed roof suddenly welcomed sunlight.
Thus, Hall abolished a rebellion,
reduced nightmarish, would-be regicides
to mere will-o-wisp spooks;
and, pretty much, solo,
concerted to hand the keys to a sub-continent—
for safekeeping—
to Empress Victoria,
her *Power* no longer apparitional,
but apportioned dread, militant *Majesty*.

We Africadian Baptists are right to concord
our brother
the gold of *Acclaim*, the symphony of *Applause*,
for his God-blessed, unmolested delivery
of *Victory*

was surely *Instantiation*
of X as his stanchion, his prop,
while the Indian sharpshooters strove
to muzzle his muzzle.
Surely, Hall ignored *Fear*, spurned all trembling,
when snapping out salvo after salvo,
calculating how to abort a fortress
by flaking, chipping, and peeling off stone—
flint and splinter and shard and boulder—
until his blaze burst through—
and sunlight could ransack—
and the British *Arms* pour into the ruin
to rout the Indo rebels.

Three cheers—loud, lusty—for our brother!

[Repressed

And yet, having been to London,
and scrutinized its worldly, earthy lords,
and parliamentarians who are *taenia*—
earthworms—
chewing up saints' corpses—
(or who are leeches—muckworms—
sacking the public *Gut*);
and for whom *Empire* is synonymous euphemism
for *Rape* and *Rob*
(no pretense of *Gentility*);
I do rue Hall's actions:
He warred to suppress a third of *Humanity*
to buttress the minority that is Great Britain.
Yet, I cannot impinge publicly
Bravery—African—
although it depreciates India.

And Whitehall is a dead-end!]

—*Rev. Richard Preston, December 1857*

[Tropea (Italia) 24 *juin* mmxxii]

Minutes of the Proceedings of the Africadian Baptist Association of Nova Scotia, Held at ?, September, 1858 A.D.

★　　★　　★　　★

Circular Letter (1858)

Dearly Beloved Brethren & Sistren:

Although we mourned expansively and incisively
all those Coloured Xian spirits drafted quickly to God—
our voices keening with the devil-slaying *Beauty*
of our spirituals—
and spurred on by the panache and *suavité*
of soloists calling out melodically to X—
even so we delighted that Believers
reside now with the Believed;
leaving us remainder not as bereaved,
but as relieved to know that our own
union with the Godhead
will neither be delayed nor denied!
　　　　Our *Happiness* has extra lustre now,
for we've witnessed the luxurious additions
of new bodies and redeemed souls
to the rosters of the churches
of our Connection....
Amen!
　　　　Assuredly, God has blessed us doubly!
So, though we grieve the loss
of our esteemed ally in our *Allegiance*—
Mr. James Shepherd
(whose surname says all that we need to know
about his biblical calibre),
we celebrate the calling to priesthood
of Bro. Abraham Clemence

(whose surname shouts *Mercy*),
who is so persuasive in speech
and expansive in spirit.
          We also welcome this year to our pulpits
the young Edward Jackson,
also stalwart in the *Faith*,
and yet another new Licentiate Minister,
to carry on, to carry on,
the work that X and John and Peter and Paul
have tasked us to fulfill.
          (We churchgoers do not imagine
that antecedent holy men and holy women
have worked miracles to last Eternity!
No! Every Believer struggles afresh
to triumph in X's *Commission*
to heft the Cross—
even if we stumble as He did—
to baptize and save, to save and worship....
No intervening accomplishments—
no previous victories—
matter one jot.
There are always sinners needing *Salvation*,
and the *Apocalypse* arrives "tomorrow.")
          Yes, our churches are poor in endowments:
Our crude, self-taught carpenters sculpt
the walls, floor, roof—
the pulpit and the pews;
our hand-me-down Bibles are flimsy
and our second-hand robes are shabby.
Our cathedrals are all pine and walnut,
elm and maple,
hardly spruced up and/or nailed down.
          Though we own zilch of the world's riches,
Faith prospers us with *Grace*—
and that empowers us us to overthrow
the *Slavery* and the *Tyranny* of *Sin*!
          Plus miracles persist!
Did not Sister Louisa Bailey—
celebrated for her sugary character

(and honeyed voice and molasses-sweet words)—
discover the perils of a constitutional stroll
just this past May?
Hardly had she stepped toe, heel, and ankle
beyond her Whylah Falls threshold,
when 20,000 bees thronged to erect
a hive in her good-quality, upswept hair.
Did not her husband, Ulysses, have to shoo
the crushing burden of that cluster
from his wife's capital,
via potentially suicidal swishing of his cane?
It was only the whirlwind that Ulysses raised
that erased the buzzing, insectile halo,
that scuppered the hiving off project.
Praise God!
        Our Ministering Brethren—
their words emerging like polished jewels—
drew nine souls to the baptismal fount
at the Association;
and so the souls saved by our sermons this year
attain number 88.
We laud God for this *Bounty*!
        Yet, we feel the *Want* of Ministers!
Still too many young men wanna run the roads,
run wild, run around on wives,
and run stills,
instead of running strong in *Faith*!
        So, Beloved Reader, we call upon thee
to pray to the Lord of the Harvest
that He summon more labourers
to the vineyard
to press more wine (strictly metaphorically).
May the Grace of Lord X be with y'all!
Amen!

—*Rev. R. Preston, D.D.*
—*Rev. James Thomas*
—*Rev. Benson Smithers*

★　　★　　★　　★

[Randall Day Responds]

Gospel gotta start with a trumpet—
tellin God's express *Distemper* re: *Sin*!

Trumpet gotta be shiny silver in substance,
but blue in its innards,

where the heart lurks, pining.
Silver gonna cry out for every black gal

descendin from the Blue Nile,
achin to hear a trumpet's blue sigh:

Silver polishin rocky places silver
via stars polka-dotting indigo-blue night.

[Montréal (Québec) 7/7/mmxviii
& Ottawa (Ontario) 17 *mai* mcmxciv]

Notes Toward a Spiritual

*D*eath disturbs us in our *Love*—
Never proof against its remove.

Dreamers gon die, eyes wide awake—
Spy no blue sky, just flamin lake.

Saints suck honey outta skulls:
God loves em, but loathes all imbeciles.

A bootlegger's *Misery* is
To call on folks where Christ's wine is.

Perfume prefaces female plagues—
Gashing nails of harlots and hags.

Mere sunflowers can direct the blind:
God looks out for his Christian kind.

Didn't X scour fishermen's feet?
In his mansion, each takes a seat.

—Louisa Bailey

[Windsor (Nova Scotia) 30 *novembre* mmxii]

Elegiac Spiritual for Father Preston

Once our Moor who travelled the English moors,
he moors us evermore; is our mooring.
His prayers—*materia poética**—

be no small-time small-talk and no double talk!
Preston maketh each syllable to swing,
so *Divinity* cometh tumblin down,

in chunks, slabs, dollops, of light..
Ain't no imitation *Brilliance* therein!
Preston's sermons, as telling as tombstones,

showcase every circumstance of sunlight,
summon him unambiguous *Prestige*.
He don't negotiate with yelpin bitches!

(Obscene, Celtic dogs, barkin doggerel,
lynchin X everytime they cry, "Nigger!,"
would be better off, God knows, as white worms,

cos they got that same unseemly pallor!)
Preston stirs *Panic* in every sinner—
who's immortally dead, due to *Nature*,

becoming as ephemeral as mould.
Preston bucks us up; he buckles us straight.
No longer King George or Queen Vic minstrels,

obliged to laugh while our babies are whipped!
How proud we be that Preston's vessel pushed
aside every paltry jump up of foam,

---

* Spanish: In poetical terms.

each light-studded shock of the Atlantic,
to sunder the ocean and arrive at
Splendour, after clashing with crashing waves

under wild clouds, to reach London and be
rendered a Baptist, after the frothing
baptism of maelstrom and Bedlam shriek

of sail, the prow hammering down each surge....
There, Preston fended off every dolled-up predator,
every doled-out rump, and slapped-down every

Babylonian-quality strumpet
(those dolorous philosophers and droll,
opium-addled, *Opprobrium*-prone,

Sapphic papists). Under London's smokestacks,
the rich—those well-bred, well-stuffed carcasses
(Caucasoid)—parade ill-got gold, no-good goods.

Preston struck em dumb with his drumming words,
Gospel, so brains and hearts split wide open,
and *Doubt* got banished, *Deceit* fell, butchered.

Back, now, among us, Preston furnishes
light that's ever brilliant, come from
on High. Father Preston proves the warhorse,

unconquerable, trampling down naysayers.
He's Byronic Christ, sardonic Samson....
To Preston, we are the Children of God:

How can we—unrefined—meet dusk or dawn?
We must forego backsliding—any, all.
Who we be is *History*, prophetic!

—*Louisa Bailey*

[Paris (France) 13–14 *février* mmix
& Bethlehem (Pennsylvania) 17 *février* mmix]

Shanghai-Capri-Serendip Blues

Sinner, why ya let Satan shanghai your soul?
Why ya let the Devil shanghai your soul?
Your blood's gonna run Parma violet
Cos your heart's viper-cold.

Xian, don't you crave the spirit of Capri?
Xian, ain't thy *Faith* as refreshing as Capri?
How else can your heart feel light—
Or like sunlight feel free?

Xian, don't ya wanna feel like Serendip?
Faith ain't capricious, but it be serendip?
Free as wind from Capri—
And as heartening as *Worship*!

Never let yourself be shanghai'd from *Caprice*!
Never stray from Serendip that wins you *Caprice*!
Serendipity ain't shanghai'd
When God appeases thy pleas!

—*Louisa Bailey*

[Leamington (Ontario) 22 *juin* mmxxi]

Regarding the Apostolic Labours of Father Preston

The pastor's a quarterly comet of every church!
When he glides in his orbit,
hovers,
his brilliance exudes and expounds and disobscures
the Gospel,
and we splurge on the *Light*
and urge on the *Gravitas*.

No wonder Tiapolo* screeches "Aiee, aiee,"
while brimstone bam-bams down the hypocrites!

Or Tiapolo (Haliburton) incarnates in the legislature,
gibbering and jerking,
stiffly animate as a Zombie,
having the scope to lie,
the largesse to bribe.

This be Father Preston's debonair foe—
always soaped, laundered, and dried in gin—
always pressed in pin-stripes
and creased with cigar smoke.

There's no way to decommission Tiapolo
except to dredge the dismal swamp,
or to buffalo through the marsh,
or to bison through the blizzard,
and then bugle him down,
trumpet blast him into lockdown,
by baptizing the very air thoroughly
with antiseptic, yet perfuming Scripture.

---

* Big Devil. Cf. Dylan Thomas.

How else to deligitimize
insidious, but ingratiating grog?
Or to cancel the pub's Beezelbub hubbub?
Or lambaste the intoxicated relics of Nero,
all too happy to shindig—
reel, puff harmonica, or cuddle fiddle,
while setting any church ablaze?

The observant know that Father Preston
galoshes through slosh and muck,
horseshoes through puddle and snowdrift and dust-storm,
and haggles and dickers—
chock-a-block—
round-the-clock—
with sodden and thus saddened unbelievers—
to materialize suddenly a solid church,
an unshaky church.

—*Louisa Bailey*

[Sheguiandah First Nation,
Lake Manitou, Manitoulin Island (Ontario)
17 *août* mmxx]

Rum-in-nation; or, Ruination?

By Randy Day

I.

To have the spectre and spectrum of rum—
the juice of aged sugar;
to dirty up a white coffee mug—
like spillin cinnamon atop rice pudding;

to take to rum and drowse
while bedbugs assault me enough
(like migratory cockroaches outta Toronto);
to be lost at the butt of my black-rot guts;

is to swallow sugar-blue-black,
a thimble-full of night-trapped moonlight;
is to end dreams—unattainable trifles—
and to be drilled by *Terror*, eh?

A lamp marks me—my visage—
as if I be the sleepy corpse in Poe's "Tell-Tale Heart"*—
and I awake. *Awake!*
To *Torment—Addiction*—itchy, lousy, unshakeable!

II.

So I'll swallow *Licor Tim Tam Tum*—
Madeira's typical—but unique—digestive—
fuses water, sugar sap, wine, plant juices,
powdered dry fruit, plus caramel syrup;

---

* The tale lacerates *Conscience*.

it's *Noctilucence,* articulate in a glass—
suggestive, entrancing—
the temptation of dirt or mud;
the creation of a *Rape*-mixed *Race*!

[Tropea (Italia) 6 *juin* mmxviii
& Funchal (Madeira) 17 & 18 *décembre* mmxv]

Martin Robison Delany Drafts "Blake"

English unfurls a *belles-lettres* alphabet—
plus terribly elastic *Grammar*—
sheer rubbery on the tongue:
My words goop out as guck, gunk,
a lot of exasperating ephemera,
a sewage ether.

My writing's no better—
just ink splatter, splotches,
a tattered typeface—
my convulsive vocabulary.

Blake (Billy) crafts each page, drafting
a watercolour cathedral.
But, my novel's hero, "Blake,"
is a philosophical *flâneur.*
My plot? A slough of lines.

(Philosophers pose as marble or bronze,
but *Philosophy* is only paper.)

Blake's book is an unearthly poem.
My "Blake" marks me as a sourpuss scribe—
unhappy and unknown—
meriting an unsavoury canonization.

I open pages of the Anglo* Blake:
I ogle an enclosing *Brilliance.*
But I drift into *Darkness*—
a droning *stupidus,*
whose heroic subjects are slaves
squabbling over pound cake and/or pig feet,
or gabbling debased platitudes.

---

* Angel.

I feel I'll end a penniless poet,
bereft of all but dreams.

My novel is a paper-weight *Pain*:
A miserable, anti-slavery *Advocate*.
Why? I'm unsatisfied as a Negro!
I'm as negative as a Negro!
My *livre* is a rhetorical shambles:
Neanderthal prattle.

Maybe I need a quill-pen mentor—
a moping preacher
with a galloping whip,
exhorting me to set poems bout the Crucifix
in the bridal bedroom!

I should follow Blake (Billy)—
alleged holyman
(or boogie man)—
the bravest of bards,
and announce *Suffering*—

roped-down mamas, raped—

befo I send my "Blake," black hero,
into the green oblivion of a jungle
(sugarcane fields, Cuba).

(Indigenous virgins go missing;
African women get kidnapped;
pallid gals get taken down.)

I'm a poetaster brought to book:
My pages exhibit not even clean-cut errors!

I invent for Blake a mistress—
a plum-faced poetess—
to be sibylline Eve
to his Homeric Adam,
a gargoyle with a six-shooter.
Neither be a *café-au-lait* Mulatto—
that asinine mixture (melee).

Still, I wish I could write like Will Blake—
he of the mystical living,
who berates *Royalty* as criminal,
who knows that diamonds come to light,
first downcast in dirt,
who insists that *Sex* be not acidic,
but sugary.

His pages are splendid windows, and again, stained-glass.

In contrast, my "Blake" endures
guttural interludes
betwixt dead-end plotting.
Inky *Pandemonium* (as in Milton)
is his *Rebellion*.

Willy Blake's angels appear anemically robust:
Their muscles look half-ether.
But their words, luminous,
constitute iridescent breath.
His *America: A Prophecy* gleams off the page
like the dragons and demons that fringe antique maps.

But my "Blake" is as distinctive as a headstone.
He cometh, black-ass, headlong from a bitch's belly,
to run the gamut of the text—
run the gauntlet of the Gothic plot—
only to re-appear as his odd, Frankenstein-like self.

He should claim a mediaeval pedigree?
Prove iron weaponry as better than bronze?
(Bronze is for statues;
iron is for cannon.)

Prove that command of *Murder*
don't require flags and smoke and horns and drums!
No, *Discipline* is *Righteousness*!

My "Blake" wields elemental *Brutality*
in a *répertoire de batailles rangées.**
He be the issue of *Slavery*,
the spawn of legalized *Barbarism*.

In compare to Great Britain's Blake,
I author unrecognizable words
and not his incomparable symbols—
those shape-shifting clouds,
authoring his dazzling signature.

I cannot imagine beings of melting *Translucence*.
I set *my* Blake against blackguard tyrants!

[Windsor (Nova Scotia) 30 *novembre* mmxii]

---

* French: Repertoire of Battle lines.

"Sam Slick" Contradicts Harriet Beecher Stowe

Regard, coldly, the streaming black ink of Homer
and the clotted, red ink of Virgil,
both agree:
Slavery improves the slave,
civilizes the master.

Hoi polloi—riff-raff—scalawags,
lack all the *Dignity*
and *Charity*
the Ancients grant th'Ethiopes.

Because of the Impeccable Institution,
Slavery,
there are no Ethiopian bastards,
no Ethiopian beggars,
no Ethiopian dregs
and drags on the public purse,
for they have toil,
may feast and drink,
and every one of em
literally
has *Value*.

But the white trash are Darwinian dogs,
the dirtiest vermin,

and all you hissing abolitionists—
bellicose as pepper,
earnest as vomit—
should attend to the piss-ass party

that be the indigent Caucasians,
whose lives mock *Civilization*.

Miss Stowe, as a political philosopher
and humorist,
but no novelist
(though critics rank me with you,
Trollope, Dickens),

I hope you'll dissociate yourself
from the smug tongues that cast *Slavery*
as an orchestra of screams,

as a gang of pale torturers
whipping the backs and buttocks
of whimpering, buck-naked blacks,

as if we were bozos enough
to damage lucrative livestock!

Those who mumble such asinine fantasies—
worthy of any opium-addled poet
(Coleridge)—
should be stuck deep in the prat
with hatpins.

Succulent conversation, heroic chatter:
That's what you Sunday School types produce.

But *Slavery* is not so trite
as a saga of do-gooders *versus* evil-doers.
Nope.

Masters are not jaunty satyrs;
slaves are not bullwhipped martyrs.

If no hypocrite, one admits earthy facts:
To eat is to murder;
Taxation is *Theft.*
The moral?
Civilization is the exercise of discreet *Violence,*
legal *Violence,*
an arrangement mirroring Divine design.

Anti-Slavery is pro-*Hallucination*—
the despotic notion that *Society*
(genteel, cultivated)
rests upon unambiguous *niceties.*

But no idyll is unprepared.

If *Slavery* is "mischievous, malicious, and ungodly,"
why, so much worse are the factories—
a Dead Sea of *Consciousness*—
where capitalists' engines, machines, tools,
blacken lily-white workers with soot, dirt, ash,
and make em stink,
and drink emselves dead.

Compared to these *avant-garde* evils—
of which only Marx mumbles a bit—
and for whom you abolitionist rabble
care not,
Slavery is operatic Venus,
comic Ceres,
and love affairs amid magnolia,
strolls amid peach trees and apple blossoms,
and much milk, much wine, much honey,
and scenes pleasing a water-colourist
decorating simple, frivolous poems.

Nor should you blame me for naming
Anti-Slavery
as bogus *Philanthropy*, ample blubber,
whose heartless speakers care zilch
for the "chillun" of Ham!

Rather, your sermons espouse the Utopian *Sadism*
of Adam Smith and his ilk.

Why don't you rescue the lowly whites
from the dirty mills?

True-blue bluebloods and bluestockings
care
for our black "help."

[Helsinki (Finland) 28 *juin* mmxiii]

Father Preston at the Beach, Winter 1860

The august *Brilliance* of the limitless sea—
the smell of salt as each seagull—
gauloise—
floats with sinuous *Whimsy*,
ushers me undeniable *Joy*.

(As incendiary as magnesium
is each bird, slicing the white foam
salving the sun-blistered ocean.)

The Atlantic's convulsive pulse sunders
thunderously
every static idea, all *Dullness*.

The seagulls observe
our besieging
by unassailable sails—

i.e. each beaching,
        beseeching broadside of foam,
the blockading cannonade of tide,
the waves—factions of mountains—massing.

Afar from this fringe,
these twinge-ing elements,
sullen autumn
culls leaves.
Gardens upthrust thorns.

Everywhere is fearsome *War*
(as per foolhardy *Policy*)—
once the Crimea,
now Harpers Ferry;

once the Light Brigade,
now John Brown;
once Cathay,
and again Cathay;
but always the prone dead
gulping a diet of snow
just as they become a diet for worms.

(*Simplicity* approves a graveyard.)

History is kaleidoscopic *Incoherence*,
tempestuous, cloudy impulses—
never as clear as this verge,
its fluxes of steeped light,
as urgent as an insurgency.

History is always an ill-defined unfolding—
as lunatic as the shifting moon.
To trust its chronicles
of treasons, liaisons,
one must vacillate like the superficial sea.
It is conspicuously ambiguous.

My Bible is as brittle as old, yellow paper.
(*Religion* is mourning,
all the time mourning,
the duty that's *Death*.)
Yet, it is more elucidating than flag-stiffening wind
or the scourging surge.

I look down:
Here's a black butterfly all washed up:
With one wing half-torn-off,
and fringed, weighted, with sand,
the insect is top-heavy,
its fuselage waterlogged.

I palm it;
The Monarch flutters violently,
praying to live.
My hand's warmth strengthens and comforts
this insect Lear,
but I cannot be its Cordelia.

Lacking animal *Animosity*,
I set it on a stone;
its gauche beauty—torn black flag—
alive to the breeze.

It drags itself off—
lumbering like a slave coffle.
Its peril also lacks *Remedy*.

To trust in *History*
is to hanker for bad weather.

A guru of boulders and pebbles—
a *loup-garou* of tides—
I ramble this shore.
Come the down-press of night,
I'm anchored in inks.

A pony's hoof—
its signature—
a splattered jellyfish.
(*Sorrow* can be got cheap.)

The contemptuous stink of dead fish
forces me to tangibly gasp.

In its repugnant wake,
as the moon's rays debut,
silver trickles upon *azzurra-negro*.

I feel an unexpected *Hunger*:
I should like to feed on her flesh,
that dove of salmon-scent,
to have unedited feasting—
the orgy of sexual gore—
seed, spit, tears—
as fragrant and as refreshing
as this strand.

The sky shows a façade of light.
The gulls glissade and glissando.

I should like an unprecedented drink—
and unabated *Lust*—
ce soir,
not traumatic church organs
struggling with recalcitrant hymns.
I should like a distinct glass of rum.

White milk at dawn,
white rum at eve,
white woman, come!

I'm your monument of bullion—
your gold standard,
bullish all night,
until that clamour of light
when darkness shatters.

Let *Ecstasy* tear us apart—
like the ocean rends a butterfly.

Unbridled, Venus is happy
to tantrum unto shining *Rapture*—
our oscillations,
like waves amid stones—
until we are as sodden
as any slobbering beach.

The moon sets a monstrous glitter
upon the dark, marbled sea:
It looks a brittle matter.

I wend toward a lovely animal,
her noble mouth,
to establish an ape's peace
as careless as the surf.

My violet shadow
is as honest as a skeleton.

[Halifax (Nova Scotia) 19 & 20 *novembre* mmxi]

Cathay Answers Europa (1860)

I.

The Anglo-French—comic-opera buffoons—
unsophisticated like all "messiahs"—

looking *clytenish*,*
and mincing—

pure eunuchs despite their gunpowder
(our invention and their loot),

descend like fussy, prissy swans
upon our harbours.

The amusing aviary, preening, crooning,
vaunt cannon like black swan swings.

II.

Let us minister our pepper—
gunpowder—

where most propitious
and skewer the French duck

and goulash the Anglo goose,
so *Mortality* trumps *Vulgarity.*

Channel our shots to *bastinado*
the pallid poultry,

---

* Sickly, pale.

skin white like plucked chickens;
our cannons savour chewing up

the pallid waterfowl;
yet, we'll also cut em by blade—

to aid the cannons' *Digestion*.
We want the Yangtze to resemble

a starry-gazey pie—
with the blond heads of the white devils

gazing upward from rivulets of rapids,
like fish-heads gaping upward from pie crust.

III.

Amid blooms of fire,
their blood must fly as sheer rain,

or flow in rubicund, jocund flood,
tiding the Yellow River orange.

Horses' green meal—pure grass—
should turn russet.

The blank-faced hordes swerve
out of the sea's blue void,

to try to thrust Cathay into Hell.
But we outnumber their mirror steel:

We'll enact immeasurable blockage,
Mass and drive the rampant rats

back into the sea—
the bone-white abyss,

the candid periphery.
Press these miserable carnivores

into crimson'd corners
where our shark-tooth-sharp blades slick.

Their phosphorescent bodies
will foam a homely botch—

a scissors-and-paste blotch—
red *papier-mâché* and Plaster of Paris.

Even their kings will end as weeds,
garbed in silk.

IV.

They crave to sic *Opium* on us—
to fashion us phthisic, jaundiced wantons.

But our *Philosophy* mandates
their morose *Biology*:

Eggs into larvae,
larvae into pupae,

pupae into mosquitoes....
Thus, blandishments and *carte blanche*

end as wave-bleached and sea-beached bones.
Picture flaming ships and charred, drifting dead.

V.

I advise the Emperor:
Cease twisty discussions,

any predilection for *Dogma*,
sermons, gargoning:*

---

* Jargon.

To plaster over shit
won't make it solid.

Edge *Statecraft* into *Warfare*.
Destroy the Caucasoid crooks

leaguing against Cathay!
Guillotine their dazzle!

Rob em of *Power*
by robbin em of breath.

Ants can swarm, yes,
but a foot crushes em.

Let *Hippomachie** replace *Diplomacy*—
with stallions, cannons, blood-washed gold-braid!

We cannot be doubtful conquerors.
Kill the Caucasians contumeliously!

Ensure all that remains
is livid, putrid garbage.

VI.

If we demonstrate diligent *Malignity*—
we'll be delirious in making *War*,

so joyous unmaking *Peace*,
til London and Paris are ruins.

Victory is a hammer
wielded against an egg!

[Annapolis Royal (Nova Scotia) 23 *mars* mmxiv]

---

* Fighting by horseback.

The Lonesome Death of Asa Crawford*

That last bled drop of lapsang souchong tea—
so redolent of smoked peat and truffle-scent Scotch
(*Verboten* to a Black Baptist,
even a singular soul of *Substance* and *Surplus*)—
plus the looming Boxer Rebellion
(all those Sino fisticuffs vs. Brit opium barons—
the iron-blood-stench of gunpowder wounds—
cannonading knuckles, bone-smashing leather)
a graphite-laden stink,
inhaled thus Asa Crawford—
that *amigo*, imago, of Red Cross
& Black Baptist *Humanity*.

Mr. Crawford took up cap-and-pipe to undertake
a dusky constitution
that Sat'day night of stove smoke, fireplace smoke,
even shut-down-for-Sunday factory wisps,
and bobbed into the lapsang-souchong-tea-smoked smelly eve
and vanished promptly into Africadian Baptist choral blues,
leaving mystery props
(befitting Poe's detective, Le Chevalier C. Auguste Dupin)—
a cap afloat like a lily pad;
a pipe afloat like a dead seahorse;
but both surfing the mud of a dirty Water Street pond
near the Burrell-Johnson Iron Foundry,
itself constantly charcoaling the air with ash
and licorice-infusing water with scum.

Did Frenchy Tars off a coal-scuttle vessel—
"blackface Frogs"—happen upon Crawford,
condemn him for being too dapper
a darky,

---

* Cf. Robart-Johnson, *Africa's Children: A History of Blacks in Yarmouth, Nova Scotia.*

too tweedy, voguing amid brogue,
his pocket-watch anchoring a gold chain,
and thus set fists and boots
to his "grotesquely bourgeois" attire,
then tossed the chap into the ship's coal holdings,
shovelled em over with smoky detritus,
and then, once aweigh, underway cross the Atlantic,
executed Mohammed bin Salman al Saud's praxis
(re: Jamal Khashoggi),
and axe-chopped-to-pieces Monsieur Crawford,
tossing chunks of human blubber
to approving sharks.

Negro Yarmouthians credited an opposing *Narrative*:
Local Proud Boys—hooligans—toughs,
also detesting Crawford's Africadian Baptist *Rectitude*
and tweed-jacket attire
and his aroma of lapsang-souchong tea
(so "suspiciously" Oriental)
beat the dude senseless
and then pitched him into the Yarmouth ooze.

As if to substantiate gossip,
a man's tan cadaver did materialize,
beached, waterlogged,
his face-flesh razored off by fish nibbles,
so he was as good as anonymous—
like rubbish mashed up in a dump.

And where were the dead thing's clothes?
The humanoid recovered from Yarmouth's beach boulders
was not a "personage," but a pauper,
denuded of even Crawford's three gold rings,

and so the salt-bleached African now wallows
in a shallow grave—
soon to be reclaimed by dandelions and daisies....

—*Septimus Clarke*

[**Marburg (Germany)** 9 *mai* **mmxxii**]

The Teachings of Mona States

Gotta go to the shit-house
fo I go to the Church.

Salvation demands
conviction in *Simplicity*.

Paradise is where saints
rock back and forth in easy chairs.

Let the hypocrite use his crucifix
fo kindling.

Tea, coffee, cigarettes, cigars,
an opaque drink or two,
keeps a marriage as flirtatious
as chalk and a blackboard.

A beautiful man?
Diamond, dead-on eyes in a coal-coloured face,
the blackness of black
and dark-tastin molasses.

A pretty gal *seems* as white as coffee is black:
Her dark allure wafts a lily scent.

[Nantes (France) 27–28 *janvier* mmix
& 7/2/9]

Abortive Effort at Scripture—I

(By Mona States)

Better that a parent tan the child's ass
than the hangman wring the adult's neck.

Bow down that insolent mule with lashing;
tremble that sassy pig with whipping!

If thou school a child
with the back of thy hand,
never will he or she yield wasteful speech.

Beware: Too much candy rots a child:
The marrow goes quirky,
and the once-upon-a-time innocent
imps into the psychopath—
a grinning cannibal, a decorous sadist—
capable of hacking down babies,
while passionately hawking out prayers.

Better to be childless
than sire bastoods* and bitches.

Rather be puissant than a piss-ant!

Better to batter a child with a broken branch
than see the stripling evolve into a viper,
mulish in wilfulness
and piggish in lusts.

---

* Newport Station (NS), Africadian pronunciation of *bastards*.

Remember: God did not tolerate mutant giants
who sinned, blasphemed;
rather, they were exterminated, stubbornly.

The righteous are like sparks setting alight a prairie.
Their *Virtue* defoliates—*via Incineration*—
all poisonous weeds
strewn—sown—by reprobates.

[Bologna & Mogliano Veneto (Italia) 10 *mai* mmxvii]

Abortive Effort at Scripture—II

(By Mona States)

1.   I, *Wisdom*, measure out the cosmos, tutor *Beauty*,
and chisel sunlight into cold, hard gold.

2.   Like roses at th'*Orangerie* (Paris), I perfume winds.

3.   I am a canal, a channel, fountaining through gardens,
drenching orchards' roots.

4.   Raw, unfiltered water = *Nirvana*.
Note the glare-splattering sea,
that wave-born, wave-borne light.

5.   (Mark the ambling *Excellence* of a Venetian canal.)

6.   A gross flood spurs on flowers.

7.   (*L'allé royale* is fragranced
by pink and white *primula sieboldii*,
the licorice-anisette scent of *le pavot bleu*,
and the pleasures fluted by *oeillet de poete*,
and the light honey'd aroma
of *oenothera glauca*—
fireworks blue-leaf sundrop—
that burning yellow flower.)

8.   I am also feathery rain, quivering,
o'er the aery cathedrals of an apple orchard
or olive grove,
the humid velvet of a lawn.

9.   Crickets' chirrups are a secret code.

10. A young girl, donning *Beauty*,
suddenly, mysteriously:
That's exactly like the arrival
of the Kingdom of God.

[Fredericton (New Brunswick) 4 *mai* mmxvii
& Paris (Ontario) 30 *juillet* mmxvii]

Abortive Effort at Scripture—III

(By Mona States)

1. I, *Wisdom*, love 3 divine graces:
Peace between nations,
Concord within families,
Amity of husbands and wives.

2. I, *Wisdom*, detest three things:
Hate broadcast and thus amped up;
citizens corralled into mobs....*

3. I hate 3 kinds of persons:
Fake beggars,
thieving plutocrats,
agèd lechers.

4. (Some of these become storied *condamnés*
in scripture [the Scrolls];
they're smothered by these leaves.

5. I, *Wisdom*, am flagrant, showy, ungovernable,
and subtle, but seditious.

6. *Envy* flees from my smarts, my *Intelligence*.

7. (Better to squat in a cellar honouring *Wisdom*
than to lounge in a palace of *Iniquity*.

8. Not even pure gold can purchase *Wisdom*!)

9. Like a lion gnawing prey,
so does *Iniquity* cancer weak-minded persons.

---

* Cf. Bony All-In, manipulating Yahoos to slag the ex-Parliamentary Poet Laureate.

10. Clarkes expose false-worded prophets;
they reveal their skulls' inadequate crevices.

11. Clerics rebuke prophets purchaseless on *History*,
who got nothing right, who are basic frauds.

[Fredericton & YFC (New Brunswick) 4 *mai* mmxvii]

Abortive Effort at Scripture—IV

(By Mona States)

1. There is nothing neutral under the sun.*

2. If you beg God's *Mercy*,
you might not bake in Hell.

3. Study bachelors and spinsters:
Their dexterous *Avoidance*
of complications
and implications.

4. *Necessity?* To vanquish
any ruddy ape-like or serpentine
demon.

5. *Time* flies like an arrow;
fruitflies like a rotten banana.
(Is your *Salvation* clearly on target,
or are you complacent, just rotting?)

6. A pie is a chorus of berries,
held together in harmonizing sugar
and flour and lemon juice—
the tart of *Truth* and the sweet of *Mercy*.

[Niagara-on-the-Lake (Ontario) 31 *juillet* mmxviii]

---

* Cf. Ecclesiastes 1:9.

The Teachings of Mona States (Redux)

I should only read and recite God's Word,
and thus not drink myself crazy,
having gone to the bank
to find all my *Capital* plundered.

I fainted in the Royal Bank, then cried and cried.

The Bible preacheth,
"Yer own chillun will do such *Evil* to ya!"

True! Everytime I turned around,
my grown pups had their claws out for money!

I can't tolerate the *Pain*!

I just want to sit and rock, sit and rock.

I wish I could turn my head,
and laugh out loud.

[Kingston (Ontario) 3 *mai* mcmxcii
& Windsor (Ontario) 5 *août* mmxviii]

Kiss-She Fells on Theology

I.

I go to church to scream my *Passion*—
whoop it up—
cos I ain't no how impressed
by meringue tears, puffed-up prayers,
or confessions ejaculated like confetti!

I prefer to scrape off shit—
to get down to the human bone and marrow—
to open the anus to inspection,
to get a clear idea of a buddy's soul.

for the body's a meat-product
(if savoury):
We's all the fruit of desperate duets—
closeted—and uncloseted—couplings.

(The happy bed's always a muddy sty,
a sweaty stew.)

II.

Only a clod carves a heart and verse in wood:
A smart fella fucks a gal spinny.

And a lady's gotta take precautions—
or she's gonna take the blame.

III.

As a slave chit down Naw Leens,
I learnt there be a worm for every skirt.
One man's wife is another man's whore.
Like that.

We're all puppets of *Lust*, toys of *Lust*:
Untouched bodies are either holy
or wholly evil, loveless, unloved.

Rotten *Sex* is plentiful,
so both man-and-woman want bravura *Fucking*—
rococo cock rocking bottomless bottom.

Every *Paradise* includes a brothel—
or it is *Hell*.

IV.

And so I've come to Halifax—
on the dirty side of town—
to erect and champion
a champion erection:
a temple of *Love*

(where there's no furniture,
there's less foopin);

to offer each adrift male
a snug cabin of flesh.

My emporium's as busy
as a navy strumpet's pussy,
for I promise every living stiff
a dick-breaking duff
or a dong-snapping muff.

And zero of my stable
is degraded snow or dirtied slush
or drastically ugly
or parades a weasel-assed, measles-poxed bod,
or slings out *queynte,* cold as a cold-cut,
or bloody
or as aromatic as piss.

Because nothing is sacred,
I take nothing for granted.
As a whorehouse goddess,
I purvey only the most gorgeous tarts
(and winter drives every whore
indoors, anyway).

Gentlemen find here belles
of a pretty coffee (toffee) shade,
supple-nippled teats
(chocolate-tipped caramel,
molasses intermingled with honey);
they unwrap ladies with mercury eyes,
ebony skin,
and an oasis for a crotch,
and whose mouthy meows
and claw-etches on backside,
cause every two-legs to bow-wow,
wag their frontal tails,
and get down on all fours,
to sniff and lick and lap.

V.

My queans create *Anarchy* via *Beauty*!
Each one's multilingual at *Cunnilingus*;
each one multitasks at "69,"
ambidextrously, dexterously,
with sincere *Dexterity*
and *Flexibility.*

And I offer baroque mixes—
precious metal combos—
copper, gold, bronze, silver—
righteously godforsaken sweets—
mint as peppermint,
buttery as peanut butter—
all supremely august,
fillies gorgeous to the nth degree
of pedigree
and filigree and capillary,
and none implacably evil,
if amiably dissolute.

VI.

I ask directly of each "associate":
"What ya got for tits?
Can ya roll a man?"

I gotta lol (cos ya yolo)
when one cocky bitch talks back,
envious of another bawd,
"So-and-so might got planets for tits,
but I know how to coddle a johnson twixt mine.

"And brown may not be a posh colour,
even on a Magdalena,
but an unfamiliar muff is priceless."

(And one can always drink coffee
to intensify *Nigrescence*.)

Amen!

Best to be half-pork in *Lechery*
than half-porcupine in *Touchiness*.

VII.

There's a petite, plush-tush, deep-throated doll—
a salaciously curvaceous,
French-kissing, Greek-septic hottie—
a redhead whose nutmeg tit
(recently lactating)
jets coconut cream....

There's also a Cleopatra with *Dignity*
as transparent and sultry as silk.
Her tart-title is "La Poitrine,"
and, dolesome but dulcet—
as creamy as Gioconda—
she likes to loll nude in mud,
to plant her pale tits in black earth.
(That's *lo strano vizio della signora.**)
Imagine the stench of that mouth,
the trench of that rear thoroughfare!

VIII.

I present "Gioconda" to the top cop,
and his face gets as shiny
as a pissed-in gutter.
Thus, I do business for another year—
unmolested.

The Mayor, that pig-headed bullshitter,
spies "La Poitrine" in a see-through sheathe,
and he must penetrate her duff and muff,
so that his *Victory* chews up *"Virginity"*—
like a knife retorting to a wound;
and the satanic "ho"
plays the devilish angel so well,
he pays out double
(half to her, half to me),
and says, "Go pout—and call some doc,
to sew up that quicksilver quim again."

---

* Italian: The strange vice of the lady.

(Queen Victoria'd be shocked
by how her minions
go on in this damned "Dominion.")

Lily is a particularly marketable muff—
a nervy beauty,
and a richly wishy-washy harlot—
spitefully loose,
and wet and tearful on cue.
She likes a dude to shovel into her
until she's dishevelled,
and he's levelled
like a hovel
(or a lover
in a novel).

Alba claps hands in joy
whenever a dude slaps her duff.
Her backbone can break a prick,
and her face can break a heart,
and her cunny can break a *bourse*!

IX.

I accept no hogwash, hooey, bullshit,
balderdash!

Man composes;
woman disposes.

Men will traipse through slush
to ogle smut—
to penetrate a tush,
ambush a slut.....

X.

My business enterprise is natural.
With my profits—royal—
I raise a family by my sweat
and on my milk.

(I still tit-feed one boy.)

I'm always set to tom-fool
and jump jim-crow
in bed;
to try new hound-and-pussy
(dog-pound and hussy)
exercises,
while drums beat down the night.

I'm no dead-end whore.

XI.

I know a pincer-lipped librarian
can jiggle briskly amid her books.

A widow, her nose stuck in romances,
will welcome loving in the sun for hours.

A virgin as stuck up as a corpse
is no less studious at being studded.

And all of us can still go to church—
and sit boldly in the front pew.

(Once sodden, a woman need not stop
at one prick,
but may ingest or swallow
another and another.)

XII.

I gobble brandy while the rain rat-tails down.

One preacher wore the Bible as camouflage,
but wanted me buck-naked.

He wore out the Bible spoutin persiflage,
but wanted me atop him, backbreaking!

(Thus Black history be dark, dark, dark,
onion-skin *noir*, I mean, a black-ink mark.)

XIII.

It's too cold for even jackrabbits
to be makin babies tonight.

I'll take Chianti
(Brondello with the straw-bottom),
then B & W whisky.

Call it a night.

[Nantes (France) 27–28 *janvier* mmix
& 7/2/9
& Ottawa (Ontario) 8 *octobre* mcmxciii
& Windsor (Ontario) 5 *août* mmxviii]

Furthermore....

By Kiss-She Fells

*H*ypocrisy is all fuss,* cosmetics,
but corrosive, corroding.

Like a gazelle leaping out a snare
is he who flees a false amigo.

Like a clay pot that splits in the kiln's heat,
so does a gossiper fail to produce *Truth*.

This sinner's flesh is like iron untreated by eel oil:
It decays, it rots, it rusts, it breaks down;
its corrupted atoms canker its surface and fault the whole.

(Rust makes iron ironic—ironically,
and so did my ancestors' dreams
of *Liberty* go awry.

mirroring
haughty steel with tufts of rust....)

[Vicenza (Italia) 7 *mai* mmxvii]

---

* Cf. Ward, *Riverlisp*.

"Sam Slick" on Preston

Preston is a Champagne character
in a charcoal suit
and chocolate shoes—
a fountain pen, black-ink,
white-shirt, D.Div.,
jigaboo!

I don't believe he quite quits
the clown style pioneered
by Uncle Tom and Aunt Jemima.

His prayers are provincial *schtick*,
stale bile,
the nigger genre
(générique),
some attempted bullshit *Putsch*.

Hog-headed, but mosquito-minded,
"nicey-nice," but a nincompoop—
authentically dubious—

the jack-o-lantern preacher sermonizing,
sounds like a broken-winged, howlin crow—
a farcical Lear.

Among his sooty society—
in the repellent, nigrescent dusk—
what wouldn't I give
to apply proud creams,
conduct an inky scrubbing,
to leach away dour black pigment!

I scrabble and muck about
this Babel of Baptist mock-ups,
but most admire that lily-lovely lady—
as virginal as snow,
as clear as vinegar,
and as healthy as milk,
though she's thoroughly, vigorously black.

(The bitch, *la belle*, is black!)

Re: the Parson?
I'd go to Hell
because I know he'll be there,
and his sermons would make me guffaw enough
to forget the unsavoury sizzling and singeing
heat.

The colourful sonority of Coloured Baptist songs
suggests super-excellent *Spirituality*.
But, I'm sure their roused saints
comprise a festival
of invalid, insect-compromised corpses—
percolating *Filth*.

After all, ain't Africa itself
a big ol *Hell*,
where hulking flies
carry off infants
to feast on em in dung heaps?

[Nantes (France) **28** *janvier* & **8** *février* **mmix**]

Mona States Re: Black Persecution

Bandits dare theologize their "rectitude"—
but these gap-toothed cockroaches
go *recto* up the rectum
and *verso* up the vagina,
and toss aside lawyers' cloaks
or priests' robes,
to vaunt at each avenue,
masculine or feminine.

There's a urine stench of oxygen—
as if the very air urinates down nostrils—
or as if the atmosphere's marinated in piss—
all round courthouses, cathedrals,
poorhouses, orphanages....

Yes, it's awesomely ugly to bruit, to air,
the satanic gospel that is clandestine *Oppression*
of children, particularly Negro chillun,
but my own daughter's a victim
of "Christian" welfare policies
and behaviour—

the residential schools,
the reform schools,
the schools for the deaf, dumb, blind,
the schools for wayward youths....

I gotta speak against em!
Churlish disregard is a saint's attitude—
to not see the sty
alongside the synagogue!

But who's gonna investigate
the unholy institutions, eh?

Will I petition imperial London—
with its needle-eye scrutiny of the globe—
to look into these *de facto* penitentiaries
for juveniles,
and lock up the jailers?

I'm a daughter's mother and her #1 guardian!

Too many "caregivers" take bribes, peddle lies,
and are ruthless in buggering even infants.

Lookit! Sodomists prevail in these *Kindergartens*!

I suspect that when my daughter returns,
she'll be brain-damaged, ass-hole damaged,
and infested with a brain-damaged fetus.

I seened everything *via* the Bible!
Why's my daughter delivered out my care?
Taken out my *Care*?

I witness bats flying among the apple and pear trees—
violet amid the mauve night—
disturbing the honey aromas of apples and pears—

and then a rat shifts, skulks, scurries—
priestly,
subtle as a bureaucrat.

That's my palaver!

I incarnate *Cacophony*.
I strum a *Grief*-stricken banjo.

I's the bastard inkling of a benighted Muse!

[Tropea (Italia) 7 *juin* mmxviii
& Berlin (Germany) 8 & 9 *mars* mmxiii]

Mona States Re: Black Persecution (II)

I do appeal to London for *Justice*!
To preserve children!

But those who hesitate?
Let em neck-dangle—or be chipped by firing squad!

(Some politicos have sworn their *Aid*,
but they change up,
they shift attitude, tone, and posture,
become as shifty as a fly,
once the ballot box is gone
and the Scotch bottle arrives;
once they're off the hustings
and on to junkets, shindigs....)

If thou art an honest *homme politique*,
thou must stop the enslavers—
the kidnappers, paleface traffickers
of black gals and lads—
tots and straplings—
whom the hustlers take by body
and break by brain-tortures,
so the children grieve, always and always,
immedicably,
even should they reach the grave as elderly souls.

(The correct order of *Civilization* is,
a babe borne lovingly from the nursery,
while the oldster's carried off in a hearse.)

The scandal—hideous—here is,
th'orphanage pimps state openly their plans
to stab open physically
boys' posteriors, girls' virginities,
but honourable judges look dishonourably away,
happy to let Africa's infants
fall prey to Europe's lecherous infantry.

To speak plainly:
Anglican, Baptist, Catholic ministries
covet, chase down, "compromise"
African and Indian children,
and then whip lads from orphanage to jail
or The Royal Navy
(same difference),
while the Lolitas get carted to the brothels.

Behind closed doors—these cloistered degenerates
cuss out Victoria Regina,
blastin her as a senile, doddering dowager,
throwing fits
and disseminating V.D.

Please, someone, anyone, plagiarize
my complaint, my plea,
to win me *Circulation*!

Too many Family Compact types are anti-family
(but pro-Ku-Klux-Klan),
with feces impacted in their mouths.

God is looking into all their faces
and is just waiting for the perfect moment
to watch em all die.

But this *Oppression* is global.

I demand *Help*!

(I don't chitchat about these necessaries.)

Truth? A rose's fragrance can't satisfy
these perverts as much as does the taste
of a child's rectum.

They shower their "disinfectant" urine
over each freshly torn-open anus.

I'm no diplomatic poet!
I lack those etiquette-aesthetic protocols.

Anyway, who's the supreme rat here,

guv'nors?

[**Tropea (Italia) 8** *juin* **mmxviii**].

Mona States Re: Black Persecution (III)

Queen Victoria is deploying capitalists—
bankers—vampires—
to entrap and exterminate black people!

She got a suction device affixed to her stomach.
It resembles an open sore—
like the wound in resurrected X's side!

When she grunts, the sucking hole glows
and churns,
vampirizing, leeching, to snare and swallow

black people! Starting with me. I seen it!
It is disgusting:
A white pus circle with a bloody hole at centre!

Affixed to the Queen's fat gut, the fetid gash
is a vacuum, a magnet,
and it expands and sucks us in, one-by-one,

brains-first, so we go into her pus-filled maw
like a lollipop sinking into a baby's mouth.
Someone must investigate this hideous empress!

Police this monster! Listen up, good people!
This device is the same that Haliburton has.
You must examine and forensically test this truth!

I am telling y'all the truth.
I seen it with my own two eyes.
It is being done to us all the way from Oxford

University.
That is where the suction is coming from—
to afflict me, all of us, here!

[Tropea (Italia) 25 *juin* mmxxii]

Kiss-She Fells Re: F.R. Langford

I woke up, was no-joke nasty,
still pasty-face with peep-eye half-sleep,
spat muck at bat-black Langford,

"Think this be a fucker's holiday?
I gotta tell ya,
no hassle intended,
there's no need for a palliative, pal,
to alleviate my groanin bed!

"Get yo black-ass up!
You're the likeness of the Loch Ness dragon—
and spectacularly dark
and particularly, sectarianly dirty
(which I like)!

"But it's time to quit the *partouze* ooze—
the extreme vodka and tepid chardonnay—
the fishy sausages and the skunky cheese;
to leave off the long gold that's ale
(the failsafe, short-stop, white cap atop)!

"I'm predisposed to dispose of
the backwash of bathtub gin,
the fished-out chowder:
the dregs can't make scrambled eggs!

"Lookit! Ya've likely had enough
of my pewter throat, moonlit,
swansong, skinny-lady singing!
Landsakes!

"Time for ya to dislodge
cos ya've already discharged
and dismounted!

"And I gave ya a discount,
lecher preacher!

"So, get up and get out!
I won't let you mute or pollute
my *Leisure* and my *Pleasure*,
ya big galoot!

"Move your slummy bum
and your clammy anatomy!
Chumminess be done!"

[Sheguiandah First Nation,
Lake Manitou, Manitoulin Island (Ontario)
22 *août* mmxx]

Louisa Bailey: Treatise on Poetics

I.

The newest poetry must be biblical.

Art is what we make of *History*.
Art is what remains of *History*.

The past is a canon of poets,
a Babel of bards,
from Homeric Milton
to Chaucerian Longfellow,
but who speaks for us—
invents a bristling, whistling script,
stifling economic—or anemic—prose,
if not a *noiriste* poet,
a black-eyed, silver-tongued, blue-in-the-face poet,
a lady-of-the-lamp poet,
a poet of blood, saltwater, and sherry—
à la Adah Isaacs Menken.
I itch for books—
Poetry and *Drama*,
kerosene and flame,
to "Think, and die."*

(The obituary bestows, really,
an honorary doctorate.)

---

* Antony and Cleopatra, 3.II.i.

II.

In Church, I hear inspired gobbledygook
by artificially-lit up Negro orators,
brilliantly sombre in Gospel-Truth-black suits,
whose *Genius* is so much smoke
and *broken* mirrors.

I dislike dialogue so black and white,
And I detest "Uncle Remus" troubadours—
these orphan versifiers—
all bad grammar, bad manners, and no wings,
dropping corpses of words,
clunk, clunk,
crow insinuations,
squawk, squawk,
unpalatable palaver....

III.

"Painting" demands light
as colossal as the sun,
not dainty candles
or fainting stars.

"Paint" rustles, hisses, on silk—
veers where it wants,
like *vers libre*
(silkworms),
but it's really ink,
blaring its triumphant passage.

So the page
breaks into blossom—
or light—

and a poem,
supreme,
replaces *History.*

IV.

The well-versed poet,
versing (pouring) inkwells,
ladles ink as strong as pitch,
pitches ink as piercing as a pitchfork,
or tunes his ink to get more pitch—
i.e., liquid, soulful music.

The blank page is pregnant
with *Poetry*,
as is unspilled ink.

The text is a pact—
eye, mouth, hand,
allied,
even if wrong.

V.

The poem is visible
and it is audible,
indivisibly.

It prompts a seesaw language,
looses ink that wrinkles in writing,
and is only as drab as *Erasure*.

VI.

Joker voices watch black ink shine—
as if a poem is merely a nameplate.

But, in reality,
no tree's real character emerges
til it's chopped, pulped,
and bleached into paper
set for poems.

A sonnet is, in short,
a custard of ink and paper.
(Cf. E.B. Browning.)

The epic is a North Star
and it is a South Sea:
a direction
and a destination.

But song is writing without words—

sunset sonnets of midnight daylight,
candled *amours* and kindled sheets,
a backfiring drum,
a backtracking rhythm,
a backtalking Moor
(the sound of *Sex*).

Writing should only be print
when it's worth repeating.

VII.

According to Nova Scotia's
museum-quality *Poetry*,
those rare-book oddities no one reads,
but keep as investments
in a locked case
(Howe, Goldsmith, and their ilk),
we Negroes must lean to the Muse
from the broken steps
of our shacks.

True: *The Book of Negroes*
is a black book
scrawled over in black ink—
prismatic *negrismo*.

And scissors cut back on ink;
sirens confiscate songs.

But stars come on like candles;
and the moon comes up roses.

And the cadence of the Africadian Baptists
is a bolt of silk—
lightning—
or white silk of rain, hissing.

Silence is a manuscript;
Prayer its illumination.

Our true preachers—
poets—
are governors
dispensing frequently sparkling rain
and occasionally appalling light.

I say every poet's a Frankenstein—
cranking out characters and causes
as galvanizing and as cranky
and as disappointing as themselves:

Yet, being administrators of *Truth*,
they are true administrators.

Thus, the T'ang Dynasty poets
brought in printing—
and toilet paper—
to accommodate constitutions....

And Mary Shelley has crafted us
a veritable, scientific devil,
the Zombie symbol of each perishing Empire....

VIII.

Because this essay mentions rain,
it rains now,
beyond ink drizzle.
Somewhere, words drip blackly
on white paper,
to suggest a canvas Venice.

IX.

This burgh ain't really Nova Scotia, finally:
It's an Africa of thistles, codfish, and rum,
Black-watched Scots, and bleached-out Moors.

I take Jamaican rum
that devils make
for angels.

I'm no *jicama*;*
yet, like roads, I have many allegiances.

Art keeps faith only with *Doubt*;
leave this *Faith*, and it turns doubtful.

How else to hemorrhage
The *Poetry* of an Age?

X.

The wind goes maniac through orchards,
uprooting, tearing down,
scattering leaves
(and leaves of books too).

---

* Mexican: An edible, turnip-like, root-vegetable—and a racial metaphor: a brown
exterior, but white interior.

A gust havocs these sheets:

Eyes, breath, find fresh *Knowing.*

My words jumble,
tumble back,
black, gleaming.

Yet, I'm suspicious of blustery voices,
their parades of unmentionables!

A *Calypso*
gait demarcates
Lingo
from *Literature.*

Poetry requires the grace of a gardener,
not the *gaucherie* of a butcher.

XI.

I want the green-inked poems of grass,
not *Pain*-poised, poison-paced elegies.

(Nor frankincense phrases
outta Frankenstein mouths!)

Let our earth-black roots
anchor star-green shoots.

Swallows freefall
through blue pigment—
a crowd of stars.

Seagulls flicker like thoughts.

XII.

In this neoclassical wilderness,
the garden communicates its interests
to bees:
Orgasmic wildness.

Their buzzing is a lot like sighing.

I'm serious in my study of sibilants—
so suggestive of *Sex*,
and I'm pretty good for a poet
(and pretty good sexually I'm told).

Tacit *Clarity*—
illicit claret—
the black-inked verse
of the drowned poet, P.B. Shelley,
finally cremated,
yields *Romance*—
the constant Eden of the beginning.

(Even an unread story
ends
fine.)

XIII.

My elemental practice?
To float pure-heart cantos,
canticles of air,

before I should face prodigious *Silence*,
be outfitted as a cemetery morsel!

My ink is my incessant—
I pray—
Residue;

my nocturnal mirror—
incandescent and as astringent
and as pungent and as true
as turpentine.

XIV.

Breath burns,
smokes out,
in winter.

Snow dismantles orchards,
erasing fruit—
and rot.

Youth also rusts out;
friends decay.
The graveyard fattens,
widens with acquaintance(s).

Soon, obituaries are more vital
than weather forecasts,
and what has been is
more vivid, vital, and alive
than anything yet to be,
including any new mortal
gasping for breath,
or grasping for a teat—

a pen!

XV.

The songs of dead poets are beguiling,
yet I prefer em already forgotten:
Their songs echo bitter *Desperation*
because they knew their voices would fade, fail,
faint, and fizzle amid *Time*'s overwhelming *Clamour*.

The living poets bark when they should trill—
caw and cackle when they should coo—
for their measures are all busted, and bastard-got,
just crackpot, monosyllabic, cuss words:
Too elementary, requiring no school!

XVI.

(I slide, land, at the bottom of the page—
with inky, slinky, squiggly, black snakes
of *Contradiction!*)

1861

[Nantes (France) 26–28 *janvier*
& 6 *février* mmix
& Durham (North Carolina) 8 *avril* / *Nisan* mmxiii
& Ottawa (Ontario) 24 *juillet* mcmxciv
& Weymouth Falls (Nova Scotia) 27 *juillet* mcmxciii
& Windsor (Ontario) 5 *août* mmxviii]

The Poetics: Redux

The line-break is a wing,
dippin a ways from us.

The edge of it—
always risqué,
thrusting into blank air
until the eye returns
(*versus*).

Every line is an uprising
marked down.

Balance?
Bores.

—*Louisa Bailey*

[**Durham (North Carolina)** 8 *Nisan* / *Aprile* **mmxiii**]

On the Apostolic Labours of Preston & Clarke: What They Themselves Say (As Reported)

Clarke: He feared neither ruffians' roughhousing nor
Dastards' upheld fists nor nagging naysayers,
Nor the howling electrical tempests
(Hellish as those that show in Lear and slow
The progress of foolish royal and royal fool).
        Usually, wherever Preston deigned pause,
The sky bristled with clouds of whistling wings,
Angelic (obviously); next, his hooves
Would bash, split-second upon split-second,
Upon stones, walloping at a gallop
Each grating bit of gravel, now travailed
As he travelled, fearless of where wharf rats
Hunker or thieves—those zealous frauds—may lurk,
So eager he was to bring *Mercy*'s light.

Preston: What is to be done to get what we want?
If God asks, I'll gnosh skunk and brood in rain,
Skulk where gnashing-jawed critters run amok.
Elsewise, all gold is slovenly, a waste!

[Oslo (NO) 20 *décembre* mmxix]

Advice to the Emperor of China (1861)

I.

Rebarbative bleeding,
be Europe's maximum *Truth*.

(If the marrow be not pure,
the bone is putrid.)

We must blacksmith our own weapons,
or be weighted down, slain, by theirs.

Reject all white-ghost entreaties—
lest we be slaves like Egypt's Jews,

and left kingless, chaotic, and pillaged
of our wives, children, wealth....

Slavery's ambassadors, ruddy jaws crying,
must be scattered—battered—from our shores.

II.

(*Patriotism* can never be *Quietism*:
        Cut out my heart if our Cathay
ever falls as defenceless as a corpse!)

        Emperor, thou must *War*, unabated,
until the assaulting apes are destroyed,
        Caucasoid cadavers left to insects,

a cemetery's fancy *Monotony*.
        Even their skeletons should be *Pollution*—
the garbage of bones.

(Empires arrive—thrive—on battlefields.
And, luckily, *Tyranny* isn't bullet-proof:
        Kings can tumble right off their saddles.)

Let Europe man—then feed—the sea!
        Treat Europe to a blades-only beating:
Furrow our frontier's fields

        with foreigners' corpses,
tearing up the grass or the dirt
        where they fall,

dyeing dry clods to red mud,
        their blood's spontaneous moisture
irrigating dusty soil.

        (Treaties are as insubstantial
and as foggy as clouds.)

        Unyoke the terrifying horses!
Pepper the French and British
        with so much shot,

their bodies look heaps of soot,
        indistinguishable from healthy turds.
Get at em, by counterpoint,

        toe-to-toe, sword vs. sword,
til maggots make a bee-line
        to their soft, sweet organs,

exposed, spewing and strewing blood.
        Unspeakable must be our *Wrath*,
too terrible for ghost poets to describe!

[Montréal (Québec) 4 *mai* mmxiv]

Preston's Xmas Critique of Imperialists

X ians, to browse the Bible is to grouse!

I've sailed beyond Washington, booted cross
Chaos to London. Everywhere cannons—
Impish—th'imperialists brandish. Like weeds
Colonizing a sewer mouth, infantry
Crowds markets and docks, to pursue orders
To befriend blast furnaces with corpses,
Or police and punish "Indian" lands,
Ready to strip "Natives" to bone, or lob
Scoured skulls like bowling balls—so gracelessly—
Or lug and fling the pitiable dead,
Unflinching, into trenches. (Nope: Ditches!)
Callous-hearted, the paleface troops, their spines
Grey-dressed, blur down roads like dust, blizzarding,
Their claws set to clasp and clutch, squash and crush,
Even "Injun" babes—juvenile as was X—
Infant who inaugurated Xmas.

[Oslo (NO) 20 *décembre* mmxix]

On the Apostolic Labours of Preston & Clarke*

The Fugitives' "farms" were deserts of wind—
Thus, useless, restless dust; or ashen snow.

Two horses clopped by, stallions, ebony,
Their sweat as bright as fire, and spurred to trot
Or prance by Preston and Septimus Clarke,
Jogging through black-souled parishes to jolt
Auditors to skip lulling lullabies,
And to startle all unvarnished *Slumber*,
And execute *Absurdity* or *Sin*.
At their hind, they left *Rejoicing*, and
Surged urgently through flurries, rattling hail,
To squat before whoever's fireplace blaze,
To crouch down and pray over the vittles,
No matter how meagre. Some shacks they toured
Were as low-down—lean—as the horizon,
Skimpy as oil-drained lamps, but the Baptists
Were always upright, even if sunflowers
Stooped, crippled, and their seeds all gone to Hell.

Indeed, *Famine* was so bad, mice all starved;
And that news hurt because folks had to chew
Even that ratty gristle! Storms knocked shacks
Right into their outhouse sewer holes! Roses
Wouldn't beautify gardens, but thorns sprouted
Easy, migrating to bramble'd berry
Patches. Dusk came down dirty and dreary.
Night was as gritty as tarpaper pitch.
The one prosp'rous settlement? The graveyard!
Each horizontal silo got loaded
As if gaping mouths stuffed with brown sugar

---

* Cf. Oliver, *History of the Colored Baptists of Nova Scotia*.

Or black jujubes. Sometimes, snow was bread loaves—
Until summer could stand up to winter,
And *Heat*—suddenly perfumed—no longer
Lurked in hearths but occupied sultry air,
And blossoms encumbered green-veined pear groves,
The rain-heavy petals soon lumb'ring down,
Plummeting like blizzarding white, while two
Black stallions, two-black cloaked preachers, two black
Saints, rambled and ambled Nova Scotia—
Preston to Yarmouth and back, Liverpool
To Africville—year-long, from the first buds
To the green-grave mounds of shucked, harvest corn;
And then the horse hooves munched up frost and ice,
After scamp'ring mice lunched on every leaf
Of August harvest. Modest were their meals.

(Wounded Knee? The black wound in the white snow.)

Contemptuous as preening pugilist
Be Preston *versus* Satan. (One imagines
The Adversary whimpering, stooping,
Simpering due to Preston's fisticuffs.)

(I'd be remiss to not recall the aid
Granted Preston by two white Baptist saints—
Messrs. Cogswell and Harding. Class-A souls
They too ranged and tramped the peninsula,
Stopping stirrup or boot at each Coloured
Chapel, to admin'ster the bread and juice
[*Not* wine]. These priests were *de souche* Baptists,
Soil-plain, not given to theatrics,
Save miracles. Never did they spit fire
And brimstone as showmanship as they rose
From baptismal waves, fishing a fresh saint.)

Preston's tally of deeds—including "Real
Estate" deeds—counts 13 churches marshalled—
Wrangled—into *Existence*, directly
Into *Fellowship*, thanks to "herding cats"—

I.e., suspicious, skittish ex-enslaved;
Plus Preston ministered to ten churches:
Headed up 23 congregations!

—*Pearl Olivier, Historian*

[ARN—Stockholm Arlanda (SE) 19/12/19
& Oslo (NO) 20 *décembre* mmxix
& Gardermoen—OSL (NO) 21 *décembre* mmxix
& London—LHR (UK) 21 *décembre* mmxix]

THE DEATH OF PRESTON*

(1861)

---

* "The dead are what move me. The various dead."—Jones, *The System of Dante's Hell.*

To Septimus Clarke

Septimus, nourish, nurture, with living water
the churches of our *Connexion*,
planted where dandelion seed can root,
so that Nova Scotia resembles
an isthmus of Ethiopia—
a landed Nile—
and we sable worshippers of olive X
(woolly haired, with feet like brass*)
require apostolic ploughing—
to uproot weeds
and refresh the earth
(each soul is earth)—
the engender the new and capacious fields,
opening on every hand—
for vineyards, orchards, dairy—
symbols of our Little Africa—
our North Atlantic Africa;

while God Himself—
voice and lightning from Heaven—
increases our harvest—
the saved souls—
fruit and flowers of The Gospel—
and thus increasing The Redeemer's Kingdom—
the fearless Empire,
defying the unfeared "Reaper."

Mr. Clarke—well-named Clerk
of our Africadian Baptist Association—
resolve to dispense every benevolent *Labour*
to our *Denomination*:
To assist our permanent flowering
amid swamp or stones
or permafrost—

---

* Revelation 1: 14–15.

to beget self-sustaining vineyards
of sweetest grapes,
orchards of fabulous apples,
and dairy kine cropping lush pastures
in a surprise, unexpected Eden.

Be it resolved, Septimus,
here at Granville Mountain—
generally at Granville Mountain—
that ye labour ever more intensively,
so that our *Connexion* encompasses
thousands.*

* * * *

Remember: Church is no good,
if you've no *Faith* in it.

And avoid governors blazed with dirt.**

(They diddle *Law*—
riddle *Law*—
with riddles.)

When whites command, "Know your place!",
know they mean, "Stay in your hellhole,
or go to your grave."

So long it's taken us
To find freedom
None take from us:
Jubilee's now come.

* * * *

---

* Ed. note: And then to enjoy sourdough bread and Manischewitz wine.
** Ricardo—the economist— / is just as incorrect / as is *Ricardo's Coconut Rum*.

For thyself to govern well,
plumb the ink well.

Love well inkwell
Also well-being—
What is well-said,
Prompts what's well-done.

Only then may thou retire
to thyme, basil, mint, spruce, pine,
blackberry bush, and crabapple tree,
at Lot 1A,
Three Mile Plains
(Municipality of West Hants).

To act like Celestine V,*
to locate *Joy* in the activities of the ant-hill,
to hear the curdly sky pronouncing rain,
to watch the mottled grey-blue-white aerial colours
furnish rain,
to hear a bluejay squawk, then see it flash—
as distracting and as attractive as the wind—
taking the colour of rain

(Rain paddles us;
sun straddles us;
for extra nothing.)

Hermits should be vintners,
gardeners, dairy herders, beekeepers,
and poets (not priests).

*   *   *   *

---

* Benedict XVI.

The pen breaks
the thin ice of the page:
ink wells up.

—Rev. Richard Preston, D.D.

1861

[San Nicola da Crissa (Italia) *22 juin* mmxviii
& Toronto (Ontario) *25 mars* mmi]

The Funeral of Rev. Richard Preston, D.D.

At the funeral, I survey
eye-catching, all-in-black sirens—
Nova Scotian *Luxury*
amid New Scottish Presbyterians.

Off to one side, rude gents
mix and match liquor.
Each shady vocal that each one vents
flows stupid, then stupider.

Death is the freezing result
of Preston's volcanic sermons.
Bet he views it as no insult,
but as rest from his burdens.

The sun seems impotent, or moist;
the light is drizzly, wet, and drab.
"Comrades, take up his coffin! Hoist
him graveward, homeward, as if glad."

The coffin is of worth:
A gold-burnished furnishing.
Soon, it'll be splinters mixed with earth.
Now, the sky twists with lightning.

Uneasy, unsettled April
washes as dull as silver.
Now, the choir sparks a canticle,
frosty as cold October.

Into the turtle dullness,
a turtle slumber,
welcoming *Darkness*,
goes Preston. Our hearts feel number.

His was a tender *Decease*—
like blossom fallen
in pale-white frost, its lease,
as extinct as its pollen.

Yes, even crowned heads feed worms:
Decorum's vulgar when each goes bust.
Steep Preston deep among germs:
The noble Xian outlives dust.

Nothing's so clarifying
as *Eternity*,
when bared bones defy dying
and parade stringent *Purity*.

Let strangers toss back blazing drink
among the little suns of candle-light:
Each of us hovers at the brink
of our personal, eternal night.

As for Preston,
he is beautiful in every atom.
Let fears now prove *Fiction*,
and we be as perfect as X's become.

Tears are agreeable—and disagreeable.
But our Church must not fall—
to flame or rust or *Hate* or *Libel*,

if our *Faith* be metaphysical.

—*Septimus Clarke*

[Halifax (Nova Scotia) 4 *mai* mmxii]

Of Father Preston

Preston merits heroic portraiture—
genre scenes—
that man spurring on a biblically black horse,
blazing through snow—
to gallop and gallivant through 40 years
to father and nurse Africadian Baptist culture—
that sacred, if out-of-the-way *Religion*—
thanks to incendiary *Poetry*,
pulpit-banger disciples following....

His ink was as brine-fine as *pinot noir*,
but infinitely blacker!

(His ink was viral, poisonous, toxic—
to do away with Haliburton—
to toy with that perfidious judge
like so much dead meat.

Preston preferred zingers—
the randomly rapturing words—
avidly heinous—
and unfeeling enough so as to curdle paper.

Thank X! Praise X!
For Preston's English of angular, chiasmatic metaphor—
all the crossings and double-crossings of crucifixions
that surpass—for gravitas—all dime-store fictions.)

Preston delivered horse-sense,
nary bullshit.

No fine-print, double-dealing *Hypocrisy*!

No *mezzatesta* (half-a-head),
Preston balanced preaching and teaching:
Never one without the other.

His incisors diced and his molars mashed.

Like a plough, he clarified
and/or divided sweetly
what had been a solid mass,
but folks—*Lumpen*—unconscious.

I don't expect him to be published
or sung in pubs;
to be caught up, echoed,
in Yahoos' yappings....

Understand:
Making means *poetry* in English,
but *Love* in Ebonics:
To give out sugar;
to give off sugar—
devoutly.

(Now, black smoke blacks out the scene—
as if Impressionist,
but fearful of light.)

—*Septimus Clarke*

[Roma (Italia) 24/6/18
& Toronto (Ontario) 13 *janvier* mmi]

Of Father Preston (II)

Father Preston galloped—nay, danced—his mount
sobrely, sombrely, the length of the Annapolis Valley
in the age of original pound cake.
He was nitpicking, not gallivanting,
as his steed's hooves shooed away grass blades
or clopped—grated—upon pebbles
or swished cross beach sand.

His hoss—*The Messenger*—shattered turf,
splattered surf—
battered dust and spattered mud.

How else to hurl down Antichrist—
slavemasters—
in Gospel fire?

Father Preston was an oval of light—
a vertical halo—
coring fatally all darkness about.

No chatter, natter, or yatter—
no chit-chat, flimflam, or yinkyank—
ever sullied his sermonizing.

Clarity is dynamic, irrepressible,
and is the most convincing *Public Relations*;
it ain't *Truth* blacked out;
it ain't *Truth* whitewashed.

Father Preston's candid *Poesy* names tyrants,
publicizes hoodlums, cranks, demons,
and brands even red-handed, red-eyed presidents
bloodying the White House.

—*Septimus Clarke*

[Kingston (Ontario) 11 *février* mcmxciii
& Roma (Italia) 26 *juin* mmxviii]

TABLE OF VERSES

*(of published works,
in order of appearance herein).*

~

AAR Centennial Roundtable: "CANTICLES: Hymns of the African Baptists of Nova Scotia." "Introduction. (To Be Read.)": *The Journal of the American Academy of Religion*. 82.3 (September 2014): 591–593.

"The Progress of Servitude": *Undocumented: Great Lakes Poets Laureate on Social Justice*. Ron Riekki and Andrea Scarpino, eds. East Lansing (MI): Michigan State University Press, 2019. 90–98.

"Deposition of Sally Bassett: Notes for the Defence (1730)": *War Canticles*. George Elliott Clarke. Vallum Chapbook Series No. 34. Montréal: Vallum Society for Education in Arts & Letters, 2022. 1–9.

"Napoléon Broods on the Saint-Domingue Revolt": *War Canticles*. George Elliott Clarke. Vallum Chapbook Series No. 34. Montréal: Vallum Society for Education in Arts & Letters, 2022. 18–23.

"John Wentworth, Governor of Nova Scotia: Libertine": *Lemon Hound*. http://lemonhound.com/2013/02/15/george-elliott-clarke-three-poems/

"Lady Wentworth, Wife to the Governor of Nova Scotia, Considers Love (1799)": *Lemon Hound*.
http://lemonhound.com/2013/02/15/george-elliott-clarke-three-poems/

"Abraham of the Seminoles: A History": *War Canticles*. George Elliott Clarke. Vallum Chapbook Series No. 34. Montréal: Vallum Society for Education in Arts & Letters, 2022. 10–17.

"Richard Preston, 'Apostle to the African Race,' Lands in Nova Scotia (1816)": *Lemon Hound*.
http://lemonhound.com/2013/02/15/george-elliott-clarke-three-poems/

"[A Chronicle of the Lord's First Africadian Miracle Affecting Richard Preston]": From "Settling Africville" (2014) in *Scripting (In)migration: New Canadian Plays*. Ed. Yana Meerzon. Toronto: Playwrights Canada Press, 2019. 107–181.

"I. The Records of Richard Preston": *The Times of African-Nova Scotians*. 3. 2011. 18.

"[Dalhousie Condemns Preston's Black Refugee Congregants]": From "Settling Africville" (2014) in *Scripting (In)migration: New Canadian Plays*. Ed. Yana Meerzon. Toronto: Playwrights Canada Press, 2019. 107–181.

"At Dover Beach": *The Beauty of Being Elsewhere: Poems of Journey and Sojourn*. Ed. John B. Lee. N.p.: Hidden Brook Press, 2021. 44–45.

"Thomas Chandler Haliburton Critiques The Black Refugees": *The Antigonish Review*. 174 (Summer 2013): 23–24.

"[Haliburton's Anatomy of the Negro]": From "Settling Africville" (2014) in *Scripting (In)migration: New Canadian Plays*. Ed. Yana Meerzon. Toronto: Playwrights Canada Press, 2019. 107–181.

"[A Rejoinder to Haliburton]": From "Settling Africville" (2014) in *Scripting (In)migration: New Canadian Plays*. Ed. Yana Meerzon. Toronto: Playwrights Canada Press, 2019. 107–181.

"Nat Türner Talks (1831)": *Tranistion*. 124: 50.

"[Notes on Ecclesiastical Presence! By Richard Preston, Lic.]": From "Settling Africville" (2014) in *Scripting (In)migration: New Canadian Plays*. Ed. Yana Meerzon. Toronto: Playwrights Canada Press, 2019. 107–181.

"Port": *Prairie Fire*. 35.4 (Winter 2014–15): 34–35.

"The Death of Alexander Pushkin." *Vallum*. 14.1 (2017): 41–42.

"Septimus Clarke Scripts Church Minutes": *Central European Journal of Canadian Studies*. 9 (2014): 26.

"Letter to the (African Baptist) Messiah": *African American Review.* 45.4 (Winter 2012): 645–647.

"Aesop of Three Mile Plains": *Parliamentary Mail-Out.* December 2016.

"'Sam Slick' Contradicts Harriet Beecher Stowe": Natalee Caple & Ronald Cummings. Eds. *Harriet's Legacies: Race, Historical Memory, and Futures in Canada.* Kingston & Montreal: McGill-Queen's University Press, 2021. 80–103.

"Cathay Answers Europa (1860)": *War Canticles.* George Elliott Clarke. Vallum Chapbook Series No. 34. Montréal: Vallum Society for Education in Arts & Letters, 2022. 24–28.

"The Teachings of Mona States": *Kola.* 24.2 (Fall 2012): 23–24.

"The Poetics: Redux": *Literature for the People.* 2 (2021): 54.

BIBLIOGRAPHICAL REFERENCES

From: *The King James Version*

Genesis X
Exodus XVIII
Isaiah XVIII
Jeremiah XIII
Revelation XXII

McKissic, Rev. William Dwight, Sr. *Beyond Roots: In Search of Blacks in the Bible*. Wenonah, NJ: Renaissance Productions, 1990.

Minutes of the African [United] Baptist Association of Nova Scotia. Halifax, NS: African Baptist Association of Nova Scotia. [All Minutes at the Eaton Archives, Acadia University, Wolfville, NS]

Oliver, Pearleen. *A Brief History of the Coloured Baptists of Nova Scotia, 1782–1953*. Halifax, NS: African United Baptist Association of Nova Scotia, 1953.

Robart-Johnson, Sharon. *Africa's Children: A History of Blacks in Yarmouth, Nova Scotia*. Toronto: Dundurn Press, 2009.

---

* Inspired by the Scofield Reference Bible, ed. Cyrus I Scofield (Oxford: University Press, 1909).

ACKNOWLEDGEMENTS

A research grant from Duke University permitted me to visit the Eaton Archives at Acadia University (Wolfville [NS]), in February 1995, where I was able to peruse and photocopy many, many *Minutes* of the African [United] Baptist Association (including those of its one-time breakaway body), 1853–1983. The Library of Parliament's Parliamentary Poet Laureateship of Canada (2016–17) ferried me to such sites as Halifax (NS) and Ottawa (ON). Dr. Sonia Labatt, Ph.D. (1937–2022), and Victoria University (*via* The E.J. Pratt Professorship at the University of Toronto), whisked me from Washington (DC) to Montréal (QC); Roissy-en-France (FR) to Helsinki (FI); Budapest (HU) to Caya Coco (CU); Malaga (ES) to Halifax (NS); Batavia (NY) to Niagara Falls (NY); Stratford-on-Avon (ON) to Niagara-on-the-Lake (ON); Unguja City (TZ) to Brno (CZ); Venezia (IT) to Funchal (PT); Dartmouth (NS) to Wolfville (NS); Nantes (FR) to Paris (FR); Windsor (ON) to Windsor (NS); Prague (CZ) to Charlottetown (PE); Mogliano Veneto (IT) to Grotto Bay (BER); St. George's (BER) to London (GB); Vicenza (IT) to Roma (IT); Corpus Christi (TX) to Tulum (MX); Fredericton (NB) to Dorval (QC); Durham (NC) to Ville de Québec (QC); Waterloo (ON) to Oslo (NO).... *et cetera*. A Harvard University travel grant, provided me as the 27th William Lyon Mackenzie King Visiting Chair in Canadian Studies (2013–14), swished me to Cambridge (MA), and London (UK), amongst other locales. Other universities also summoned: Acadia (Wolfville [NS]), Ain Shams (Cairo [EG]), Bolognà (IT), Dalhousie University (Halifax [NS]), Universität Duisburg-Essen (DE), Università Ca' Foscari Venezia (Venezia & Grottammare [IT]), Goethe-Universität (Frankfurt [DE]), Helsinki (FI), John Cabot University (Roma [IT]), Marburg (DE)— severally, Monrovia (Bethlehem [PA]), New Brunswick (Saint John [NB]), Salamanca (ES), and Universidade Federal de Santa Catarina (Florianópolis [BR]), Università degli Studi di Udine (IT), University

of Toronto—Berlin (Berlin [DE]). Reading Series [Mesic Autorskeho
Cteni: Nejvesti Tuzemsky Literarni Festival (2008), Calgary Spoken
Word Festival (2011), III. "Sea and Word that Separates and Connects"
International Poetry Festival (2011), Pordenonelegge Festa del Libro
con gli Autori (2012), Saskatchewan Writers Guild (2014), Lorenzo
(2015), Hackmatack Children's Choice Award (2017), Emancipation
Day Celebrations (2018); Wild Threads Inspired (2019)] landed me in
Brno (CZ); Calgary (AB); Szentendre, Budapest, and Isaszeg (HU);
Pordenone (IT); Regina (SK); Saint John (NB); Fredericton (NB); and
Windsor (ON); and Charlottetown (PE). Hon. Mayann Francis,
Lieutenant-Governor of Nova Scotia, hosted me at Province House,
Halifax (NS), in February 2011. Officiating the common-law wedding
between Linda Warley and Alan Filewood, at St. Agatha, ON, June 18,
2011, transported me to Waterloo (ON). The Quick as a Wink Theatre
Society brought me to Windsor (NS) in November 2012. The border
shutdowns and quarantine restrictions enacted in Spring 2020 to try
to curtail the transmission of the 2019–edition Coronavirus global
pandemic urged Pratt-supported, intra-Ontario travel, especially to
London and Leamington and Manitoulin Island. If my verses deserve
curses, I am to blame. If my pressings seem blessings, my benefactors
own your applause.

The usual suspects—*The* John Fraser and M.R. Haapio—inspired.
Michael Mirolla and Giovanna Riccio edited, here and there. Paul
Zemokhol corrected my "scripture." Any *faux pas* are my missteps alone.

Michael Mirolla okayed this project, way back in 2011. I'm proud to be
associated with Guernica Editions, and I anticipate, with relish, the
return of this epic poem in *Canticles III (MMXXIII)*, which will also
mark the conclusion of a project begun in Zanzibar in February 2008.

David Moratto executed the design of this book. The titular font and
section titles reflect the artistry of William Clarke (1935–2005). Digitized
in 2011 by Andrew Steeves of Gaspereau Press, *Bill Clarke Caps* is a
font my late father drafted—with yardstick, pencil, and ink—in 1969.
The body text is *Garamond*, however.

continuation:
CANTICLES
III
(MMXXIII)

ABOUT THE AUTHOR

To strive to descant Haligonian, Black voice *via* blank verse. (A decasyllabic line be just bunk if there be no slam-dunk adjunct so that iambs kerplunk, kerplunk, kerplunk!)

Sho nuff, the Ivory Tower wanna indoctrinate *moi* in veddy British jabberwocky. So what? Still I learned to Frankenstein-suture "Blind Jack" Milton to Milton Acorn and Little Milton! Make vowels howl and screech! Consonants crunch and crack!

I hear Africadian speech as pseudo-Shakespeare. Dem voices come at me like sumpin outta Chaucer—Blake—Burns, and then Dylan Thomas (shadowin Bobby Dylan).

Poetry be my breath passed through (black) ink....

Since 1983, I've published 10 lyric collections—
  [*Saltwater Spirituals and Deeper Blues* (1983)
  Lush Dreams, Blue Exile: Fugitive Poems, 1978–1994 (1994)
  Blue (2001)
  Illuminated Verses (2005)
  Black (2006)
  Blues and Bliss: The Poetry of George Elliott Clarke (2008)
  Red (2011)
  Lasso the Wind: Aurélia's Verses and Other Poems (2013)
  Gold (2016)
  White (2021)]

5 book-length poems (2 novels, 3 bios)—
  [*Whylah Falls* (1990)
  I & I (2009)

Traverse (2014)
Portia White: A Portrait in Words (2019)]
J'Accuse...! (Poem Versus *Silence) (2021)]—*

4 narrative-lyric sequences—
    [*Execution Poems* (2000)
    Illicit Sonnets (2013)
    Extra Illicit Sonnets (2015)
    The Gospel of Tobit in *These Are the Words* (with John B. Lee) (2018)]—

5 volumes of epic poetry—
    [*Canticles I (MMXVI)* (2016)
    Canticles I (MMXVII) (2017)
    Canticles II (MMXIX) (2019)
    Canticles II (MMXX) (2020)
    Canticles III (MMXXII) (2022)]

6 verse-dramas—
    [*Whylah Falls: The Play* (1999)
    Beatrice Chancy: A Passional (1999)
    Québécité: A Jazz Fantasia in Three Cantos (2003)
    Trudeau: Long March / Shining Path (2007)
    The Merchant of Venice (Retried) (2017)
    "Settling Africville" in *Scripting (Im)migration* (2019)]—

3 translated works—
    [*George Elliott Clarke: Poesie e Drammi.* Trans. & Ed. Giulio Marra
        (2012): Italian
    Whylah Falls. {*Many Kinds of Love: Earthy, Heavenly, and Hellish.*}
    Trans. Tong Renshan (2006): Chinese
    Poeme Incendiare. {*Burning Poems.*} Trans. Flavia Cosma (2006):
        Romanian]—

and 3 opera libretti
    ["Beatrice Chancy: A Libretto in Four Acts" (1998)
    "Québécité: A Libretto in Three Cantos (First Draft)" (2002)
    "Trudeau: Long March / Shining Path" (2006)].

Yet, I'm still a songwriter, makin vowels yowl and consonants go kermash! (Hear Shad's "Storm"! That's my voice—lyric—in the background!)

In Bridgetown, Barbados, in February 2007, I saw half a rainbow. A month later, in Rodos, Greece, the answering spectrum appeared. Likewise, *Poetry* traverses my life, bridging always *Beauty* and *Pain*, *via* "vernacular formalism" (Kevin McNeilly), "majestic euphony" (Terrance Hayes), or "exuberantly beautiful excess" (Shane Neilson), or "Poundian melopoeia" (Marjorie Perloff). So, I gotta sound "Compendious and baroque" (Fiona Sampson), maybe non-stop, eh?

Awards? Prizes? Honours? Laurels?

Basta!